Advance Praise for *Standing at the Edge*

"Roshi Joan Halifax's new book, *Standing at the Edge,* is a reflection of her enormous courage, compassion, and wisdom. In her willingness to cozy up to the great mystery, she transforms fear into wonder. But most of all it is her great love that shines through the pages of this wonderful book and gives us a clear path to a graceful life."
— Ram Dass

"Reading *Standing at the Edge*, I am struck by Joan Halifax's honesty and hard-won humility. This is an unusual, courageous, and inspiring work, a true guide to keeping one's footing in these unstable and perilous times."
— Mark Epstein, M.D., author of *Advice Not Given*

"Joan Halifax knows of what she speaks. *Standing at the Edge* is powerful, honest, wise, and personal." — Sharon Salzberg, author of *Real Happiness* and *Real Love*

"In this moving and timely reflection on embracing life with passionate care, Roshi Joan shares her insights from Zen Buddhism, social engagement, neuroscience, and, above all, from half a century of living fearlessly."
— Stephen Batchelor, author of *After Buddhism*

"There is no easily accessible education on how to stay well in the midst of stress and suffering—our own or of the people around us—until now. Halifax lays out a clear map for how to transform the challenging states we all experience to those of growth—building the foundation of our desperately needed ability to become more stress-resilient and compassionate. There is nothing abstract here. Through science and contemplative wisdom, through examples of courageous lives, and especially the powerful exemplar of Halifax's own life and immense service to humanitarian causes, you will see how your own courage can overcome your fear to live your best life possible."
— Elissa Epel, Ph.D., professor, University of California, San Francisco, and coauthor of the *New York Times* bestseller *The Telomere Effect*

"*Standing at the Edge* is a book that inspires us to rise into our better selves and gives us the tools to do that." — Jane Fonda

"In this beautifully written volume, Joan Halifax combines a spiritual master's depth, the insight of a psychologist, and the vision of a prophet to help us fulfill our humane duty toward others while maintaining respect and care for our own body, mind, and soul."

—Gabor Maté, M.D., author of *In the Realm of Hungry Ghosts*

"The wisdom that Roshi Joan Halifax has distilled from her work with cancer patients, clinicians, teachers, disaster-relief workers, CEOs, and Zen students is all here, recast into a guide to the way we live now that is urgent, principled, practical, and deftly psychological. An astonishing gift."

—Anthony Back, M.D., professor, University of Washington, Cambia Palliative Care Center of Excellence, Fred Hutchinson Cancer Research Center, and founder of VitalTalk

"I thought I knew these words: *altruism, empathy, integrity, respect*, and *engagement*. Not until I read this book did I realize that I have not really understood the words thoroughly. This book is a result of the author's long years of spiritual practice and service. It is a book in which one needs to anchor oneself in order to survive the stormy sea of our present reality."

—Dhammananda Bhikkhuni, the first bhikkhuni in Theravada Buddhism in Thailand and abbess of Songdhammakalyani Monastery

"I love this book. *Standing at the Edge* places Roshi Joan alongside our greatest teachers and practitioners—Pema Chödrön, Thich Nhat Hanh, Gandhi, Dorothy Day, Thomas Merton, and Dr. King. Reading it, I was reminded of the old adage 'Don't just do something—stand there!' By exploring the big themes of altruism, empathy, integrity, respect, engagement, and compassion, she helps us take a stand in a bad time, and to know where we stand, and to stand there in the fullness of wisdom and compassion. Given our violent, inhuman world, this timely book will help us become more nonviolent and more human, to do our part for a more nonviolent world. With Roshi Joan as our guide, we, too, can stand at the edge, learn to see a new vision of humanity, and enter into universal compassion, nonviolence, and peace. What a gift!"

—Father John Dear, author of *The Nonviolent Life* and *The Beatitudes of Peace*

"*Standing at the Edge* is a must-read not only for all clinicians but also for anyone who is caring for others in their suffering. Roshi Joan has a gift to transform the complexity of scientific, theological, and philosophical theories into practical models for everyone to express compassion to others. She enables us to being able to sit in the midst of the other's suffering—offering presence and love." —Christina Puchalski, M.D., OCDS, professor of medicine, director of the Institute for Spirituality and Health, George Washington University

"Roshi Joan defines and explores in her book *Standing at the Edge* human qualities that are essential for living a fulfilling life while serving a larger human community—integrity, respect, altruism, empathy, compassion, and engagement. She calls them edge states, because each of them has a potential shadow side or 'near-enemy' that represents a pitfall on the spiritual journey. Showing how to differentiate between them, she draws on decades of meditation practice, her rich life story, and personal study with shamans, Zen masters, Tibetan lamas, and Native American elders. Written in a clear, engaging style, and illustrated by many moving stories, *Standing at the Edge* is a source of invaluable information for spiritual seekers." —Stanislav Grof, M.D., author of *Psychology of the Future, The Cosmic Game*, and *When the Impossible Happens*

"Joan Halifax has been an 'edge' adventurer all her life. I am astounded by what she has accomplished, in so many fields and in so many places, simply by following her curiosity and love. But even more astonishing to me is her ability to digest and conceptualize what she has seen and done, so that we, her readers, can learn how to grow in courage and wisdom as we face the precipitous 'edges' that loom in our own lives. Combining personal stories with a wide range of studies and techniques, *Standing at the Edge* is a valuable sourcebook for anyone trying to cope in this tragic world, with eyes and heart wide open, and with hands willing to help." —Norman Fischer, poet, Zen priest, author of *What Is Zen?*

"In this exquisite work Roshi Joan Halifax takes us on a tour of the checkered landscape of compassion, exploring with acute psychological insight the precious qualities—the edge states—that contribute to the success of compassionate action and their dark underbellies that can lead to frustration and burnout. Especially useful to those in the care-giving and helping professions, this book will prove an essential guide for all who aspire to make the world a better place." —Bhikkhu Bodhi, founder, Buddhist Global Relief

"Defining moments arise in all our lives when we least expect them. These moments are ones in which the decisions we make and actions we take can have resounding impacts on ourselves and others near and far. Often at these times we are 'standing at the edge'—we might feel overwhelmed, fearful, protective, and act from these self-protective motives, or we might find the capacity to care, have compassion, patience, and generosity. In this moving and inspiring book, Roshi Joan Halifax deeply explores these edge states and with openness and grace provides us with a road map and practices to support us in these defining moments. Wisdom abounds in a time in which it is greatly needed!"
—Mark T. Greenberg Ph.D., Bennett Chair of Prevention Research, Edna Bennett Pierce Prevention Research Center, Penn State University

"With the mastery of an adept mountaineer, Roshi Joan Halifax nimbly guides the reader along the razor's edge that leads to the high places of kindness and wisdom. This is a profound, nuanced, and eminently instructive meditation on spiritual balance." —Pir Zia Inayat-Khan, author of *Mingled Waters*

"In *Standing at the Edge* Joan Halifax has created a panoramic, yet detailed view of those human qualities that afford deep meaning to life. Drawing on decades of engagement with suffering in many forms, her lucid, reflective prose communicates wisdom, honesty, and a hopeful sense of our self-renewing capacity to heal when our aspirations and intentions exceed our grasp. She leaves the reader with a palpable sense of the value to be gained by moving to the edge of, and sometimes beyond, the limits of our vision to make the world a better place." —Clifford Saron, Ph.D., research scientist, Center for Mind and Brain, University of California, Davis

"Roshi Joan Halifax has a simple yet daunting challenge: to live fully we must live at the edge. Some may think that means pushing ourselves toward ever more busy action to somehow take care of the suffering we encounter. She offers a different lens. Compassion requires us to recognize a hidden gift. Standing at the edge affords us a place from where we can both embrace the vista of great light and live into awareness that the precipice of our own deep shadow is but a step away. The wisdom of Roshi's life experience and writing could not arrive at a more opportune time for our divided world and for those of us who seek to live in ways that embody healthy, compassionate lives." —John Paul Lederach, professor emeritus, University of Notre Dame and senior fellow at Humanity United

"Our journey into a meaningful life is guided by such positive qualities as altruism, empathy, integrity, respect, and engagement. However, as Joan Halifax clearly illustrates in her book, these qualities have shadow sides, which can push our life into turmoil. Nevertheless, we can learn a lot from suffering and find boundless possibilities from it. *Standing at the Edge* reminds us that working skillfully with suffering can bring us new life, and with compassion our life will be firm on the path of fulfillment. I found that this book is very inspiring, it brings us hope, and cultivates compassion in our hearts."
—Phra Paisal Visalo, abbot of Wat Pasukato, cofounder of Sekiyadhamma, and recipient of the Asian Public Intellectual Fellowship of the Nippon Foundation

"*Standing at the Edge* is a guide to help us cultivate the courage and creativity to face the reality of these life challenges as the world changes and confronts us with troubles and turmoil. Offering us a unique and powerful framework for understanding the edge states of altruism, empathy, integrity, respect, engagement, and compassion, exploring their important upsides and helping us navigate their inherent downsides, Joan Halifax has created an essential reading guide to bring a sanctuary of clarity to our inner lives and to this magnificent world we all share. This is a work of heart filled with the hard-earned wisdom of a master teacher and our loving guide, Joan Halifax, that will provide you, no matter your place in life's journey—young and starting out on your journey, in the midst of your professional and personal life, or senior in your position in the world—with life-changing insights, cutting-edge science, and a comprehensive, in-depth view of how we can embrace the fullness of life as we bring resilience to our inner world and service to those around us. This is a life-affirming, life-transforming work that is a gift to us all."
—Dan Siegel, M.D., clinical professor of psychiatry, UCLA School of Medicine

"Understanding the intricacies of the edge states offers a courageous approach to engaging in today's uncertain and perilous world. It is an invitation to embrace our strength and our suffering with compassion, insight, and wisdom. A primer for preserving integrity in the midst of confusion, complexity, and conflict."　　　　　—Cynda Rushton, Ph.D., RN, FAAN, Bunting Professor of Clinical Ethics, Johns Hopkins University

ALSO BY JOAN HALIFAX

Being with Dying: Cultivating Compassion and Fearlessness in the Presence of Death

The Fruitful Darkness: A Journey Through Buddhist Practice and Tribal Wisdom

Shamanic Voices: A Survey of Visionary Narratives

Shaman: The Wounded Healer

A Buddhist Life in America: Simplicity in the Complex

Seeing Inside

STANDING AT THE EDGE

Finding Freedom Where Fear and Courage Meet

JOAN HALIFAX

FLATIRON
BOOKS
NEW YORK

www.flatironbooks.com

Grateful acknowledgment is made for permission to reproduce from the following:

"Birdfoot's Grampa" from *Entering Onondaga*, copyright © 1975 by Joseph Bruchac.

"Although the wind" from *The Ink Dark Moon: Love Poems by Ono no Komachi and Izumi Shikibu, Women of the Ancient Court of Japan*, translated by Jane Hirshfield with Mariko Aratani, copyright © 1990 by Jane Hirshfield. Used by permission of Vintage Books, an imprint of Knopf Doubleday Publishing Group, a division of Penguin Random House LLC. All rights reserved.

Designed by Steven Seighman

The Library of Congress Cataloging-in-Publication Data is available upon request.

ISBN 978-1-250-10134-1 (hardcover)
ISBN 978-1-250-10136-5 (ebook)

Our books may be purchased in bulk for promotional, educational, or business use. Please contact your local bookseller or the Macmillan Corporate and Premium Sales Department at 1-800-221-7945, extension 5442, or by email at MacmillanSpecialMarkets@macmillan.com.

First Edition: May 2018

10 9 8 7 6 5 4 3 2 1

For Eve Marko and Bernie Glassman
Mayumi Oda and Kazuaki Tanahashi
with boundless gratitude

CONTENTS

FOREWORD

I'VE WALKED WITH Roshi Joan Halifax on the old traders' trails through the Tibetan plateau and straight up the pathless sides of mountains in New Mexico into the high country of clear streams and summer thunderstorms. I know she's circumambulated the great pilgrimage mountain of Kailash many times, wandered alone in the deserts of North Africa and northern Mexico, walked all over Manhattan, done walking meditation in her own Zen center and in many temples on both sides of North America and throughout Asia. She has broken glass ceilings on her journey as a medical anthropologist, Buddhist teacher, and social activist, and she's brought many along with her. She's a clearheaded and fearless traveler, and in this book she recounts what she's learned in journeys through areas many of us are just beginning to map or notice or admire on the horizon of individual and social change.

We have undergone a revolution in our understanding of human nature in the past few decades. It has overthrown assumptions laid down in many fields that human beings are essentially selfish and our needs essentially private—for material goods, erotic joys, and family relationships. In disciplines as diverse as economics, sociology, neuroscience, and psychology, contemporary research reveals that human beings originate as compassionate creatures attuned to the needs and suffering of others. Contrary to the 1960s "tragedy of the commons" argument that we were too selfish to take care of systems, lands, and goods owned in common, variations on such systems—from grazing rights in pastoral societies to Social Security in the USA—could and in many places does work very well. (Elinor Ostrom, whose work explored successful economic cooperation, became the only woman to date to win a Nobel Prize in economics.)

Disaster sociologists have also documented and demonstrated that during sudden catastrophes such as earthquakes and hurricanes, ordinary human beings are brave, improvisationally adept, deeply altruistic, and often find joy and meaning in the rescue and rebuilding work they do as inspired, self-organized volunteers. Data also shows that it is hard to train soldiers to kill; many of them resist in subtle and overt ways or are deeply damaged by the experience. There is evidence from evolutionary biology, sociology, neuroscience, and many other fields that we need to abandon our old misanthropic (and misogynist) notions for a sweeping new view of human nature.

The case for this other sense of who we really are has been building and accumulating, and the implications are tremendous and tremendously encouraging. From this different set of assumptions about who we are or are capable of being, we can make more generous plans for ourselves and our societies, and the earth. It is as though we have made a new map of human nature, or mapped parts of it known through lived experience and spiritual teachings but erased by Western ideas of human nature as callous, selfish, and uncooperative, and of survival as largely a matter of competition rather than collaboration. This emerging map is itself extraordinary. It lays the foundation to imagine ourselves and our possibilities in new and hopeful ways; and suggests that much of our venality and misery is instilled but not inherent or inevitable. But this map has been, for the most part, a preliminary sketch or an overview, not a traveler's guide, step by step.

That is to say, most of this work points to a promised land of a better, more idealistic, more generous, more compassionate, braver self. Yet the hope that merely becoming this better self is enough may be naïve. In our best self, even on our best days, we run into obstacles, including empathic distress, moral injury, and a host of other psychic challenges that Joan Halifax charts so expertly in *Standing at the Edge*. She shows us that being good is not a beatific state but a complex project. This project encompasses the whole territory of our lives, including our fault lines and failures.

She offers us something of extraordinary value. She has traveled these realms, learning deeply from her own experiences and those of others, including both those who suffer and those who strive to alleviate suffering, and she has come to know how the attempt to alleviate suffering can bring on its own pain and how to steer clear of that misery and draining of vitality. She has gone far and wide in these complex human landscapes and knows that they are more than lands of virtue shining in the distance. She has seen what many only point to from afar—the dangers, pitfalls, traps, and sloughs of despond, as well as the peaks and possibilities. And in this book she offers us a map of how to travel courageously and fruitfully, for our own benefit and the benefit of all beings.

—Rebecca Solnit

A VIEW FROM THE EDGE

THERE IS A SMALL CABIN in the mountains of New Mexico where I spend time whenever I can. It is located in a deep valley in the heart of the Sangre de Cristo Range. It's a strenuous hike from my cabin up to the ridge at more than twelve thousand feet above sea level, from where I can see the deep cut of the Rio Grande, the rim of the ancient Valles Caldera volcano, and the distinctive mesa of Pedernal, where the Diné say First Man and First Woman were born.

Whenever I walk the ridge, I find myself thinking about edges. There are places along the ridgeline where I must be especially careful of my footing. To the west is a precipitous decline of talus leading to the lush and narrow watershed of the San Leonardo River; to the east, a steep, rocky descent toward the thick forest lining the Trampas River. I am aware that on the ridge, one wrong step could change my life. From this ridge, I can see that below and in the distance is a landscape licked by fire and swaths of trees dying from too little sun. These damaged habitats meet healthy sections of forest in borders that are sharp in places, wide in others. I have heard that things grow from their edges. For example, ecosystems expand from their borders, where they tend to host a greater diversity of life.

My cabin sits on the boundary between a wetland fed by deep winter snow and a thick spruce-fir forest that has not seen fire in a hundred years. Along this boundary is an abundance of life, including white-barked aspen, wild violet, and purple columbine, as well as the bold Steller's jay, the boreal owl, ptarmigan, and wild turkey. The tall wetland grasses and sedges of summer shelter field mice, pack rats, and blind voles that are prey for raptors and bobcats. The grasses also feed the elk and deer who graze in the meadows at dawn and dusk. Juicy raspberries, tiny wild strawberries, and tasty purple whortleberries cover the slopes holding our valley, and the bears and I binge shamelessly on their bounty come late July.

I have come to see that mental states are also ecosystems. These sometimes friendly and at times hazardous terrains are natural environments embedded in the greater system of our character. I believe it is important to study our inner ecology so that we can recognize when we are on the edge, in danger of slipping from health into pathology. And when we do fall into the less habitable regions of our minds, we can learn from these dangerous territories. Edges are places where opposites meet. Where fear meets courage and suffering meets freedom. Where solid ground ends in a cliff face. Where we can gain a view that takes in so much more of our world. And where we need to maintain great awareness, lest we trip and fall.

Our journey through life is one of peril and possibility—and sometimes both at once. How can we stand on the threshold between suffering and freedom and remain informed by both worlds? With our penchant for dualities, humans tend to identify either with the terrible truth of suffering or with freedom from suffering. But I believe that excluding any part of the larger landscape of our lives reduces the territory of our understanding.

Life has taken me into geographically, emotionally, and socially complex geographies. Organizing within the Civil Rights and Antiwar movements of the sixties, working in a big county hospital as a medical anthropologist, founding and leading two practice and educational communities, sitting at the bedsides of dying people, volunteering in a maximum-security prison, meditating for extended periods, collaborating with neuroscientists and social psychologists on compassion-based projects, and running health clinics in the remotest areas of the Himalayas—all have introduced me to complex challenges, including periods of overwhelm. The education I've gained through these experiences—especially through my struggles and failures—has given me a perspective I could never have anticipated. I have come to see the profound value of taking in the whole landscape of life and not rejecting or denying what we are given. I have also learned that our waywardness, difficulties, and "crises" might not be terminal obstacles. They can actually be gateways to wider, richer internal and external landscapes. If we willingly investigate our difficulties, we can fold them into a view of reality that is more courageous, inclusive, emergent, and wise—as have many others who have fallen over the edge.

Edge States

Over the years, I slowly became aware of five internal and interpersonal qualities that are keys to a compassionate and courageous life, and without which we cannot serve, nor can we survive. Yet if these precious resources deteriorate, they can manifest as dangerous landscapes that cause harm. I call these bivalent qualities *Edge States*.

The Edge States are altruism, empathy, integrity, respect, and engagement, assets of a mind and heart that exemplify caring, connection, virtue, and strength. Yet we can also lose our firm footing on the high edge of any of these qualities and slide into a mire of suffering where we find ourselves caught in the toxic and chaotic waters of the harmful aspects of an Edge State.

Altruism can turn into *pathological altruism*. Selfless actions in service to others are essential to the well-being of society and the natural world. But sometimes, our seemingly altruistic acts harm us, harm those whom we are trying to serve, or harm the institutions we serve in.

Empathy can slide into *empathic distress*. When we are able to sense into the suffering of another person, empathy brings us closer to one another, can inspire us to serve, and expands our understanding of the world. But if we take on too much of the suffering of another, and identify too intensely with it, we may become damaged and unable to act.

Integrity points to having strong moral principles. But when we engage in or witness acts that violate our sense of integrity, justice, or beneficence, *moral suffering* can be the outcome.

Respect is a way we hold beings and things in high regard. Respect can disappear into the swamp of toxic *disrespect*, when we go against the grain of values and principles of civility, and disparage others or ourselves.

Engagement in our work can give a sense of purpose and meaning to our lives, particularly if our work serves others. But overwork, a poisonous workplace, and the experience of the lack of efficacy can lead to burnout, which can cause physical and psychological collapse.

Like a doctor who diagnoses an illness before recommending a treatment, I felt compelled to explore the destructive side of these five virtuous human qualities. Along the way, I was surprised to learn that even in their degraded forms, Edge States can teach and strengthen us, just as bone and muscle are strengthened when exposed to stress, or if broken or torn, can heal in the right circumstances and become stronger for having been injured.

In other words, losing our footing and sliding down the slope of harm need not be a terminal catastrophe. There is humility, perspective, and wisdom that can be gained from our greatest difficulties. In her book *The Sovereignty of Good* (1970), Iris Murdoch defined humility as a "selfless respect for reality." She writes that "our picture of ourselves has become too grand." This I discovered from sitting at the bedsides of dying people and being with caregivers. Doing this close work with those who were dying and those who were giving care showed me how serious the costs of suffering can be for patient as well as caregiver. Since that time, I have learned from teachers, lawyers, CEOs, human rights workers, and parents that they can experience the same. I was then reminded of something profoundly important and yet completely obvious: that the way out of the storm and mud of suffering, the way back to freedom on the high edge of strength and courage, is through the power of compassion. This is why I took a deep dive into trying to understand what Edge States are and how they can shape our lives and the life of the world.

No Mud, No Lotus

Thinking about the destructive side of the Edge States, I recall the work of Kazimierz Dąbrowski, the Polish psychiatrist and psychologist who proposed a theory of personality development called *positive disintegration*. This is a transformational approach to psychological growth based on the idea that crises are important for our personal maturation. Dabrowski's concept is similar to a tenet of systems theory: living systems that break down can reorganize at a higher and more robust level—if they learn from the breakdown experience.

Working as an anthropologist in Mali and Mexico, I also observed positive disintegration as a core dynamic in "rites of passage." These are ceremonies of initiation that mark important life transitions, and are intended to deepen and strengthen the process of maturation. This notion of positive disintegration was also reflected in the work I did as a co-therapist with the psychiatrist Stanislav Grof, using LSD as an adjunct to psychotherapy with dying cancer patients. In the process of this contemporary rite of passage, I learned much about the value of directly encountering our own suffering, as a means for psychological transformation.

Years later, I was to hear the Vietnamese teacher Thích Nhât Hạnh—or Thây (as his students call him)—echo this wisdom as he spoke of the suffering he experienced while being in the midst of the war in Vietnam and then later on as a refugee. Quietly he would say: "No mud, no lotus."

Reflecting on the difficulties we can experience in serving others, from pathological altruism to burnout, the toxic side of Edge States can be viewed from the perspective of positive disintegration. The rotting mud at the bottom of an ancient pond is also food for the lotus. Dąbrowski, Grof, and Thây remind us that our suffering can feed our understanding and be one of the great resources of our wisdom and compassion.

Another metaphor for positive disintegration relates to storms. I grew up in southern Florida. Every year of my childhood, hurricanes turned our neighborhood upside down. Electric lines crackled in the wet streets, old banyan trees were uprooted from firm earth, and terracotta tile roofs were blown completely off the Spanish-style stucco houses in our neighborhood. Sometimes my parents would take my sister and me to the beach to watch the hurricanes come in. We would stand at the water's edge, feeling the force of the wind, the slap of the rain. And then we would quickly return home, open all the windows and doors, and let the storm blow through.

I once read about a geologist whose special area of research was the study of beaches. He was being interviewed during a massive hurricane that was slamming into the Outer Banks of North Carolina. The geologist told the journalist, "You know, I'm excited to get out to that beach as quickly as I can."

After a pause, the journalist asked, "What do you expect to see out there?"

Reading this, my attention sharpened. I expected the geologist to describe a scene of total destruction. But he simply said, "There will probably be a new beach."

A new beach, a new coastline: gifts of the storm. Here at the edge, there is the possibility of destruction, suffering—and boundless promise.

Edge States are where great potential resides, and working skillfully within these states, understanding can be quickened. Yet Edge States are a fickle territory, and things can go in any direction. Freefall or solid ground. Water or sand. Mud or lotus. Being caught in strong wind on a beach or a high ridge, we can try to stand strong and enjoy the view. If we fall off the edge of our understanding, maybe the fall can teach us how important it is to keep our life in balance. If we find ourselves in the mud of suffering, we can remember that decayed matter feeds the lotus. If we are pulled out to sea, perhaps we can learn to swim in the middle of the ocean, even in the midst of a storm. While there, we might even discover how to ride the billowing waves of birth and death, alongside the compassionate bodhisattva Avalokiteśvara.

Vast View

Sometimes, I imagine Edge States as a red-rock mesa. Its top is solid and gives us a vast view, but at its rim is a sheer drop-off, with no rocks or trees to slow our fall. The edge itself is an exposed place where a lapse in concentration can cause us to lose our footing. At the bottom is the hard ground of reality, and the fall can injure us. Or sometimes, I imagine that we have fallen into a dark swamp, where we can get stuck for a long time. Whenever we try to extract ourselves, we are sucked deeper and deeper into the mud of suffering. But whether our fall ends in solid rock or a nasty cesspool, we are a long way from the high edge of our best selves, and the descent and landing take their toll.

When we find ourselves on the precipice—on the high side of altruism, empathy, integrity, respect, and engagement—we can stand firm there, especially if we are aware of what could happen if we lose our footing. This recognition can fuel our determination to act from our values, as well as our humility about how easy it is to make mistakes. And if we do trip and fall, or if the earth collapses beneath our feet, we have to somehow find our way back to the high edge, where our balance and ballast can keep us firmly rooted and the view includes the entire landscape. Ideally, we can learn to keep ourselves from falling over the edge—most of the time. Yet the itinerary is subject to reality, and sooner or later, most of us will fall over the edge. It is important that there is no judgment in that. It's what we do with that experience, how we use the fall as a place of transformation, that really matters.

I believe that we have to work the edge, expand its boundaries, and find the gift of balance among the diverse ecosystems of the Edge States, so that we can make a greater range of human experience available to us. At the edge is where we can discover courage and freedom. Whether we are encountering the anguish and pain of others or our own difficulties, we are invited to meet suffering head-on so that hopefully we can learn from it—and cultivate perspective and resilience, as well as open the great gift of compassion.

In one sense, the Edge States are all about how we see things. They are a fresh way of viewing and interpreting our experiences of altruism, empathy, integrity, respect, and engagement—and their shadow sides. Through nurturing a wider, more inclusive, and interconnected view of these powerful and rich human qualities, we can learn to recognize when we are standing at the edge, when we are in danger of going over the edge, when we've gone over the edge, and how to make it back to the high edge of the best of ourselves.

From there, we can discover how to cultivate a view that is embracing—a view within ourselves that we develop by nurturing deep awareness into how our hearts and minds operate in the midst of life's great difficulties. And also seeing the truth of impermanence, of interconnectedness, of groundlessness.

Vast view can open when we talk with a dying person about their wishes, when we hear the prison door clang, and when we listen deeply to our children. It can open when we connect on the streets with a homeless person, when we visit the wet tent of a Syrian refugee stuck in Greece, and when we sit with a victim of torture. It can open as well through our own experience of anguish. View can open almost anywhere; without it, we cannot see the edge before us, the swamp below us, and the space within and around us. View also reminds us that suffering can be our greatest teacher.

Interdependence

Many influences have shaped my way of seeing the world and have contributed to my perspective on the Edge States. During the sixties, I was young and idealistic; it was a difficult and exciting time for many of us. We were outraged by the systemic oppression in our society—racism, sexism, classism, ageism. We could see how this oppression fed the violence of war, economic marginalization, and consumerism, as well as the destruction of the environment.

We wanted to change the world. And we wanted a way to work with our good aspirations—to not lose them, nor get lost in them. In this atmosphere of social and political conflict, I began reading books about Buddhism and teaching myself to meditate. I met the young Vietnamese Zen master Thích Nhất Hạnh in the midsixties, and through his example, I was drawn to Buddhism because it directly addresses the causes of individual and social suffering, and because its core teaching says that transforming anguish is the path to freedom and the well-being of our world. I also liked that the Buddha emphasized inquiry, curiosity, and investigation as tools of the path and that he did not recommend we avoid, deny, or valorize suffering.

The Buddhist concept of *interdependent co-arising* also gave me a new way of viewing the world: seeing the intricate connections between seemingly separate things. As the Buddha explained this concept, "This is, because that is. This is not, because that is not. This comes to be, because that comes to be. This ceases to be, because that ceases to be." Looking into a bowl of rice, I can see sunshine and rain and farmers and trucks driving on roads.

In a sense, a bowl of rice is a system. Soon after I started studying Buddhism, I began exploring systems theory, which is a way of seeing the world as a collection of interrelated systems. Each system has a purpose; for example, a human body is a system whose purpose (on the most basic level) is to stay alive. All parts of the system must be present for it to function optimally—without a working heart or brain or lungs, we'll die. The order in which parts are arranged matters; you can't mix up where the organs are.

Systems range from micro to macro, from simple to complex. There are biological systems (the circulatory system), mechanical systems (a bicycle), ecosystems (a coral reef), social systems (friendships, families, societies), institutional systems (workplaces, religious organizations, governments), astronomical systems (our solar system), and more. Complex systems are typically composed of numerous subsystems. Systems peak, move toward decline, and finally collapse, leaving room for alternative systems to emerge.

I mention this because, together, the Edge States are an interdependent system, influencing each other and forming our character. And systems are the ground in which Edge States develop—interpersonal relationships, the workplace, institutions, society, and our own bodies and minds. As systems decline, so also can we encounter ruin. Yet often, from collapse, a new and more robust perspective on reality can emerge.

Futility and Courage

I have a friend who was a dedicated and skillful psychologist, but after years of practicing, he had caved in to futility. In a conversation with me, he confessed, "I just can't bear to listen to my patients anymore." He explained that at a certain point in his career, he had begun to feel every emotion his patients were going through, and he was totally overwhelmed by their experiences of suffering. The constant exposure had eventually dried him up. At one point, he couldn't sleep, and he was overeating to relieve stress. Gradually, he had moved into a space of helplessness and emotional shutdown. "I just don't care," he said. "I feel flat and gray inside." Worst of all, he had begun to resent his clients, and he knew this meant he needed to get out of his profession.

His story exemplifies the negative outcomes of a combination of all the Edge States: what happens when altruism goes toxic, empathy leads to empathic distress, respect collapses under the weight of sensitivity and futility and turns to disrespect with a loss of integrity, and when engagement leads to burnout. Suffering had crept up on the psychologist, and he began to die inside. He could no longer absorb and transform pain to find meaning in his work and his world.

My friend is far from alone in his suffering. Many caregivers, parents, and teachers have confided similar feelings to me. Part of my work has been to address the devastating epidemic of futility, which leads to a deficit of compassion in people who are expected to care.

I have another friend, a young Nepali woman who bucked the odds and turned adversity into strength. Pasang Lhamu Sherpa Akita, one of the country's greatest woman mountain climbers, was an hour's walk from Everest Base Camp in April 2015 when the 7.8 earthquake hit. She heard the thundering avalanche that killed many at Base Camp. She immediately set off to help but was forced to turn back when an aftershock hit.

Pasang's home in Kathmandu had been destroyed by the quake—but she and her husband, Tora Akita, realized that they had to respond to the loss of life, home, and livelihood that many in Nepal were facing. "I could have been killed at Everest Base Camp," Pasang said. "But I was safe. I survived. There had to be some reason why I survived. I told my husband, 'We have to do something for the people who are in trouble.'"

In Kathmandu, Pasang and Tora began to organize young people, and hired trucks to bring rice, lentils, oil, salt, and tarps to people in Sindhupalchowk, the region of the quake's epicenter. She returned week after week to the Gorkha area with roof tin, tents, medicine, and more tarps for the survivors in a number of villages. She hired local people to make new trails across and over landslides that had destroyed existing pathways. She employed hundreds of villagers to bring food and supplies to people who were completely isolated by the effects of the quake and facing the monsoon season without food or shelter.

Pasang was acting from altruism, an Edge State that can easily enough tip toward harm. But in speaking with Pasang during her months of intensive service following the earthquake, I never detected anything in her voice but unlimited goodwill, energy, and dedication. She also expressed a tremendous sense of relief that she and her husband were able to help.

My psychologist friend went over the edge and never found his way back. My Nepali friend stood on the best edge of her humanity. How is it that some people don't get beaten down by the world but are animated by the deep desire to serve?

I think compassion is the key. The psychologist had lost his connection to his compassionate heart; burnout had deadened his feelings. Cynicism had sent down a deep root. Pasang, though, was able to remain grounded in compassion and let those feelings guide her actions. I have come to view compassion as the way to stand grounded and firm on the precipice and not fall over the edge. And when we do fall over the edge, compassion can be our way out of the swamp.

When we learn to recognize the Edge States in our lives, we can stand on the threshold of change and see a landscape abundant with wisdom, tenderness, and basic human kindness. At the same time, we can see a desolate terrain of violence, failure, and futility. Having the strength to stand at the edge, we can draw lessons from places of utter devastation—the charnel grounds—of refugee camps, earthquake-destroyed areas, prisons, cancer wards, homeless encampments, and war zones, and at the same time be resourced by our basic goodness and the basic goodness of others. This is the very premise of coming to know intimately the Edge States: How we develop the strength to stand at the edge and have a wider view, a view that includes all sides of the equation of life. How we find life-giving balance between oppositional forces. How we find freedom at the edge. And how we discover that the alchemy of suffering and compassion brings forth the gold of our character, the gold of our hearts.

1. ALTRUISM

May I do a great deal of good without ever knowing it.
—*Wilbur Wilson Thoburn*

In the early seventies, my passion for biology and the sea led me to serve as a volunteer at Lerner Marine Laboratory in the Bahamas. I assisted a biologist from Brandeis who was researching the ever-so-brief life cycle of the intelligent and wondrous Octopus vulgaris, which we know as the common octopus.

My work afforded me the rare chance to witness a captive female octopus spawn her eggs after she was fertilized. Hundreds of thousands of translucent, teardrop-shaped eggs, each the size of a grain of rice, were spun out of her mantle into long, lacy strands that hung in the water of the aquarium where she was captive. As the weeks passed, she floated like a cloud above them, not hunting or eating, just gently moving the water around the knotted thread of eggs that were slowly maturing. Hovering over her eggs, keeping them aerated, she hardly budged, and her body slowly began to disintegrate, becoming food for her brood as they hatched. The mother octopus died to feed her offspring, her flesh the communion meal for her hatchlings.

I was puzzled and moved by the strange sight of this beautiful creature dissolving before my eyes. Although her sacrifice was not altruism per se, but part of the natural life cycle of her species, this octopus mother brought up a lot of questions for me about human behavior—questions about altruism, self-sacrifice, and harm. When is human altruism healthy? When do we give so much to others that we can harm ourselves in the process? How do we recognize when our altruism might be self-centered and unhealthy? How do we nurture the seeds of healthy altruism in a world where being hurried and uncaring is so often the order of the day? How does altruism go off the rails, over the edge?

In my later work with dying and incarcerated people, and as I listened to the stories of parents, teachers, lawyers, and caregivers in my capacity as a Buddhist teacher, I began to understand altruism as an Edge State. It is the narrow edge of a high cliff, one that allows us a vast view but also one that can erode under our feet.

To act altruistically is to take unselfish actions that enhance the welfare of others, usually at some cost or risk to our own well-being. When we are able to stand firm in altruism, we encounter each other without the shadow of expectation and need lurking between us. The recipient of our kindness may discover trust in human goodness, and we are ourselves enriched by the goodness of giving.

However, when our physical and emotional safety is at risk, it can be challenging to keep our feet planted on solid ground; it's all too easy to lose our footing and free-fall into harmful forms of serving. We might help in a way that undermines our own needs. We might inadvertently hurt the one we're trying to help by disempowering them and taking away their agency. And we might "appear" altruistic, but our motivation is not well grounded. These are forms of pathological altruism, as we'll explore.

Standing at the edge of altruism, we gain a view of the vast horizon of human kindness and wisdom—so long as we avoid falling into the swamp of egoism and need. And if we do find ourselves stuck in the swamp, our struggle doesn't have to be in vain. If we can work with our difficulties, we might be compelled to figure out how we got there and how we can avoid falling off the edge again. We might also get a good lesson in humility. This is hard work—but it's good work that builds character and helps us become wiser, humbler, and more resilient.

I. AT THE HIGH EDGE OF ALTRUISM

T HE WORD *ALTRUISM* WAS COINED in 1830 by French philosopher Auguste Comte, who derived it from *vivre pour autrui*, or "live for others." An antidote to the selfishness of living for ourselves, altruism became a new social doctrine based on humanism rather than religion. Altruism was an ethical code for nonbelievers, one detached from dogma.

Those who act from the purest form of altruism are not looking for social approval or recognition, and they are not looking to feel better about themselves. A woman sees a child she doesn't know wandering into the path of a car. She doesn't think, *Saving this child would make me a good person*—she just rushes into the road and grabs the child, putting her own life at risk. Afterwards, she probably doesn't praise herself too much. She thinks, *I did what I had to do. Anyone else would have done the same.* She feels relieved because the child is alive and well. As this example illustrates, altruism is a step beyond ordinary generosity; it entails self-sacrifice or physical risk.

In 2007, Wesley Autrey (not far from *autrui*), a construction worker, jumped onto the Manhattan subway tracks to save Cameron Hollopeter, a film student who was having a seizure and had fallen from the platform onto the tracks. Autrey saw the oncoming train and leapt down to haul Hollopeter out of the way. But the train was coming too fast, so Autrey threw himself over Hollopeter in the foot-deep drainage trench between the tracks. As he held down the seizing man, the train passed over them both, grazing the top of Autrey's knit cap. No thought to self, just an unmediated impulse to save a fellow human's life.

Later, Autrey seemed bewildered by all the attention and praise he received. He told *The New York Times*, "I don't feel like I did something spectacular; I just saw someone who needed help. I did what I felt was right."

I see Autrey's story as an example of pure altruism. We all have altruistic impulses, but we don't all act on them at all times. Other people on that subway platform no doubt saw Hollopeter seizing and recognized the need to help—but they also understood that they could get killed in the process. Altruism happens when our impulse to serve others overrides our fear and our instincts of self-preservation. Thankfully, Autrey was resourceful enough to save a life and to survive as well.

All over the planet, every day, people are acting from unmediated altruism to serve one another. Like the unidentified Chinese protester who stood resolutely in the pathway of the tanks heading toward Tiananmen Square. Like the doctors in Africa who so courageously treated Ebola patients. Like the Parisians who opened their homes to those escaping the 2015 terrorist attacks. Like the three thousand courageous Syrian volunteers who serve as first responders rescuing survivors after the bombs fall on civilian neighborhoods. Like Adel Termos, who tackled one of the suicide bombers heading toward a crowded mosque in Beirut the day before the Paris attacks in 2015. When Termos caused the bomb to detonate away from the crowd, he lost his own life—but he saved the lives of countless others. Like Ricky John Best, Taliesin Myrddin Namkai-Meche, and Micah David-Cole Fletcher, who fearlessly intervened in a racial attack on two teenage girls riding the MAX Light Rail train in Portland in May 2017. Ricky and Taliesin lost their lives; Micah survived. As Taliesin was bleeding out, he offered these words: "Tell everyone on this train I love them." In our fraught world, I feel that it is important to hear stories like these to keep our faith in the beauty and power of the human heart and to remember how natural altruism is.

Self, Selfish, or Selfless?

Let's return for a moment to the woman who pulls the child out of traffic. If she later thinks, *I'm a good person for doing that,* does this self-congratulatory thought negate the altruism of her action? The strictest definitions of *altruism* do not allow for ego involvement, either before or after the action. Altruism is characterized as an act of selflessness that is about benefiting others, free of expectation of an external reward (such as gratitude or a quid pro quo), and free of internal rewards like higher self-esteem or even better emotional health. Pure altruists have "no gaining idea," to quote Zen master Shunryū Suzuki-rōshi—they gain nothing from their beneficial actions. They are fundamentally unselfish.

Great contemplative practitioners and some naturally compassionate human beings have the kind of boundless heart that is open to serve in all circumstances. No self, no other; just unbiased goodness toward all. But most of us are merely human, and it's very human for us to feel some sense of fulfillment from serving others.

Whether pure altruism even exists is a subject of debate among psychologists and philosophers. According to the theory of *psychological egoism,* no act of service or sacrifice is purely altruistic, because we are often motivated by at least some small feeling of personal gratification, or we feel a little ego enhancement after helping others. This theory might hold that in the real world of human psychology and behavior, there is no such thing as pure altruism.

Buddhism takes a more radical position; it says that altruism and its sister, compassion, can be totally free of the ego, the small self. Altruism can arise spontaneously and unconditionally in response to the suffering of others, as it did for Autrey. Buddhism also suggests that selfless concern for the welfare of others is part of our true nature. Through contemplative practice and ethical living, we can resist the pull of selfishness and come home to the place inside us that loves all beings and holds them in equal regard; the place that fearlessly aspires to end their suffering and is free of biases.

Thích Nhất Hạnh writes, "When the left hand is injured, the right hand takes care of it right away. It doesn't stop to say, 'I am taking care of you. You are benefiting from my compassion.' The right hand knows very well that the left hand is also the right hand. There is no distinction between them." This is the kind of altruism that is *non-referential*, meaning that it is not biased toward family members, friends, or other in-group affiliations.

A poem by Joseph Bruchac conveys this deep and humble sensibility to care for all beings equally:

Birdfoot's Grampa
The old man
must have stopped our car
two dozen times to climb out
and gather into his hands
the small toads blinded
by our lights and leaping,
live drops of rain.
****
The rain was falling
a mist about his white hair
and I kept saying
you can't save them all
accept it, get back in
we've got places to go.
But the leathery hands full
of wet brown life
knee deep in the summer
roadside grass
he just smiled and said
they have places to go
too.

Here, the grampa is a good example of a living *bodhisattva*, in Buddhism, someone who freely saves all beings from suffering. Grampa keeps stopping to rescue those toads, though it means scrambling along the rainy, dark road. Smiling, he seems to be experiencing what Buddhists call "altruistic joy," joy in the good fortune of others.

Altruistic joy is considered to be a truly nourishing quality of mind. In this way, Buddhism agrees with Western psychology that feeling joy about the good fortune of others is good for us. I know I feel better mentally and physically when I am doing good things for others, although feeling better isn't what motivates me. Recent studies in social psychology suggest that being less self-centered and more generous is a source of happiness and contentment for the giver. One study showed that very young children, even those under two years old, tend to experience a greater sense of well-being when they give treats than when they receive them. Another found that adult participants who spent money on others experienced greater satisfaction than those who spent money on themselves. And the neuroscientist Tania Singer has discovered that compassion (a close companion of altruism) triggers the brain's reward centers and pleasure networks. She believes that humans are wired for kindness. When we act from kindness, we feel aligned with our deepest human values. We take joy in our actions, and life feels more meaningful.

Conversely, when our actions harm others, we don't feel well; we often lose sleep, become irritable, and worse. With more and more research documenting the positive health outcomes for people who help others (e.g., enhanced immune response and increased longevity), we might soon face a wave of pseudo-altruists who help others just to live a longer and healthier life. Of course, this might not be a bad problem to have.

Forgetting the Self

For me, one of the most moving examples of altruism is the story of the late Englishman Nicholas Winton. In 1938, as the Nazis were in the process of occupying Czechoslovakia, Winton organized the transport of 669 children, most of them Jewish, from Czechoslovakia to Britain. He ensured their safe passage through Europe by train and found a home in Britain for each and every refugee. This was an incredibly risky, selfless act. He didn't even tell his wife for fifty years. He wasn't interested in fame, though in the end he did become famous when his wife told the BBC about this extraordinary endeavor, after she discovered his scrapbooks when cleaning their attic in 1988.

That year, the BBC invited Winton to the airing of a show called *That's Life*. Unbeknownst to him, people whom he had saved, now in their fifties and sixties, had also been invited. The presenter said, "Is there anyone in our audience tonight who owes their life to Nicholas Winton? If so, could you stand up, please?" Everyone in the studio audience stood up. Winton hugged the woman next to him and wiped away tears.

We can ask if we can really know Winton's precise motivations, and whether his actions may have reified his sense of self in some way. In 2001, when a *New York Times* reporter asked why Winton did what he did, Winton modestly replied, "One saw the problem there, that a lot of these children were in danger, and you had to get them to what was called a safe haven, and there was no organization to do that. Why did I do it? Why do people do different things? Some people revel in taking risks, and some go through life taking no risks at all." An interesting personal assessment of his extraordinary courage.

Winton saw the need, saw that he could serve, and had an appetite for positive risk. If he felt any "fulfillment" from his actions, would that change the way we regard him? I think not. Saving the lives of 669 children earns our profound appreciation. His actions had such a powerful long-range effect, through generations, that we simply rest in the wonder that this happened, and that so many people benefited. Winton lived a long life, passing away in 2015 at age 106.

As Auschwitz survivor and psychiatrist Viktor Frankl said, "Being human always points, and is directed, to something or someone, other than oneself. . . . The more one forgets himself—by giving himself to a cause to serve or another person to love—the more human he is."

II. FALLING OVER THE EDGE OF ALTRUISM: PATHOLOGICAL ALTRUISM

IT'S SOMETIMES CHALLENGING TO KEEP altruism healthy; as we stand at this cliff's edge, we can be vulnerable to falling into harm. When we help excessively and ignore our own needs, we can begin to resent the person we are helping and the situation in general. I knew a woman who cared around the clock for her cancer-ridden mother. Worn out, frustrated that she couldn't do more to alleviate her parent's pain, and feeling guilty for being so frustrated, she ended up turning anger toward her mother, and then later toward herself. She felt she had lost heart and failed both her mother and herself.

When our altruism shifts out of selfless goodness into obligation, duty, or fear . . . or we simply feel burned out from giving, we may start to churn with negative emotions. I remember listening to a schoolteacher who was angry at himself for spending "too much time" helping a needy student. And a nurse who came to resent her patients, then felt ashamed for feeling so negative toward those whom she had once enjoyed serving.

We may also believe that helping a patient, student, or relative gives us permission to offer unsolicited advice or to control their actions. Once, when I was in the hospital very sick with sepsis, I became the recipient of so much kindness that I was almost done in. Finally, one of Upaya's chaplains wisely advised me to have a sign put on my door: "No visitors." Struggling through fever and chills, I was hosting an overwhelming number of visitors who were giving me copious counsel on how to recover my health. These kind people had taken time out of their day to visit me and were trying to be helpful—but clearly, I needed my own energy to heal, and not theirs. I couldn't even mentally track what they were saying, my fever was so high. Their need to help seemed to overwhelm their capacity to feel into my situation and to realize that I could not be receptive. Altruism's edge in these situations can easily crumble when our anxiousness or need to fix take the lead.

If we can learn to view altruism as an edge, we will become more aware of the risk and peril of this geography, and can realize what's at stake: harming others, ourselves, and even the institutions in which we serve. If we find ourselves on shaky ground, we can learn to sense when our actions are likely to send us over the edge. In the best of circumstances, we can pull ourselves out of precarious situations and move back to solid ground.

Help That Harms

When altruism goes over the edge and into the abyss, it becomes *pathological altruism*, a term used in social psychology. Altruism that is sourced in fear, the unconscious need for social approval, the compulsion to fix other people, or unhealthy power dynamics easily crosses the line into harm. And there can be tough consequences, from personal burnout to the disempowerment of entire countries. It is important to unmask situations where we see pathological altruism operating, whether in the lives of parents, spouses, clinicians, educators, politicians, aid workers, or one's self. Recognizing and naming this phenomenon has opened the eyes of many who have found themselves slipping down the precarious slope of good intentions gone awry.

In their book *Pathological Altruism*, Dr. Barbara Oakley and her colleagues explore help that harms. They define *pathological altruism* as "behavior in which attempts to promote the welfare of another, or others, results instead in harm that an external observer would conclude was reasonably foreseeable."

A familiar example of pathological altruism is codependency, in which we focus on the needs of others to the detriment of our own, often enabling addictive behavior in the process. I knew a married couple who let their twenty-five-year-old son, alcoholic and unemployed, live in their basement for a while. They didn't want to kick him out onto the street with no job or home—but his presence strained their finances and, as their resentment grew, tested their marriage. They tried to make him go to AA and to inpatient rehab, and they found temporary jobs for him, but their attempts to control his behavior and modulate his addiction always backfired. For their son, having a free place to stay wasn't a good thing either, because he had no incentive to change his situation.

Alongside codependency, Dr. Oakley cites other manifestations of pathological altruism, including animal hoarding and "helicopter" parenting. We all know the cat lady who can't say no to taking in one more stray, and the father who makes a federal case to school administrators about his son's well-deserved C in chemistry class as a way to "help" his son.

In my own work, I have observed many people who are caught in the grip of pathological altruism: a nurse who worked too long without food or sleep in order to care for her dying patient; a social activist who camped out in her office so she could be on call 24-7; the CEO of a social relief organization who was chronically jet-lagged from flying all over the world; a volunteer helping refugees in Greece who experienced empathic distress from all the suffering she was witnessing.

Parents, teachers, health care professionals, employees within the justice system, and activists working in crisis situations are especially at risk of pathological altruism from exposure to others' suffering. The consequences can manifest as resentment, shame, and guilt, and also as the toxic sides of the other Edge States: empathic distress, moral suffering, disrespect, and burnout.

Also, viewing ourselves as "saving," "fixing," and "helping" others can feed our latent tendencies toward power, self-importance, narcissism, and even deception of ourselves and others. A particularly troubling story of pathological altruism involves an organization which claimed to be doing health and humanitarian relief work in Asia and Africa. The organization not only misrepresented itself to its funders about the scope of its work—it also failed to pay their local staff in various countries. Ethical violations like this are sourced in self-delusion. My hunch is that in the beginning of their work, they probably wanted to be of service, but they eventually got caught in the need to represent the organization as doing good in order to raise money. Of course, the funder finally realized what was going on and the funding stream stopped, but in the meantime, there was harm all around.

Pathological altruism on a systemic level occurs when helping actually harms the organizations or peoples who are supposed to be served, such as in situations of foreign aid gone wrong. There are abundant examples of this—from my experience, they include clinicians doing medical service in refugee camps where there is no incentivizing or training of local people to offer follow-up care, so refugees become dependent on outside sources for medical help; NGOs that bring in Western products or services rather than giving grants and training to local entrepreneurs who could meet the demand; and "toxic charities" that give money without providing opportunities for skill development, creating more dependency on outside sources for support.

When we Westerners think we can save the world, we might do so not only from a place of goodwill but from hubris. Writer Courtney Martin notes that from afar, other people's problems seem exotic and easily solved. She says that while this tendency is not usually malicious, "it can be reckless. There is real fallout when well-intentioned people attempt to solve problems without acknowledging the underlying complexity."

Martin urges us instead to "fall in love with the longer-term prospect of staying home and facing systemic complexity head on. Or go if you must, but stay long enough, listen hard enough so that 'other people' become real people. But, be warned, they may not seem so easy to 'save.'" Bearing witness to the problems of another culture, and really listening, may be the only way to stay on the healthy side of altruism.

Some people become so obsessed with helping others that their own well-being is compromised. In her book *Strangers Drowning*, Larissa MacFarquhar profiles American "do-gooders" who make helping strangers their life's mission. Her subjects forgo everyday luxuries such as restaurant meals and concert tickets so they can send the money to families in developing countries, tallying up how many lives they are saving through their frugality. Mac-Farquhar examines this phenomenon without judging it; she documents uplifting moments of generosity and disturbing moments of pride and guilt. Some of her subjects are part of the effective altruism (EA) movement, which uses data analytics to predict where donations will have the greatest impact on people in need. EA urges its followers to divorce their giving from emotion, arguing that "sentimentality" gets in the way of financial efficiency.

In *Pathological Altruism*, Dr. Oakley also cautions about getting our emotions mixed up in giving. "The bottom line is that the heartfelt, emotional basis of our good intentions can mislead us about what is truly helpful for others," she writes. Oakley implies that "tough love" approaches, like the parents who kick out their basement-dwelling son, can be more truly altruistic.

I think it depends on the situation. From a Buddhist perspective, caring, love, kindness, compassion, and altruistic joy are highly valued qualities. And yet, sometimes help harms. And here, wisdom is essential. Buddhists do not separate wisdom from compassion. These qualities are two sides of the same coin of our basic humanity.

Healthy or Not?

In Buddhism, the Jataka tale of the hungry tigress is usually considered to be a meme of selflessness as an expression of generosity, altruism, and compassion. In another interpretation, however, it could be a story of pathological altruism.

In a dense forest, a bodhisattva (who will one day incarnate into Gautama Buddha) and his two brothers encounter a starving tigress who is preparing to feed on her own cubs. The brothers go off looking for food for the tigress, but the bodhisattva, in an act of pure and unconditional altruism, lies down before the weak mother cat. He pierces his own neck with a bamboo splinter so that she and her cubs can more easily feed on his body.

We can view this story as inspiration for us to engage in radical acts of kindness; as a legend, it isn't supposed to be taken literally. But looked at another way, it could serve as a rationale for actions that violate the First Precept of Buddhism, which says that we should not harm living beings, including ourselves. This story also might encourage martyrdom. The bodhisattva in this tale gives his life, if taken literally, and seems to cross a dangerous line.

The Buddhist canon contains many stories of martyrdom. Records from as early as the fifth or sixth centuries C.E. tell of respected Chinese monks and nuns immolating themselves as protest and offering. Even as I write this, in Tibet, young men and women are immolating themselves in resistance against Chinese oppression. Once, I attended a large service in Dharamsala led by His Holiness the Dalai Lama. His Holiness's eyes were filled with tears as he conducted the service for those who had martyred themselves. His young colleague, His Holiness the Gyalwang Karmapa, has urged Tibetans to stop this extreme and deadly practice. I have asked myself again and again what immolation has to do with Buddhism, which exemplifies nonviolence and non-harming. But then I remember Thích Quảng Đức.

Fire Lotus

In 1963, several years into the Vietnam War, I saw a newspaper photograph that burned itself into my psyche. It was an image of the Vietnamese monk Thích Quảng Đức, who, in protest against the persecution of Buddhist monastics by the government of South Vietnam, had turned himself into a human torch on a busy intersection in Saigon. On a cushion right on the street, in lotus position and in utter stillness, gas can behind him, this stoic monk sat still and silent as raging flames consumed his body.

I was stunned and horrified. I wondered, what had motivated this monk to set himself on fire? How had he developed the quality of character and mind that allowed him to stay upright as flames consumed his body? I remember thinking, *This war must stop.* It was because of this image that I was moved to speak out against the war, and it has been a psychic trigger for me ever since as I continue to uphold nonviolence as the only path to peace. The irony is that the trigger—no, the inspiration—for my work as a peacemaker was an act of extreme self-violence.

The photograph of Thích Quảng Đức in flames, for which the API photojournalist Malcolm Browne won a Pulitzer, became one of the most iconic images of the Vietnam War. It is an image that epitomizes suffering and transcendence; it also exemplifies, for many, an ultimate act of altruism. In the months and years that followed, other Buddhist monastics followed Quảng Đức's example, including Sister Nhất Chi Mai, a student of my teacher Thích Nhất Hạnh. Thích Nhất Hạnh spoke of Sister Nhất Chi Mai often and repeated her words: "I offer my body as a torch to dissipate the dark."

Several years after Thích Quảng Đức's immolation, I met the young journalist David Halberstam, who was one of the few reporters present when Thích Quảng Đức set himself on fire. As Halberstam recounted to us the details of what he had witnessed, I could see that he was deeply disturbed by almost every aspect of the event. I don't remember his precise words that evening, but I do remember his hollow, tired eyes. He seemed shut down and numbed by all he had seen. Later, he wrote:

I was to see that sight again, but once was enough. Flames were coming from a human being; his body was slowly withering and shriveling up, his head blackening and charring. In the air was the smell of burning human flesh; human beings burn surprisingly quickly. Behind me I could hear the sobbing of the Vietnamese who were now gathering. I was too shocked to cry, too confused to take notes or ask questions, too bewildered to even think. . . . As he burned he never moved a muscle, never uttered a sound, his outward composure in sharp contrast to the wailing people around him.

Thích Quảng Đức's self-immolation spurred much controversy among Buddhists and non-Buddhists alike about the ethics of taking one's life to benefit others. Sister Mai's martyrdom raised the same questions, such as, where is the line that separates benefit from harm? Who draws that line?

Does the great harm that came to their bodies negate the good they did in bringing international attention to the war? What motivated their actions— was it the conviction that this act would ultimately save the lives of others? Or was it extreme intolerance of the experience of the suffering of others? Is martyrdom of value to social transformation—or is it deluded and harmful?

Buddhism explores the connection between self and other. I have a sense that Thích Quảng Đức and Sister Mai acted from the space where there was no self and there was no other. They perceived injustice and suffering, felt they had the power to change it, and took action—self-sacrificing action. In that space, there are no boundaries between what we do for others and what we do for ourselves.

In my opinion, the actions of Sister Mai and Thích Quảng Đức in one way transcend categories of help and harm. They galvanized protests around an unjust war, likely saving many lives; yet two people died in a shocking and excruciating way. After nearly fifty years of thinking deeply about their immolations, I now feel that when viewing their ultimate sacrifice, we must recognize the heroism and the harm, the benefit and the costs. I have come to understand the profound value of altruism as an act of selflessness, and I have also gained some insight into its shadow. Holding both of these perspectives prompted me to see altruism as an Edge State. And it occurs to me that not only the intention but also the outcome affects whether we judge an action as pathological or not. If Wesley Autrey had died trying to save Cameron Hollopeter from the subway car, we might call his action pathological or foolish.

The real work we must do is to hold both perspectives, so we can have true depth of field—because often, we are not able to make out the whole picture at any given moment. Our view really depends on where we are standing. This is why turning toward any act of seeming altruism entails a practice of deep inquiry and openness. In the best of worlds, altruism and our perception of it is grounded in the ability to rise above self-interest, to be context-sensitive, and to be comfortable with ambiguity and radical uncertainty.

Altruism Bias

As the actions of Thích Quảng Đức and Sister Mai reveal, martyrdom could be considered an extreme form of altruism; some would call it pathological. The more common forms of pathological altruism—the ones we know from our everyday lives—are less complicated, but they can also be treacherous.

When we do good for others, we must take care that it's not about our own emotional gain. Religions warn against this motivation. In the Sermon on the Mount, which was a source of inspiration for me as a young woman, Jesus condemns doing good works for the purposes of recognition. In Buddhist terms, when we serve others to gain social approval, it can reify our sense of self and foster attachment to an identity as a "good person."

I remember my first Zen teacher, Zen master Seung Sahn casually asking me how I had been spending my time. I listed all my recent "good" deeds. He paused after my recitation and growled, "You are a bad bodhisattva!" I felt like I had been struck by lightning. With not a little bit of shame, I saw that by working to exhaustion for causes related to social justice, I was burning myself out and disempowering others by taking away their agency. Moreover, I was probably trying to gain approval from my teacher and from others. I felt chagrined but also grateful for the tough lesson he had given me.

On the other hand, is it really bad to feel good about helping people? Maybe feeling joy about serving others is important. So much depends on our values, motivations, and intentions. If our motivation is to feel good about ourselves, or to accrue the admiration or respect of others, our actions will be compromised by ego needs. Instead of asking, "Will this action prove I'm a good person?" or "Will doing this make me feel good?" we need to ask, "How will this serve?"

The late Tibetan Buddhist teacher Chögyam Trungpa Rinpoche coined the term *spiritual materialism*, in which seekers try to amass "spiritual" credentials through various means, including appearing "altruistic" in order to enhance one's spiritual identity. Aspiring to benefit others is an important aspect of the spiritual life—it helps align priorities and can deepen practice. And yet, if we start using altruism as a way to boost our sense of self, this becomes a trap. A little reality-based humility can be useful in tempering the need for approval and appreciation.

Some aspects of pathological altruism correlate with gender. When I was growing up, my mother was a Gray Lady, volunteering with the Red Cross in a military hospital in Miami. The day she died, she was a Pink Lady, delivering magazines and books to hospitalized seniors in North Carolina. All her life she served others. She was an altruist. At the same time, her altruism was mediated by a subtle need for social recognition that she was a good person. I believe it was her identity as a woman that put this small warp into her motivation. I learned from my first Zen teacher, through his tough lesson, that I had that warp too.

Women have often gained purchase and power in society by being altruistic—whether in their role as wives and mothers or as caregivers. Many women also have family, social, and cultural histories of oppression, or are subject to religious values that encourage self-sacrifice. And listening to women clinicians, social workers, teachers, lawyers, and executives speak about the challenges of their professions, I have come to understand the role gender identity can play in how altruism is lived and how it can harm through overdoing. Granted, many men share the same issue of needing to gain social approval through what I call "service martyrdom," but I've observed that women often carry an extra burden that results in harm to self and others.

Oakley has a term for this: *altruism bias.* This is the social, cultural, and spiritual expectation to be empathetic and caring. Many of us are biased toward acting altruistically even when it might not be appropriate to the situation. We may ignore signs that our help isn't serving and bail our addicted spouse out of jail again, because we believe it is our role to help our loved ones conquer addiction. Or we might become caught in self-righteousness or the role of rescuer in which we unconsciously seek social approval for our attempts to care.

And yet, altruism bias is hardly a bad thing. Saving a seizing young man from being killed by a subway train, or bringing medical services to vulnerable villagers in the Himalayas, or defending girls against a racist attack, or reaching out to a neighbor who is dying, or saving children from Nazi death camps may be what is called for, even though risky and hard. Experience tells us that altruism bias is a necessity. If our parents didn't lean toward some degree of altruism, we wouldn't have survived our infancy. And without altruism bias, we each are less of who we really are.

Yet there are other interesting considerations to altruism bias. Ethical systems, like those we find in spiritual and religious traditions—as well as the humanistic concept of altruism itself—reinforce altruism bias. These cognitive and cultural systems, coupled with our personal values and histories, can create unconscious tendencies that may blind us to what will truly serve. Due to the influence of these systems, we can be fooled into discounting alarm signals sounded by our intuition, our conscience, our body, and our mind. Even if we get feedback from observers such as friends or colleagues, we may still push ahead with selfishly based altruism at a great cost to all. In the aftermath, these unconscious biases and processes of self-deception can also help us to rationalize actions that go sidewise. "I thought it was the right thing to do," or "It made me feel like a good person," we might say in retrospect.

I learned from working in Nepal, Tibet, Mexico, and Africa that altruism bias can negatively affect not only individuals but also systems, playing into institutional and systemic violence. International aid organizations often fail to conduct adequate studies on the impact of their programs and therefore may not understand the complexity of suffering in the situations they are trying to serve and heal.

At Upaya Zen Center, we were determined to take a different approach when we responded to the catastrophic earthquake in Nepal in the spring of 2015. We knew from our years of work in health care projects in Nepal that smart and motivated young Nepalis were already on the ground and ready to serve earthquake survivors. They knew the territory, could communicate with each other and with us through social media, and had the energy and inspiration to serve. We also suspected that the usual pathways of aid to Nepal through large, international NGOs would be less effective in getting help to the remote areas of Gorkha, the earthquake's epicenter, than through the emerging cadre of local young leaders who were already doing the work. We remembered the 2010 earthquake in Haiti, which inspired an outpouring of international aid that remained outside the control of Haitians themselves. One person described Haiti as a "republic of NGOs," failing to focus on Haitian resilience and autonomy. Funds were mismanaged, and to make matters worse, cholera was introduced into the water supply by UN peace-keepers. We did not want to repeat this kind of foreign aid mistake, and so we turned toward our young and trusted Nepali colleagues.

Through our years of medical service in Nepal, we had collaborated with many dedicated people in remote areas of the Himalayas. They were tough and efficient, and they knew the ropes. We knew they had little to no over-head expenses, had intimate connections with the people, and knew what would serve. We also thought that their involvement in aid work might be an opportunity for them to develop leadership capacities and that the earth-quake tragedy could open a door for leadership training for the next genera-tion of Nepalis.

As we suspected, millions of dollars of humanitarian aid funneled into the government's coffers, and as of this writing, much of it is still there due to political squabbling.

While other foreign aid supplies languished at the airport or were seized at the Indian border, Upaya's team, including mountain climber Pasang Lhamu Sherpa Akita, her husband, Tora Akita, and many other young Nepalis, was able to get tons of food, medical supplies, and building materials into the affected areas right away. With our support and the support of other well-known mountain climbers, Pasang hired out-of-work porters to build trails in the quake zone, so people could be employed and supplies could be transported by foot to impacted villages. With funds raised by Upaya, she also hired a helicopter to evacuate kids from Lho monastery; these kids had been stranded and without adequate food for weeks.

Her husband, Tora, and his team organized and delivered thousands of tarps, blankets, food, and clothing for quake survivors. Over time, they have rebuilt schools, a nunnery, a monastery, a women's center, and an old-age home. Whole villages were reroofed with safer building materials. Medical services were and continue to be offered to quake survivors, as well as for a group of Rohingya refugees from Burma. The work continues inside Nepal, with these young people taking the lead.

But when a U.S. aid program brings in a U.S. contractor to build houses in Haiti, South Sudan, or Nepal instead of employing local workers, this can become an example of colonialism, paternalism, and patronization rather than of wise altruism. I am remembering a well-known saying that Anne Isabella Thackeray Ritchie coined in her nineteenth-century novel *Mrs. Dymond*: "If you give a man a fish he is hungry again in an hour. If you teach him to catch a fish you do him a good turn." I believe that true altruism teaches people to fish. Our Nepali youth network can fish, and they taught others to fish. I continue to ask, how can we, as activists, educators, clinicians, parents, and politicians teach people to fish? I believe this question is important to understanding altruism as an Edge State. When our reasons for serving others are self-oriented or ill-informed, when our help creates an unsustainable situation, we go over the edge into pathological altruism.

III. ALTRUISM AND THE OTHER EDGE STATES

EDGE STATES INFLUENCE EACH OTHER directly and indirectly, and they resonate with each other to support or sabotage us. Healthy empathy for those who suffer can inspire kindness, concern, and altruism. If we encounter someone who is being bullied or subjected to systemic violence and direct abuse, our altruism and integrity compel us to intervene. Altruism is also a powerful platform for dedicated engagement. However, if we can't regulate our empathy, we may suffer personal distress and be unable to serve, or we may react defensively and unskillfully and cause harm to others and ourselves.

If our altruistic actions are not congruent with our moral sensibilities, we are bound to be caught in moral suffering. If we get stuck in pathological altruism, disrespect and disdain for those we were originally trying to help often follow. When altruism is unhealthy, then burnout is not infrequently the outcome. Yet courageous insight into misaligned altruism, what Cassie Moore has called "the delusional highway of helping," can transform a person's life toward the good and toward compassion.

In the early winter of 2016, Upaya's community visited a Santa Fe homeless shelter to make dinner and serve two hundred homeless people. The following day, Cassie had an experience that inspired her to write about what she had learned about altruism:

The day after the shelter dinner, on Marcy Street, I cross paths with a homeless man. We meet eyes, mid-crosswalk. We meet hearts somehow, too, in the crossing. I realize how unafraid of him I am. That feels new to me. I don't mean I'm unafraid in a careless throwing-caution-to-the-wind manner; I'm aware of the wise discernment it requires to engage the world from a 5'2" female body. The man smiles. His long Santa beard moves with his smile, and I nod back as if it were a bow. This feels normal, humane—totally non-magic, but profound. As I walk on, I feel guilt like a cold metallic pearl grow in my gut: Hello, shame. What does it mean that the ability to see my own face in a homeless person is a thing that, for me, feels new? This shame feels warranted. It's not that I've ignored homelessness, not at all. It's that I've othered it. I've not seen myself in it. I've seen myself as a fixer, as coming to meet it with the heart of a rescuer.

Suddenly this feels to me to be a brand of meanness, a sly and convincing story about helping which conceals a deep discomfort with suffering, and has at its root the fundamental belief that I am on a higher level than those who would need helping. I've distanced myself from suffering by believing I can help fix it. In no small way, this makes me sick to my stomach. It seems to me that "fixing" has been my delusional highway meant to transport me to the equally delusional land of Problem Solved. More than anything, it prevented me from seeing anything but difference between myself and someone living on the street.

When Cassie met the eyes of the homeless man, they shared a moment of connection that opened up a portal of insight for Cassie. She recognized that helping, fixing, and rescuing are unhealthy forms of altruism. She experienced moral suffering (in the form of shame) when she realized that she had "othered" him. The tendency to "other" involves a measure of disrespect, another Edge State. Cassie is not alone; homeless people are "othered" by most in our society. Realizing her small part in this system of oppression took Cassie past pathological altruism and into compassion.

Cassie's story reminds me of an important teaching by Dr. Rachel Naomi Remen: "Helping, fixing, and serving represent three different ways of seeing life. When you help, you see life as weak. When you fix, you see life as broken. When you serve, you see life as whole." Remen explains that helping is based on inequality: "When we help we may inadvertently take away from people more than we could ever give them; we may diminish their self-esteem, their sense of worth, integrity and wholeness. When I help I am very aware of my own strength. But we don't serve with our strength, we serve with ourselves. We draw from all of our experiences. Our limitations serve, our wounds serve, even our darkness can serve. The wholeness in us serves the wholeness in others and the wholeness of life."

Altruism at its best is a radical expression of connection, concern, inclusivity, and a sense of responsibility regarding the well-being of others. It is about consciously *not* robbing others of their autonomy by "helping" or "fixing" them. It is about the realization that our own survival is not separate from the survival of others. Like Nicholas Winton's courage in saving so many children during WWII, altruism is characterized by selflessness, unselfishness, courage, generosity, a sense of mutuality, and a deep regard for all of life.

I believe that our deep work is to build a strong internal infrastructure of character, recognize the perils that are disguised as goodness, and have the wherewithal to step out of the trap before it closes around us. Yet we can also fall prey to self-deception, misguided motivations, and the need for praise at one time or another. And when this happens and we recognize it, here is where we open the great gift of humility borne of failure.

IV. PRACTICES THAT SUPPORT ALTRUISM

O N ROSHI BERNIE GLASSMAN'S FIFTY-FIFTH birthday, in 1994, he and his wife, Jishu Angyo Holmes, and friends sat on the steps of the U.S. Capitol in the dead of winter, contemplating their next steps in working to solve the AIDS crisis. They had successfully established the Greyston Mandala, a large social services complex in Yonkers, New York, that includes the Greyston Bakery, an HIV clinic, child care, after-school programs, low-income housing, community gardens, and more. Yet anyone who knows Roshi Bernie knows that he is beset by a restless and revolutionary kind of altruism that has him always moving on to something new and radical.

Sitting on the freezing Capitol steps, Roshi Bernie and Jishu began to envision what would become the Zen Peacemaker Order (ZPO), an organization of socially engaged Buddhists. They grounded ZPO and the practice of Three Tenets of Not-Knowing, Bearing Witness, and Compassionate Action, a path that fosters altruism of the bravest kind. *Not-Knowing* is the practice of letting go of fixed ideas about ourselves and the universe. *Bearing Witness* is the practice of being present for the suffering and the joy of this world. *Compassionate Action* is action that arises out of Not-Knowing and Bearing Witness, and which fosters the healing of the world and ourselves as a path of practice.

ZPO went on to create courageous programs that continue today. In ZPO Street Retreats, participants live as homeless people on the streets for days at a time, bearing witness to homelessness. In their Auschwitz Bearing Witness Retreat, hundreds gather in Auschwitz in the cold of November to practice Not-Knowing, Bearing Witness, and Compassionate Action as a way to meet the historical and present-moment suffering of this world.

I joined ZPO as a cofounder in the midnineties. Roshi Bernie, Jishu, and I, along with several other Zen practitioners, worked intensively to make the practice of the Three Tenets a central part of our own lives and to offer this possibility to our students. Some years later, I incorporated the tenets into Upaya's Buddhist Chaplaincy Training Program, and they serve as a foundation for how we train chaplains in view, meditation, and action.

Using the tenets as a frame of reference, we ask: How can we sit with Not-Knowing when the suffering we are experiencing is close to overwhelming? When does Bearing Witness verge on being a bystander? When Compassionate Action is called for, how do we keep "helping" and "fixing" at bay, and altruism balanced and healthy so we don't fall over the edge? And if we do find ourselves teetering toward pathological altruism, how can we make our way back to the solid ground of healthy altruism, so we aren't done in by the downward slide?

My sense of altruism was tested repeatedly during the years when I worked as a volunteer in a maximum-security prison. When I first walked into the Penitentiary of New Mexico to teach meditation to the prisoners, I really understood what the practice of the First Tenet, Not-Knowing, was about. I was literally afraid of being inside a maximum-security prison. I was concerned about working with a population of men who were gang members, all of whom had committed multiple murders. To make matters more challenging, in the volunteer orientation, we were told that if we were taken hostage by a prisoner, the prison officials were not responsible for rescuing us.

In spite of all this, I had long wanted to serve in this particular charnel ground. I had worked with dying people for decades, and I realized I needed to learn from a world that seemed far from what I was familiar with. I was also keenly aware that our economic system, racism, and cultural exclusiveness have fed the systemic oppression of the prison-industrial system. I wanted to plunge more deeply into the psychosocial suffering associated with justice and injustice in our country, and to serve those who were victim to crushing social ills.

The first meeting I had with my group of "students" turned out to be quite a lesson in Not-Knowing. The men were brought into the meeting room by a prison guard, who then left my female colleague and me alone with a dozen very rough-looking, tattooed individuals. Most of them wore dark glasses and had shaved heads with hairnets tight over their foreheads. All of them slouched low in the plastic chairs and were seriously "manspreading."

As a Zen priest, I had a shaved head too, but no hairnet—and I had my legs neatly crossed!

Sitting uncomfortably in their midst, I was struck by how my fear was getting in the way of interacting with this silent and glowering group of men. I had to quickly give up my preconceptions about what it was like "inside," or I was not going to have a very easy time. I asked the group if they would be okay with a check-in (i.e., to share how they were doing), and one of them growled an affirmative. I had to shift my attention to my breath to get myself grounded, and then we began.

The first man just glared at me. It was unnerving. The second man had shades on, and I couldn't see his eyes. I asked him politely if he would mind removing his sunglasses, and he popped them up and down so quickly that I caught only a brief glimpse of his bloodshot orbs. I had to smile, as did a few of the other men in the circle.

Eventually the next fellow took off his shades and began to talk, and things began to warm up. Man after man offered a few more words, until the last man reached into his shirt pocket, pulled out a small package, and handed it to me. It was a hairnet. I unwrapped the little package, took out the net, and slowly put it on my head. The room went into a meltdown of laughter, and thus began six years of practicing Not-Knowing in one of the toughest prisons in the United States.

I saw then and know now that being a so-called "expert" could have easily separated me from these men. We too often build a wall of expertise because of our fears. I learned from this experience about the value of clearly seeing my biases and story—and how these were obstacles to meeting the moment in an unmediated way. In the end, I learned that the practice of Not-Knowing is the very ground of altruism, because it opens us up to a much wider horizon than our preconceptions could ever afford us and can let in connection and tenderness.

The Second Tenet, Bearing Witness, is the practice of being fully present and connected with our whole being to the full catastrophe, neutrality, or joy of whatever is arising. Even more deeply, the practice of Bearing Witness is about being in an unfiltered relationship with others and the world around us, as well as ourselves, and coming alongside with open hands and heart.

When I am in Nepal serving in Upaya's Nomads Clinics, I am bearing witness to many people who are materially impoverished, and injured or ill. I also have to bear witness to the consequences of a corrupt government, environmental degradation, and the marginalization of Tibetans. I cherish the Tibetan people, and I have sat with the truth of their situation, again and again, in order to learn what might serve their communities. I could not do this without the practice of Bearing Witness.

From Not-Knowing and Bearing Witness, the Third Tenet arises, Compassionate Action—or what the Zen master Yúnmén Wényǎn called "an appropriate response." This means taking action (or consciously refraining from taking action) with the clear intention of benefiting others. The philosopher Jiddu Krishnamurti once wrote, "Action has meaning only in relationship, and without understanding relationship, action on any level will only bring conflict. The understanding of relationship is infinitely more important than the search for any plan of action." In traveling to Nepal and supporting Upaya's medical clinics for decades, I have done this work from a base of Not-Knowing and Bearing Witness, and from a grounding in the relationships my team and I have developed with Himalayan people.

Practicing the tenets runs counter to the path that most of us are comfortable walking. Caregivers might want to get things done. So might educators, lawyers, activists, and parents. So do I. We also tend to rely on our expertise, our knowledge base, our past experience in helping others. But if we are to fully meet the present moment, the Three Tenets can be invaluable guides. For me, the Three Tenets are among the most powerful *upayas* (skillful means, or tools of practice) that I use to work with the energies of the Edge States. In this book, as I explore each Edge State and other practices that support them, I will return to the Three Tenets as skillful means, as practices, for encountering our own suffering and the suffering of others, and as a path of cultivating wisdom and compassion, and of finding freedom.

Practicing Not-Knowing

So how do we actually practice the Three Tenets? Here, I will offer a few practice points for each tenet, starting with Not-Knowing.

When I recognize the need to serve someone who is suffering, I usually take an in-breath to get grounded and settle the body on the exhalation. Then I might ask myself as I encounter this person's suffering, *How can I keep an open mind and not jump to conclusions or actions?* I also can ask, *Why, really, do I want to be of service in this situation? Am I caught in the trap of pathological altruism? Do I have what it takes in this moment not to harm but to serve?* If I experience fear, judgment, or aversion to suffering, ideally, I notice this and let go again into openness by bringing my attention back to my breath, grounding myself, and then being present to whatever is arising.

Recently, I was sitting with a dying friend when suddenly his wife climbed into the bed and rather vigorously plumped up the pillow his head was resting on. She then tapped his arm, again and again, telling him that he was all right. At that moment, no one was all right, as far as I could see. And I had to drop into Not-Knowing, holding a space of love for both of them. She was terrified. He was in mental and physical agony. After a while, they both quieted down, but my impulse to pull her out of his proximity was not easy to resist. Pausing and getting grounded helped me refrain from rescuing and advising, and to just be present.

Practicing Bearing Witness

Not-Knowing supports me in Bearing Witness. Equanimity and compassion are important to embody as I come alongside the suffering of others and as I become aware of my own responses in the face of their suffering. Returning again and again to grounding helps. Watching how the mind makes a case for things and against things is also essential. Bearing Witness is not about being a bystander—rather, it's about being in relationship, and it's about the courage to face the whole catastrophe. This isn't always easy to do, but practice enhances our capacity.

Then there was Rita. On a rainy day in downtown San Francisco, I left my hotel and took my place in line for a taxi when a tiny African American homeless woman, with a long sweatshirt covering just the tops of her naked legs, approached me and asked if I was standing in line. I said I was, and she responded, "Now you know that I am a good person." She then pointed at my *rakusu* (a garment worn by Zen Buddhists who have taken the Bodhisattva Precepts) and asked, "Are you a nun?" I paused, then nodded an affirmative as I looked into her eyes. At that moment, I felt like I had the wherewithal to be with her, to not turn my eyes away or hurry past her, and not to objectify her. I spontaneously wanted to connect with her and just be with her. I wasn't thinking about this; it just happened, with rain falling on both of us.

She then asked me for money. I had none on me, and gently told her I was cashless. Again, I did not look away or try to pull myself out of her field; I just tried to stay gently present with her for a few brief moments. Then, all of a sudden, she broke down in anguish, dissolving into tears and shouts. She then lunged at me, and the hotel's doorman rushed up to us, saying, "Rita, it's okay. You can go now." But Rita wasn't going anywhere. Nor was I. She had me cornered, and I had me cornered as well, as I realized that the intimacy of the moment might have not only broken down the wall between us but also the wall protecting her from herself.

I stood there truly Not-Knowing, and I had to bear witness not only to her suffering but also to my own quandary. Her suffering was obvious; my ability to relieve it was nil. My action, skillful or not, was to get grounded, take an in-breath, and bear witness to the grip of her chaotic energy.

I learned a lesson from Rita that day. Intimacy without enough time to process it might contribute to suffering. To the extent that I could, I practiced the Three Tenets as a way of being with the encounter. Later, I remembered the words of my teacher Roshi Bernie: "When we . . . bear witness to life on the streets, we're offering ourselves. Not blankets, not food, not clothes, just ourselves." That means the whole of ourselves, including our confusion; including love and respect. Meeting Rita, I could not control the outcome, nor could I predict it. I only knew that I could not turn away from her suffering.

I have asked myself what Compassionate Action I might have taken to really serve Rita. I don't have a pat answer. Maybe we both were served. I feel that part of our practice is to revisit our seeming less-than-perfect interactions and ask how we could have been more skillful. How can we bring together our intuition, insight, and experience in a way that reduces harm and may even, in the best of worlds, be useful? And perhaps needing an obvious positive outcome is also a second-level problem. Bearing witness means being with the whole of the situation, just as it is.

Compassionate Action

Grounding ourselves, coming back to the body, is important to the practice of all Three Tenets. That is what I did in meeting Rita's distress. When it's time for Compassionate Action, grounding helps us discern which action might best serve the situation—and when doing nothing could be the most compassionate response. I remember many times when I was about to jump in and help or fix, and taking an extra few seconds to inhale, exhale, and drop into the body led me to a choice that was more aligned with the needs of the moment. Stopping and getting grounded, we give ourselves the time to let go of ourselves.

The body often signals to us that there is a lack of alignment between what we want to do and why we want to do it. Or that what we are doing might violate our sense of morals or ethics. Or that it is probably better to do nothing. Or that we are serving because we have a need to be needed.

Through sensing into the body, we can also learn what it feels like physically when we are going over the edge: the paralyzing tightness in the gut or chest; tension around the heart, throat, eyes, or head; jitteriness, tingling, or pain; cold hands, sweating, feet moving as if we want to flee; or feeling dissociated from the body as we watch ourselves do things we don't really want to do. We may be able to rationalize our behavior in our minds, but the sinking feeling or tension in the body will give the truth away. If we shift our attention to the breath and body, we can bear witness to what the body is saying, and we might avoid falling off the edge into the mire of pathological altruism.

Practicing the Three Tenets can also surface the shadow of altruism by helping us see our spiritual materialism, self-deception, and our need for recognition. If we slow things down and reflect on our motivations, we might notice that we are acting from a desire for acknowledgment and appreciation. We can say hello to the small self, with a touch of nonaggression, as we recognize our self-importance or unmet emotional needs—and take this as a good lesson learned. Our motivation for serving others must be at least a little bit unselfish, and reflecting on the Three Tenets before we act can help us discern when we are serving and when we are helping and fixing.

V. DISCOVERY AT THE EDGE
OF ALTRUISM

A T THE CORE OF BUDDHIST philosophy is nonattachment, which is an important principle to remember in relation to altruism. When we see others suffering—whether a family member, colleague, client, animal, an entire group of people, our earth—we hopefully try to meet suffering honestly and intimately, so we can serve. We also put Not-Knowing into practice by recognizing that really, we are always in free fall. It's not like we will find some moral high ground where we are finally stable and can catch all those falling around us. It's more like we are all falling above the infinite groundlessness of life, and we learn to become stable in flight, and to support others to become free of the fear that arises from feeling unmoored. The final resting place is not the ground at all but rather the freedom that arises from knowing there will never be a ground, and yet here we are, together, navigating the boundless space of life, not attached, yet intimate.

Nonattachment doesn't mean we don't care—in fact, it can be a way to show we care. "Detach with love" is a slogan from twelve-step programs that packs a lot of wisdom. Detaching with love can liberate us from the constraints of expectations. Our attempts to serve others may fail, causing disappointment, guilt, or shame. The dying person whom you hoped would have a "good death" had a messy and difficult one instead. The prisoner whom you helped get early release shoplifted an expensive watch and ended up incarcerated again. You worked for five years raising funds to educate kids in the Sudan, and the project collapsed because the headmaster never paid the teachers. And on and on. Practicing the Three Tenets gives us ballast as our attachment to outcome tries to grab us and pull us off the high edge of goodness.

Another part of altruism is to explore how our culture, race, gender, sexual orientation, education, class, and personal history create biases and values that shape our behaviors, and how our privilege and power relative to others influence the expectations we have about serving others. Not-Knowing does not mean that we turn away from our biases. Rather, it provides the open ground where our social conditioning can become more visible to us. We see the fact that unconsciously objectifying others makes them objects of our pity or power and feeds unhealthy forms of altruism.

Another important interpersonal skill is setting boundaries. This is not a selfish act, and it doesn't mean pushing people away or "othering" them (objectifying those whom you think are in a separate, often subordinate, category from you). Good boundaries protect us from empathic distress; we remember that, from one point of view, we are not the suffering person. If we start to overidentify with someone who is suffering, practicing the Three Tenets is a powerful method for recognizing this slide and transforming empathy into compassion by remaining open (Not-Knowing), coming alongside suffering (Bearing Witness), and responding with care (Compassionate Action).

Being part of a community is another skillful means that helps to keep us grounded and realistic. Dr. Oakley says we need external observers— whether a family, a team of colleagues, a spiritual community, or even the community of those whom we serve—who can bear witness to us and help us correct our course before (or after) our seemingly altruistic actions cause harm. We also can benefit deeply from a relationship with a skilled teacher who can remind us of the power of the Three Tenets and save us and others a lot of trouble.

If we apply these practices and perspectives, at some point our response to the suffering of others might become selfless and simple. Until that time or that moment, you and I have to keep showing up, practicing the Three

Tenets, and learning from our experience. Being honest and vigilant with ourselves can keep us on the healthy side of altruism.

It's also important not to engage in self-judgment but rather to be friendly and curious about ourselves. In the *Vegetable Roots Discourse*, Ming Dynasty philosopher Hong Zicheng writes, "Soil that is dirty grows the countless things. Water that is clear has no fish. Thus as a mature person you properly include and retain a measure of grime." These are wise words, as few of us, if any, are perfect altruists. Altruism might take us to our edge. Standing at that edge—and even falling off it, if that's what happens—can ultimately nourish our humility and basic humanity. These words capture the essence of altruism: "May I do a great deal of good without ever knowing it." Indeed, may we practice Not-Knowing, along with Bearing Witness and Compassionate Action, with a whole, open, and humble heart.

I have learned a thing or two from the falls I have taken into the lesser territories of helping and fixing, as well as from the mishaps I have contributed to in the name of altruism. And perhaps, I have been able to serve with a little more wisdom earned from surviving the failures of overwork, from too much empathy, from moral conflicts and moral suffering, and from the power struggles I have experienced.

We should never try to fall over the edge, of course. But when we do, our struggle will bring its own gifts as well as its own suffering. And the stories of those who fall over the edge—and learn from that journey—can be just as inspiring as the stories of those who have stood on solid ground. I wrote earlier in this chapter about the married couple who let their alcoholic son live in their basement. Both parents had definitely fallen over the edge and were mired in a swamp of codependency. They fought with their son and with each other. But they were able to come back from that morass.

During a meditation retreat, the mother had an epiphany that she and her husband had been enabling their son's behavior for years. She got her husband on board with a plan to change the situation. They stopped giving their son money, asked him to move out, and changed the locks. This was, in a way, an act of love. Their son couch-surfed with friends until he had burned those bridges too. For several months, he was homeless, in and out of jail, in a downward spiral. Things looked bad. When his mother heard news of him, she was genuinely concerned, but she didn't cave in—she knew that enabling him would harm herself, her husband, and also her son. Eventually, the young man hit bottom and became desperate enough to seek help.

Now, her son has eighteen months of sobriety and counting. He has his own apartment and is working at a recovery center. His mother told me she is incredibly grateful not only for his sobriety but also for her own journey through codependency to health, because she learned so much. "I thought that as his mother, it was my job to do everything I could to make him quit drinking," she said. "I thought it was my job to make sure he had food and shelter. When I realized that my job was actually to detach with love, every-thing shifted. I'll never forget that lesson. I knew nothing about addiction before. Now I know so much. I have more compassion now for addicts and their loved ones." Empathy and wisdom are what she learned at the edge.

The Wooden Puppet and the Wounded Healer

Altruism can give our lives purpose and depth. Our deep aspiration to serve others helps us remain steadfast and committed during difficult times. The bodhisattva's vow, to save all beings from suffering, can guide us away from self-centeredness. We take a step away from the small self and touch into the realization of our boundless interconnectedness with others.

Ultimately, we may learn that there is no self, no other—no one serving, no one being served. We can be like a wooden puppet responding to the world, her limbs pulled by strings attached to the world's suffering. Our in-clination toward altruism can transform naturally as snow melting into water with the coming of spring. The moisture of kindness may have done its work, and the seeds of unconditional altruism begin to sprout. When our aspirations are dedicated to the welfare of *all* beings, including ourselves, our busy mental projections can come to rest, allowing us to dwell in the present without thought of self or other, without expectations or attachment to outcome.

In Greek mythology, there is the story about the centaur Chiron, who was wounded by Hercules' poisoned arrow. Chiron's wound sent him looking for a cure, and his journey inspired him to serve the less fortunate. His wound became the gateway to his transformation. Jung cited this myth in his writings about the archetype of the wounded healer, which personifies the experience of altruism rooted in the experience of suffering that has been transformed into boundless compassion.

A wounded healer tries to exclude nothing from her heart. This requires bringing together effort and ease as we stand upright at the edge. It takes both effort and ease to spend hours doing nothing by the bedside of a dying child or in the tent of a frightened refugee. It takes both to serve others and not expect something in return. It takes both to return the mind to our practice; to keep showing up, even when the outcome looks miserable. Effort and ease mean letting go of fear and "opening the hand of thought," to quote Uchiyama Roshi. These two qualities in combination give us the courage and stamina to stay stripped to the bone and come face-to-face with what is. They help us manifest wholeheartedness and wholeness in the midst of the tight knot of suffering.

Love

After a talk I gave recently on altruism and compassion, an older woman named Sarah asked if she could speak with me. Sarah told me that her husband of thirty-seven years had Alzheimer's disease. Every night, as she was putting her husband to bed, he gazed up at her, not recognizing her, and said slowly and guilelessly, "You are a very nice woman."

As Sarah told me this, her eyes seemed completely without self-pity, sorrow, or grasping. We both paused, and then she added in a quiet voice, "I have been waiting to hear those words our whole married life."

I am quite sure that Sarah was not taking care of her husband in order to elicit this response from him. His words seem to accurately express her extraordinary kindness. She later confided in me that caring for her husband has been the happiest time of her life.

Our deepest values can point us toward serving others not out of ego or desire for payback—but out of love. I'm reminded of a passage from *The Mysterious Affair at Styles* by Agatha Christie: "You know, Emily was a selfish old woman in her way. She was very generous, but she always wanted a return. She never let people forget what she had done for them—and, that way she missed love."

Sarah did not miss love. Neither did Cameron Lyle, an athlete at the University of New Hampshire. Two years after he was swabbed in the national bone marrow transplant program, Be The Match, Lyle received a call that his bone marrow was needed immediately in order to save a life. A month before championship matches, he had to go into surgery to have his bone marrow extracted. This was his last year at the university and his last opportunity to compete. For Lyle, there was no question. Wouldn't anyone do something like this rather than chase a gold medal? he asked. His main concern was that his coach would be disappointed. As it turned out, his coach and teammates gave him their unqualified support. Later, he was bewildered by the attention he received for his selfless act. I believe that Cameron Lyle did not miss love, although he missed the games.

Wesley Autrey, Nicholas Winton, Sarah, and Cameron Lyle did not miss love. Nor have the great altruists Rosa Parks, Malala Yousafzai, and Rigaberta Menchú Tum—women who have served the world courageously and selflessly and who have stared down death as they stood in their resolve to meet suffering.

Maybe the stories that you and I have lived are not so dramatic and life-threatening. And that is not a bad thing. But we don't want to miss love and shrink away from the precious opportunity to benefit others.

Last year, the poet Jane Hirshfield shared with me that her life broke open when she first read a *tanka* (short poem) by Izumi Shikibu, a tenth-century

Japanese poet. This beautiful tanka is about risk, suffering, permeability, tenderness, and courage, the invisible limbs supporting altruism.

> Although the wind
> blows terribly here
> the moonlight also leaks
> between the roof planks
> of this ruined house.

Referring to this poem, Jane related in a talk she gave in 2016, "Wall up your house too well, and you will stay dry, but also stay moonless." I believe that we have to let life into our lives, let others into our lives, let the world into our lives, let love into our lives, and also let the night into our lives and not let the roof over our heads—our knowing, our fear—keep out the moonlight. Altruism is exactly this permeability, this wall-less wilderness, this broken roof that lets the moonlight flood our ruined house, our suffering world.

I believe that what is important is our ability to recognize when we are at risk of slipping over the edge into selfishness and to learn from the utter fragility and mystery of life. When our altruism is morally grounded, wise, and unselfish, it's because we are able to stand on the edge, a place of Not-Knowing, accompanied by compassion, wisdom, and love. With these companions of altruism, we build the strength to respond spontaneously to the deep pull of goodness inside the human heart, like moonlight leaking through the roof planks of a ruined house.

2. EMPATHY

Empathy is always perched precariously between gift and invasion.
—Leslie Jamison

I was serving in a small medical facility in Simikot, Nepal, years ago during one of Upaya's medical clinics. In the early morning, a weary man, dressed in tattered clothes, walked into this rural Himalayan hospital with a grimy, reeking bundle in his arms. The lead doctor on our team approached the man, who wordlessly began to unwrap the knot of rancid rags to reveal a little girl who had suffered severe burns on her head, arms, back, and chest. Her name was Dolma.

When we examined Dolma, we saw that some of her burns were filled with writhing white maggots, and that other burn sites were raw, red, and badly infected. Her father was mute, but his eyes conveyed unbearable sadness and total resignation. Our intercultural medical team of Nepalis and Westerners immediately mobilized, taking the child into a small wooden room, where local nurses began to clean her wounds.

I slipped into the room behind the team to support them as they did this tough work. We had no pediatric anesthesia, and Dolma's sharp cries filled the clinic halls. The cleanup seemed to go on for a very long time as I stood on the edge of the tight circle of Nepali and Western nurses and doctors who were managing this critical situation.

From the beginning, I was not only observing the clinicians and the child—I was also observing my own mental and physical state. I had worked as a consultant in the burn unit at the University of Miami Leonard M. Miller School of Medicine in the seventies, and I was aware of how painful debridement is. This process entails the removal of infected or dead tissue from a wound site, and our clinicians were doing a massive and masterful job on this little girl.

My heart went out to Dolma, who cried throughout the procedure, her tears reflected in her father's anguished eyes. As I stood there, my heart rate increased, my skin grew cold and clammy, and my breath was shallow and rapid. I was pretty sure I was going to faint, and I thought about leaving the room, but I also felt it was my responsibility to hold the space for the men and women who were performing this difficult procedure. Within another few seconds, my own internal space had closed down into a small tight fist of distress, and passing out became an even more imminent possibility. Dolma seemed to have slipped into my skin, and I was overwhelmed with my perception of her pain.

In some way, this experience of distress was also a wake-up call. I saw I was on a dangerous edge—one not unfamiliar to me. I realized that getting through this was not a matter of avoiding what I was witnessing; it was not a matter of shutting down, or walking out of the room, or letting go into a dead faint. I recognized that my identification with the child's experience had spiraled out of control, and if I were to stay in the room, I needed to shift from hyper-attunement to care, from empathy to compassion.

I was experiencing empathic distress, a form of vicarious suffering that comes with feeling the pain and suffering of another. When I realized this, I used an early version of GRACE, an approach I created for moving out of such distress and into compassion. I unpack the process in chapter 6, but in brief, GRACE is a mnemonic for:

GATHERING OUR ATTENTION
RECALLING OUR INTENTION
ATTUNING TO SELF AND THEN OTHER
CONSIDERING WHAT WILL SERVE
ENGAGING AND THEN ENDING THE INTERACTION

As I stood in that tight little room in the clinic in Simikot, I used this approach as a way to regulate my reaction to empathic distress and to open myself to compassion. Catching myself in this fraught and fragile moment, I took a mindful in-breath and shifted my attention to my feet, to the simple sensation of the pressure of my feet on the floor. I gave myself a few seconds to get grounded. I then recalled briefly that I was there to serve, as were all who were working with the child. I kept my awareness on my body and stayed firmly rooted to the earth. When my heart rate shifted and my head began to clear, I lent my attention again to Dolma, and I could sense how resilient this little one was. All of this occurred in a matter of a minute or so.

I also recognized that although this procedure was an incredibly hard thing for little Dolma to go through (and for the clinicians as well), the doctors and nurses and aides were saving her life. As soon as that thought passed through my mind, I was flooded with warmth and a deep sense of gratitude that her father had brought her to the clinic and that our team, including these compassionate Nepali nurses, was there to keep her from death. I took in the whole room and sent love and strength to all who were there, most especially Dolma.

I saw Dolma and her father hours later, as he departed the clinic with his little daughter in his arms. Dolma's face was bright and relaxed, and her eyes were luminous, as were the eyes of her father; years had dropped from his face. I felt admiration for him; he had walked such a long way to bring her to us. I lightly hugged them both, bowed, and saw in her father's hands medicines that would support his daughter's further healing.

I turned my back on the afternoon and returned to the clinic to sit with a dying grandmother, my right hand on her forehead as she struggled for breath. Then I sat with a woman who had chronic obstructive pulmonary disease. She, too, had not long to live. And so it was that day of work in the clinic, life and death flowing back and forth on the shore of the moment.

Night finally fell, the clinic closed, and I returned to my tent in the guesthouse yard. I felt I had been a small boat coming alongside lives that *were somehow sent to us to learn from. In the Himalayan darkness and silence, I slept.*

Empathy—our ability to include another's experience into our own—is a fundamental human capacity, one that is important to the healthy functioning of friendships, family structures, societies, and our earth. Empathy can bring the best of the human heart forward. If we can stay with our experience of empathy, keeping ourselves open and upright, we will stand solid on the earth of empathy.

Yet balance is delicate on the edge, and empathy can so easily tip toward distress. If we fuse too strongly with another's physical, emotional, or mental state, we can easily fall over the edge and into the murky swamp of empathic distress. But if we recognize empathy as an Edge State, we are more likely to notice when we're feeling empathic distress and correct our course before we fall too far or get stuck in the swamp for too long.

I. AT THE HIGH EDGE OF EMPATHY

THE WORD *EMPATHY* IS DERIVED from the ancient Greek *empatheia*, which was formed from the words for *in* and *pathos*. A century ago, German philosophers borrowed *empatheia* to create the German word *Einfühlung*, "feeling into," which was later translated into the English word *empathy*. Interpersonal empathy describes the capacity that nearly all of us have to include another being into our awareness in a way that enables us to sense what they might be experiencing physically, emotionally, and cognitively.

Empathy, literally taken, is feeling *into* another, while compassion is feeling *for* another, accompanied by the aspiration to take action that benefits the other. Empathy is often a precursor to compassion and part of compassion, but it is not compassion. Whereas empathy is a good thing in the right dose, I believe that we cannot overdose on compassion.

Caregivers often complain of "compassion fatigue," but in my experience, there is no such thing. This term confuses compassion with empathy. In fact, some neuroscientists and social psychologists say that "compassion fatigue" is empathic overarousal and distress. Compassion does not fatigue us—it is a source of strength, and supports our thriving and benefits others. And yet, empathy is an essential feature of our basic humanity. Without empathy, our lives become small and exclusive to the point of narcissism and solipsism.

Empathy extends our world as we lay aside the self, and enriches us through the power of our imagination.

Essentially, empathy is our capacity to merge with, include, understand, or identify with the experience of another. Walt Whitman described empathy beautifully when he wrote, "I do not ask the wounded person how he feels, I myself become the wounded person."

Being empathic, we can internally share not only the emotional experiences of another; we might also resonate with the physical and cognitive experiences of another. In my view, then, empathy can take three forms: it can be somatic, emotional, or cognitive. Social psychologists have focused on emotional and cognitive empathy. Yet from my experience as a meditation practitioner and caregiver, I have seen that we can experience somatic empathy as well, and there is increasing research on this area.

Somatic Empathy

Somatic empathy describes the experience of strong physical resonance with another, such as a mother feeling her baby's hunger, a nurse sensing her patient's pain, or a bystander doubling over as he watches someone get punched in the stomach. I believe that somatic empathy is also present between friends who are close. I remember walking in the mountains with my assistant Noah. A tree branch flicked me in the face, and we both said, "Ouch!" as though both of us had been hit by the branch. Although science hasn't deeply explored this phenomenon, there is some evidence that shared experience between people who are close occurs quickly and automatically.

I first learned about somatic empathy years ago from Buddhi, the yak herder who has walked with me for years in the Himalayas. Buddhi and I share no common spoken language. He is from a small village in the Humla region of Nepal. He has no formal education, just the knowledge he has gained from the mountains that are his home. For years, he has herded yaks on the high ridges above his village.

Buddhi was asked by my colleague Tenzin Norbu to be my "minder" as

I walk the narrow, high-altitude trails of Nepal. He is charged with keeping me safe and free from falls. After walking hundreds of miles together over daunting passes and along thread-thin mountain trails, he has somehow become so physically attuned to me that he seems to catch me even before I fall. It is uncanny that this silent yak herder gliding beside me has included me in his somatic awareness so seamlessly.

I believe that somatic empathy and lack thereof occurs on a wide spectrum. Some people experience little to nothing somatically when presencing the physical experiences of others, while a small percentage of people are hypersensitive to the somatic sensations of others, as though it were happening to them.

Dr. Joel Salinas, a neurologist at Massachusetts General Hospital, has what is called "mirror-touch synesthesia," which allows him to sense the somatic experience of others. According to researchers Michael Banissy and Jamie Ward, mirror-touch synesthetes have more gray matter in areas of the brain associated with social cognition and empathy, and less in areas associated with the capacity to distinguish self from other. This certainly makes sense from the point of view of what mirror-touch synesthetes subjectively experience, who report being easily overwhelmed by their vicarious experience of the physical sensations of others.

In order not to be overcome by his patients' physical experiences, Dr. Salinas learned to ground himself by bringing his attention to the sensation of his own breath. He also recalls his role as a clinician, and that his intention is to be of service to others. In order to control his arousal level, he might notice subtle differences between his vicarious mirrored somatic experience and the way his body typically feels in response to physical stimulation. Using meta-awareness, he knows that the vicarious physical sensations he is experiencing will pass. Sometimes, he reallocates his attention to a person or object that is neutral. And he considers how to use his experience of mirrored somatic resonance for the benefit of his patients. What Dr. Salinas does to cope with his hypersensitivity to the physical experience of his patients is not dissimilar to what I did when approaching overwhelm as I stood close to Dolma, the burned Nepali child as her wounds were being debrided.

Physical attunement can be a medium for our understanding of and care for others. If our identification with someone who is suffering physical pain is too great, however, we may fear the assaults of the other's misery on ourselves and be flooded with so much sensory information that we cope by getting totally scattered or shutting down, protecting ourselves by hermetically sealing ourselves off from the overwhelm of suffering and becoming shut-ins of sorts.

It seems to be a matter of finding a middle way between the extremes of too much sensitivity, on the one hand, or being numb or unaware on the other. It is also important to consider the profound benefit of the practice of "strong back, soft front," the physical metaphor of bringing together the mental qualities of equanimity and compassion, as we attend to, absorb, and then release another's somatic experience.

Emotional Empathy

The most familiar form of empathy is *emotional empathy*. Sharing the emotional experience of others requires the ability to take in the experience of another person without objectifying them. It is allowing ourselves to be inhabited by another's feelings—although sometimes at a great cost to our own well-being.

Every year, I have the opportunity to meet many Nepali villagers who come to our Nomads Clinics in the Himalayas. In the fall of 2015, near the village of Yalakot in Dolpo, Nepal, I sat with a young woman whose name was Pema. Her husband had carried her on his back down a steep, winding, and dusty trail to Upaya's medical clinic in this remote Himalayan region. She had fallen off the roof of her home some weeks before and had been seriously injured. Unable to move from the neck down, Pema was deeply withdrawn; futility seemed to have flattened her face into a blank mask.

During our team's long and careful assessment of her situation, I felt my own chest tighten when we proposed that she be evacuated to Kathmandu, where she could receive medical support for her injury. I seemed to be feeling her resistance, fear, and despair. As our medical team discussed her options, she and her husband talked quietly with each other; they then told us the story of a villager with a similar injury who had been evacuated to Kathmandu and died there. Also she was worried about the cost, although we offered to cover all expenses.

Barely speaking above a whisper, she also let us know that she did not want to eat or drink, as it was difficult for her to pass urine and to defecate. Learning this, we gave her meds to help her appetite, and a nurse on our team taught Pema's husband how to catheterize her and give her an enema. The nurse also taught him how to care for Pema's bedsores and shared with him ideas for how to ease her physical and emotional suffering.

An hour later, we offered to help Pema back to her village, but she and her husband said a quiet "no." Pema was then picked up by her fellow villagers and lifted onto the back of her anxious husband, and this tiny group slowly walked up the trail toward their home. I stood in our camp as this humble entourage disappeared into the distance in the dim light of late afternoon. In a way, I went with them.

I could have been overwhelmed by what I experienced as Pema's futility. My heart was heavy, but I also felt very present, and I had only one thought: How could we best serve her in these circumstances? In the end, I felt our team had done their best by slowing down, staying grounded, being honest and caring, and by not overreacting or pressuring Pema to relieve our own concerns in response to her circumstances. We gave her the medical help we could, and we supported the decision that she and her husband made.

I remained grounded throughout with Pema and made a clear distinction between what I sensed was going on inside of her and what was happening in my own experience. This distinction between self and other can make it possible to avoid being overwhelmed by the feelings of another. I also knew that I could not really know what Pema was experiencing, but I could sense and imagine. Clearly, I could assume nothing, and needed to respect what I could never know.

Two years later, in the fall of 2017, our team returned to Yalakot. Near the village, the trail by the river took a sharp right turn into a pine grove, and, to my astonishment, there was Pema, tiny and leaning on a cane. Her eyes were wet as she greeted me. Her husband had deserted her, but with the return of her appetite, her spirits had lifted. Her brother took her to India for surgery, and some functionality had returned. We both shared joy on seeing each other.

Internalizing someone else's pain and suffering can help us understand them or it might overwhelm and wound us. Empathy of the kind I experienced with Pema was a mixture of both love and suffering. With Pema, my response was characterized by concern and care, and I was able to distinguish Pema's experience from my own.

Healthy emotional empathy makes for a more caring world. It can nurture social connection, concern, and insight. But unregulated emotional empathy can be the source of distress and burnout; it can also lead to withdrawal and moral apathy.

Empathy is not compassion. Connection, resonance, and concern might not lead to action. But empathy is a component of compassion, and a world without healthy empathy, I believe, is a world devoid of felt connection and puts us all in peril.

Cognitive Empathy

Cognitive empathy, also known as *perspective taking* or *mind reading*, is often described as our ability to see through the eyes of another, to stand in their shoes, to be in their skin. But my sense is that we actually expand our awareness and way of thinking to include the experience of another as though we incorporate their views, their mind-set, their way of seeing the world, their reality.

While perspective taking is often a good thing, it also can be used for negative means by those who wish to seek out the vulnerabilities of others and use this knowledge to manipulate them. At its extreme, perspective taking can lead to a loss of our own point of view, our conscience, our moral compass. This kind of mental experience may have been a factor in what happened in Hitler's Germany, where people began to see society from the führer's point of view and lost their independent moral grounding. Or what happens in cults and even political parties. Despite these dangers, perspective taking is an important skill for living in society because it helps us view others as individuals rather than stereotypes or outsiders.

I remember one precarious situation when I was able to make a connection with someone rather than "othering" him, and perspective taking might have saved my life. In 1969, I drove a Volkswagen bus across the Sahara. It was a long and arduous journey of driving hour after hour through slippery, sinking sand, half the time not knowing where I was going.

At the frontier between Algeria and Mali, I found myself surrounded by angry Algerian soldiers. It was more than a little bit scary. I realized that a Western woman with long blond hair was a perfect target if they wanted to cause trouble. My adrenaline surged when one of the soldiers shouted out to his superior to come and look at this strange lady in her Volkswagen bus. As the man approached my vehicle, I spontaneously included him into my awareness. Suddenly, I felt like I was looking through his eyes as he began interrogating me. I did not have time to think through the situation. Strategizing was not an option. Instead of succumbing to negative projections about him in which he might regard me as a victim and treat me accordingly, I felt he was part of me, and I felt safe. We seemed to make a fragile connection as I responded to his questions respectfully, telling him in my broken French that I was an anthropologist and crossing the Sahara to get to Mali. Within minutes, to my relief, he released me to drive on through the night and into that vast, sandy world.

About an hour later, I was stopped dead in this trackless expanse. I could drive no further without digging the bus out of the sand. Fortunately, I was far from the desolate army post and alone in the darkness. I had time to reflect on what had just transpired, and I realized that this intimate moment with the lead officer had probably averted an unfortunate situation. I realized that the best thing had happened by not "othering" him or viewing him as a threat or enemy. And this was possible because of the uncanny moment when his eyes became my eyes. I did not want him to perceive me as a victim but rather as an ally, and I wanted to be on my way. And so I was.

Take a Knee

I recall another story of perspective taking, this one from the Iraq War—and one that prevented a massacre. On April 3, 2003, Lieutenant Colonel Chris Hughes (now a brigadier general) led two hundred soldiers from the 101st Airborne into the holy city of Najaf to liberate the town and protect Grand Ayatollah Ali al-Sistani, the spiritual leader of Iraqi Shia Muslims, whom Saddam Hussein had put under house arrest. The American soldiers were marching down a street near the Imam Ali Mosque, the holiest Shia mosque in all Iraq, its golden cupolas a crown against the dusty sky.

A crowd of Iraqi civilian men had gathered to watch. The crowd seemed friendly—until suddenly, the mood changed radically. The crowd surged toward the troops, shrieking with rage; fists waved, rocks flew. As Hughes later learned, Ba'athist agitators had spread the false rumor that the Americans were there to invade the mosque and arrest the cleric. Hughes's troops, who hadn't slept in days, were heavily armed and frightened by this sudden turn of events.

Hughes sensed that if anyone fired a shot, a massacre would ensue. He also immediately understood that from the Iraqis' point of view, the Americans seemed to be disrespecting their most sacred mosque. The obvious solution to him was to show them a gesture of respect—and peace.

So he did something remarkable. He pointed the barrel of his rifle at the ground and raised it high in the air, showing the crowd that he did not intend to fire it. He ordered his troops, "Everybody smile! Don't point your weapons at them. Take a knee, relax!"

His soldiers looked at Hughes and each other, wondering if he'd lost his mind. Still, they followed orders. In their bulky body armor, they each got down on one knee, pointed their rifles at the ground, and smiled. Some Iraqis continued to yell, but others backed off and sat down. Some even returned the smiles, in a moment of empathic resonance.

Hughes ordered his troops through a loudspeaker to stand up and back away. "We're going to withdraw out of this situation and let them defuse it themselves," he said. Placing one hand over his heart in a traditional Muslim gesture meaning, "Peace be with you," he told the crowd, "Have a nice day," and he led the regiment away.

Hughes and his regiment marched back to their compound in silence. After tempers had calmed, the Grand Ayatollah issued a decree asking the people of Najaf to welcome Hughes's soldiers.

Later, Hughes told CBS News, whose embedded cameraman had captured the whole incident, "In terms of scale of significance, that is the mosque that would have probably not just have caused every Shia in that country to rise up against the coalition. It probably would have at least brought in the Syrians, if not the Iranians."

Hughes's ability to take the perspective of the Iraqis in a moment of extreme pressure avoided the loss of countless lives, and it earned him high praise as a war hero "who won a big battle by never firing a shot."

Hughes must have sensed in his gut and heart that he had to avert suffering on all sides. But the action he took was not one he had trained for (imagine military commanders teaching "Take a knee!"), nor did he have time to craft a response strategy. Healthy empathy leads us toward connection and skillful action, as it did for Hughes. It extends our view as we open ourselves to the experience of others, letting empathy and intuition, rather than calculation, be our guides. I also believe that Hughes's actions were inspired in part by imagination, the ability to see things differently; obviously, in this case, the benefits were incalculable.

Throughout the Body, Hands and Eyes

A *koan* is a Zen story or phrase that can reveal a practitioner's mind. The koan below is a dialogue between the two Zen masters Daowu and Yunyan. It is a powerful teaching on empathy and compassion. It goes like this:

> YUNYAN: What does the bodhisattva of great compassion do with so many hands and eyes?
> DAOWU: It's like someone reaching for a pillow at night.
> YUNYAN: I understand.
> DAOWU: What do you understand?
> YUNYAN: All over the body, hands and eyes.
> DAOWU: You only got 80 percent.
> YUNYAN: What about you?
> DAOWU: Throughout the body, hands and eyes.

This exchange may seem a little puzzling, but first we have to remember that a bodhisattva is a Buddhist archetype exemplifying empathy, altruism, compassion, and wisdom, an awakened being who has vowed to come back lifetime after lifetime in order to save others from suffering. Bodhisattvas could leave our world of pain and anguish behind forever, but they choose to be reborn into the terrible and beautiful wilderness of this life to serve others.

The bodhisattva of compassion, Avalokiteśvara, is often depicted with many arms and hands, and in the palm of each hand is an eye. The hands represent skillful means, and the eyes represent wisdom.

In the koan, the younger teacher, Yunyan, asked what a bodhisattva does with all these hands and eyes. Daowu doesn't give a conventional answer. He goes deeper into how empathy, compassion, and wisdom emerge spontaneously from the heart of this very moment. He replies that it is like what happens when we adjust our pillow at night. There is no thought to moving our pillow. We just do it easily and naturally.

Shantideva wrote in chapter eight, verse ninety-nine (VIII: 99) of *A Guide to the Bodhisattva's Way of Life* that if someone is suffering and we refuse to help, it would be like our hand refusing to remove a thorn from our foot. If the foot is pierced by a thorn, our hand naturally pulls the thorn out of the foot. The hand doesn't ask the foot if it needs help. The hand doesn't say to the foot, "This is not my pain." Nor does the hand need to be thanked by the foot. They are part of one body, one heart.

Daowu is hinting that for a bodhisattva extending compassion to another is instinctual; it is natural, and his image of night is so fitting, as the darkness of night obscures all differences between self and other. We are all one body indeed . . .

Yunyan seemed to get it. But Daowu tested him, asking what did he really understand. Yunyan replied that the bodhisattva of compassion's body is covered with hands and eyes.

Daowu immediately saw that Yunyan had missed the point. This was a superficial answer, only skin deep. So Daowu corrected him, saying, "*Throughout* the body," meaning that the whole of the physical and psychic organism of a bodhisattva *is* hands and eyes.

When I heard Dolma's cries, beheld Pema, or gazed into the eyes of the Algerian military man, I did not say to myself, *In order to be a good bodhisattva, I'd better be empathic.* Rather, I was immediately and thoroughly suffused with the experience of each of these people. Empathy was unprescribed.

In what I experienced with Dolma, however, I had to deliberately regulate my experience in order not to be overwhelmed by empathic distress. When I did this, compassion was given the space in which to arise. This is why empathy is an Edge State. Its value in our lives cannot be measured. But what might need measuring is the height and depth of our empathic response, so overwhelm does not follow.

II. FALLING OVER THE EDGE OF EMPATHY: EMPATHIC DISTRESS

WE MIGHT ASK, WHAT could be the consequences of becoming Whitman's "wounded person," of merging with the sufferer through over-identification? I am not talking about a fleeting moment of sensing or understanding but about an experience of deeply fusing with the suffering of others physically, emotionally, and/or cognitively and not releasing the experience.

When we identify too strongly with someone who is suffering, our emotions can push us over the edge into distress that might mirror the anguish of those whom we are trying to serve. If our experience of his or her suffering overwhelms us, empathic distress can also cause us to go numb, to abandon others in an attempt to protect ourselves from suffering too heavy to bear, and to experience symptoms of stress and burnout.

Close relatives of empathic distress are *secondary trauma* and *vicarious trauma*. Both refer to the acquired and indirect trauma that a doctor, lawyer, humanitarian aid worker, or chaplain can experience when sitting with another's suffering and becoming overly saturated with it. Secondary trauma can happen suddenly; vicarious trauma happens accumulatively. Both occur as a result of unregulated empathy.

A chaplain and close colleague of mine listened to the stories shared by relief workers and survivors of the 9/11 attacks on the World Trade Center. Sleep deprived, in the thick of chaos and confusion, chaplains like my colleague did their best to serve survivors and workers. The hardest part for my colleague was supporting those who were pulling apart the rubble to find human remains. Traumatized by listening to their stories, for years she couldn't get the scenes of suffering out of her mind. In the years following the 9/11 attacks, she told and retold stories as if she were reliving the events of that terrible day and its aftermath.

Humanitarian workers and people in the helping professions are especially prone to empathic distress. They might begin to manifest the same physical and mental symptoms of those whom they serve. This phenomenon is not uncommon. Clinical psychologist Yael Danieli wrote a review paper in 1982 about the emotional reactions experienced by therapists who worked with Holocaust survivors. Several therapists told her that they frequently had nightmares similar to those of their patients. One therapist shared that when he saw the identification tattoo on his patient's forearm, he had to remove himself quickly in order to vomit. Dr. Danieli reported that several therapists began to avoid their survivor clients, and if they did meet with them, they dreaded hearing about their experiences in the camps.

I have also heard about this phenomenon from lawyers and social workers supporting survivors of domestic violence, sexual abuse, and natural disasters. After Hurricane Katrina, a chaplain associate of mine traveled to New Orleans to work with hurricane survivors. When he shared his experiences with me, he reported feelings of deep disgust about what had happened to some of the men and women in the Superdome. Anxiously, he said he felt like he himself was a survivor, and he said he was afraid to return to New Orleans ever again, as the horrors the survivors experienced seemed to have flooded him.

In April 2008, three years after Hurricane Katrina, I visited the Superdome and found myself thinking about this chaplain's reaction to what had transpired in that hellhole, where thousands were incarcerated in what some called the "shelter of last resort." I was there as part of a gathering produced by writer Eve Ensler to mark the tenth anniversary of her global V-Day movement to end violence against women and girls. Some thirty thousand people made their way to the gathering, among them several thousand who had been caught in the confines of the Superdome in the aftermath of Hurricane Katrina.

During my time there, I met with a number of women who had been subjected to sexual assault in the Superdome's confines; others had to empty their bowels on the Superdome floor, as the toilets were overflowing. Many were humiliated, ashamed, and enraged by what they had experienced. And most of the women I met with had not returned to New Orleans since they had been "rescued" from the Superdome; they had resettled in cities around the country.

As I listened to woman after woman tell her story, I became more and more sensitized to what they had gone through. I felt like I was living through something out of a Hieronymus Bosch painting. I soon realized that I was beginning to slip down the slope of empathic distress into the greasy waters of Hurricane Katrina.

Before my trip to New Orleans, I had made a commitment to stand on firm ground and to bear witness to what had happened in the wake of Katrina. If I was to sustain myself in the midst of this flood of suffering, I had to not abandon the ship but ride the waves by remembering that I had not in fact experienced this catastrophe. I had to ground myself in my intention, which was to be a resource for women who had survived the hurricane and its aftermath, and I had to sustain my energy by getting adequate sleep, eating decently, and taking walks in a park near the Superdome.

I also suggested that the women tell me their stories more slowly, so together we might be able to transform these narratives. I always asked these remarkable women how they had gotten through it; what had served their strength; how was it that they had not given into despair but kept their kids safe, and how was it that they could be there for their mothers, sisters, brothers under these frightening circumstances? The act of recalling their inner and interpersonal resources seemed to inspire some of them as they shared these painful stories with me. I saw that if we manipulate others into not sharing so we don't have to hear, so we don't have to listen, or if we react with horror or abandon the scene, we stifle our empathy and rob ourselves of this fundamental virtue of humanity.

I am aware that we have to be careful about not retraumatizing those who have suffered when we listen to their stories. Sometimes recalling these narratives of suffering can serve both teller and listener; sometimes not. When sitting with people who have experienced and survived deep harm, I always ask a person to find what aided them, how they have managed to rebuild their lives, what has been their greatest resource in times of great difficulty.

The experience of empathic distress and its siblings, secondary and vicarious trauma, often arouse a storm of reactivity and fear within us— one powerful enough to shatter us and our world. But if we are patient and careful with ourselves and others, the narratives can shift from dreadful to heroic, and what was traumatizing in the past can become medicine for the present and the future.

Empathy Is Not Compassion

My friend Matthieu Ricard, a Tibetan Buddhist monk who has spent decades practicing in the Himalayas, has collaborated with scientists over the years in experiments that explore the effects of meditation practice on the mind and body. One experiment in particular provides an excellent illustration of empathic distress, as well as of the distinction between empathy and compassion.

In 2011, under the guidance of neuroscientist Tania Singer and her team at the Max Planck Institute in Germany, Matthieu climbed into an fMRI machine and was asked to generate empathy when contemplating the suffering of others. The night before, Matthieu had watched a BBC documentary about orphans in Romania. He was deeply disturbed by their plight. Although the children were fed and washed, they failed to thrive, as they received little to no human affection.

Matthieu shared that for these orphans, "the lack of affection had caused severe symptoms of apathy and vulnerability. Many children were rocking back and forth for hours and their health was actually in such a bad state that deaths were regular in this orphanage. Even when being washed, many of these children winced with pain and the slightest hit could lead to a broken leg or arm."

While in the fMRI machine, Matthieu mentally immersed himself in the suffering of these children, visualizing them vividly and sensing into their horrendous situation as though he were one of them. Rather than modulate his experience of their suffering, he allowed himself to feel their pain and suffering as deeply as possible. Before long, he felt overwhelmed, drained, and exhausted.

After an hour of this intense practice, Matthieu was given the choice to continue with the empathy practice or to switch to compassion meditation. He said, "Without the slightest hesitation, I agreed to continue the scanning with compassion meditation, because I felt so drained after the empathic resonance."

He proceeded with compassion meditation, continuing to focus on the suffering of the children. During this phase of the session, however, Matthieu intentionally generated feelings of love, kindness, concern, and altruism as he brought to mind the extreme human suffering of these orphans.

As the experiment concluded, Matthieu described his experience during the compassion meditation as a warm, positive state coupled with a strong desire to be of service to the children. This was in distinct contrast to his earlier experience with empathy (actually empathic distress), which was completely draining and debilitating.

His brain reflected these remarkable differences as well. Brain scans showed that his experience of empathy had registered in the neural networks associated with pain. These areas have been shown to be associated with both the emotional component (but not the sensory component) of experiencing pain oneself and with observing another in pain. Whereas the compassion phase of his experience had registered in different neural networks—those associated with positive emotion, maternal love, and feelings of affiliation. The dramatic difference between empathy and compassion surprised the researchers.

Later, Matthieu shared with me that during the compassion meditation, he had been flooded with feelings of love and tenderness, and afterward he felt fresh and inspired. He wrote, "Subsequently engaging in compassion meditation completely altered my mental landscape. Although the images of the suffering children were still as vivid as before, they no longer induced distress. Instead, I felt natural and boundless love for these children and the courage to approach and console them. In addition, the distance between myself and the children had completely disappeared."

What Matthieu experienced was similar to my experience with Dolma, the little Nepali girl who had suffered from terrible burns. At that time, I was unaware of the neurological differences between empathy and compassion—but I knew I had to shift out of my identification with the child's agony and into a state where I was grounded and full of gratitude for those who were saving her life. After I made that shift, like Matthieu, I felt revitalized by the compassion that had arisen in me.

Tania, Matthieu, and their colleagues reported that this experiment was a turning point in their research on compassion. Not only had they gathered compelling evidence of the neurobiological distinction between empathy and compassion, but Matthieu had also confirmed a significant difference in his subjective experience of these states.

Empathic Arousal

Several years before these experiments with Matthieu, social psychologist Nancy Eisenberg participated with me in a Mind and Life Institute dialogue in Washington, D.C., with His Holiness the Dalai Lama and specialists in education, neuroscience, and social psychology. Eisenberg presented an interesting model that maps the elements that give rise to empathic arousal. She then analyzed the ingredients that propel the experience into either personal distress or healthy compassion.

From her research on children, Dr. Eisenberg identified three braided streams of experience that, when we encounter the suffering of others, come together inside us to foster a level of arousal that initiates action. Essentially, her research revealed that when we're in the company of someone who is suffering, we hopefully can sense into their emotions, view the situation from their perspective, and remember parallel experiences from our past. This results in an arousal experience that, if not regulated, can cause empathic distress. Dr. Eisenberg observed that empathic distress is an aversive emotional reaction that can lead us to avoid, rather than serve others.

From empathic distress, several responses might unfold. Dr. Eisenberg identified one response as "helping" behavior based on the need to protect ourselves from unpleasant or difficult experiences that are threatening. (Pathological altruism is a good example.) Other aversive responses include avoidance behavior (i.e., denial and apathy) and abandoning the suffering person because it is too painful to be in their presence, a kind of flight reaction that is fear-based. After the conference, I adapted Dr. Eisenberg's model to share with clinicians, educators, and others as a tool for working with empathy and empathic distress. I realized that there are at least two other fear-based reactions that can occur as a result of personal distress: moral outrage (fight) and numbing (freeze).

Dr. Eisenberg explained in the meeting that if the arousal response is regulated, healthy concern is activated, and from there, sympathy and compassion can arise. In collaboration with the social psychologist Daniel Batson, she found that those who are feeling compassion in a given situation are more likely to take action to serve than those who are suffering from empathic distress.

I know how important it is to allow ourselves to include the experience of others into our own experience. Yet also recognizing that we are not the other gives us the space to stay grounded and to experience at least a little humility as well. Finding that balance between identification and distinction is essential. Without making this distinction between self and other, empathic distress is inevitable.

Dr. Eisenberg's model and Dr. Batson's research have been invaluable to me, helping me better understand the complexity of our responses in our encounters with suffering. It also reinforced for me that empathy needs to be well modulated in order to avoid or transform distress.

Emotional Blunting and Blindness

But sometimes there is no arousal in response to another's suffering. Power, for example, can blunt our capacity for empathy, as if our brain had sustained serious damage. An article in the July–August 2017 issue of *The Atlantic* summarized it this way:

> *The historian Henry Adams was being metaphorical, not medical, when he described power as "a sort of tumor that ends by killing the victim's sympathies." But that's not far from where Dacher Keltner, a psychology professor at UC–Berkeley, ended up after years of lab and field experiments. Subjects under the influence of power, he found in studies spanning two decades, acted as if they had suffered a traumatic brain injury—becoming more impulsive, less risk-aware, and, crucially, less adept at seeing things from other people's point of view.*

Then there is emotional blindness, the inability to read our own and others' emotions. Neuroscientist Tania Singer and her colleagues researched an autism-related disorder known as *alexithymia*, which is characterized by difficulties recognizing and describing one's emotions and visceral processes. People who suffer from alexithymia also have challenges distinguishing the emotions of others. The work in this area confirmed what I had intuited from working with clinicians—that our ability to sense into our own somatic experience might relate to our capacity to sense into the emotional and physical experiences of others. Conversely, the inability to sense into our own visceral processes might be connected to a diminished capacity for empathy.

In another important study, Tania and her colleagues learned that the act of tuning in to our own visceral processes (heart rate, breathing, etc.) lights up the neural networks associated with empathy. This particular study suggests that the ability to focus on our somatic experience, a skill that meditators may take to a high level of development, might in turn nourish our ability to be more empathic.

For years, I had observed how doctors and nurses often ignored their own physical needs, such as hunger, bathroom needs, and sleep, as they cared for their patients. As well, many shared with me that in their training they were basically discouraged from being empathic (it was not "professional"!); yet, at the same time, they knew that they weren't really connecting with those whom they were serving and felt uncomfortable about how they were as clinicians. Hearing this so often, I realized that it might be important to give people the skills to develop healthy empathy. Because of the findings about the relationship between somatic awareness and empathy, I modified the curriculum of Upaya's clinician training program to include a stronger component of physical practice and attunement to the body in order to enhance the capacity for healthy empathy.

Between Gift and Invasion

Leslie Jamison writes in *The Empathy Exams*, "Empathy is always perched precariously between gift and invasion." In the case of empathic distress, the invasion goes both ways, potentially affecting both the receiver and the giver of empathy. Not having clear boundaries between self and other can cause harm to both parties. At the same time, if our boundaries between self and other create too much distance, we might objectify the other or lose our sense of caring.

In an interview with *Harper's*, Jamison said,

> I'm interested in everything that might be flawed or messy about empathy—how imagining other lives can constitute a kind of tyranny, or artificially absolve our sense of guilt or responsibility; how feeling empathy can make us feel we've done something good when we actually haven't. . . . [W]e start to like the feeling of feeling bad for others; it can make us feel good about ourselves. So there's a lot of danger attached to empathy: it might be self-serving or self-absorbed; it might lead our moral reasoning astray, or supplant moral reasoning entirely. But do I

want to defend it, despite acknowledging this mess? More like: I want
to defend it by *acknowledging this mess.*

Developmental psychologist Paul Bloom expands on how empathy can lead our moral reasoning astray. We can identify with and have empathy for our so-called "in-group" at the expense of those who are not like us. "Empathy leads somebody like me to prefer . . . people in my neighborhood over strangers. . . . It's easy to see upon reflection that's a really bad guide to policy."

Another moral issue is whether we are "allowed" to feel empathy for people widely regarded as villains. After writing and posting a poem that mused about the feelings of Boston Marathon bomber Dzhokhar Tsarnaev, blogger Amanda Palmer received death threats and widespread rebuke from both conservative and liberal journalists. On the other hand, it's a mark of good art when writers and filmmakers are able to make us feel empathy for unsavory characters, such as in the novel *Lolita* or the TV show *Breaking Bad*. And understanding how others think, especially those who are very different from us, is an important factor in creating social change.

One messy thing about empathy is that we can't be sure whether our connection to another's experience might be just our own projection, desire, aspiration, or delusion—or whether it's kind of real. As Jamison writes, "Imagining someone else's pain with too much surety can be as damaging as failing to imagine it."

Maintaining humility is important as we navigate our relationship with someone who is suffering. Rowan Williams, a former archbishop of Canterbury, spoke at Harvard about empathy and its grounding in humility: "The ethically significant expression of . . . empathy would be in saying not, 'I know how you feel,' but, 'I have no idea how you feel.' " When we come from this place of Not-Knowing, we realize that we cannot truly embody the experience of another, and we can better modulate our empathic response.

Eve Marko, my friend and the wife of Roshi Bernie Glassman, has written eloquently about receiving empathy from those who thought they understood her experience. Bernie suffered a stroke in January 2016. Consolation and advice poured in from everywhere. In the midst of carrying so much, for Bernie and for herself, Eve wrote: "The biggest lesson I've learned over these past 34 days since Bernie's stroke is how hard it is to simply bear witness and listen. So many people are ready to tell me how I feel or felt, i.e., 'You must have been so scared!,' 'How awful this must be for you,' etc. I feel like telling them . . . How do you know?"

She continues, "I also make assumptions about what other people must be thinking and feeling. Maybe I picked it up in Empathy 101: Imagine how someone may be feeling and right away empathize, i.e., 'How terrible this must be for you!' Maybe it is, and maybe it isn't. How do I know how you're feeling till I ask, and then listen to the answer?"

Eve describes the experience she would rather have. "I am most grateful for the silence that deep listening affords me, when someone sits across from me or else is quiet at the other end of the phone line, patiently letting me think things out, waiting for me till certain emotions finally surface and I can speak them out loud. . . . Don't cover up the uneasy silence by apologizing, backtracking, second-guessing, noticing that it's begun to rain, or thanking her for the coffee. Let the silence be while s/he is considering your request, wait for them to give an answer."

Eve is asking us to listen and to not assume we know anything about another's suffering. She is suggesting that we practice Not-Knowing and Bearing Witness, the first two tenets of the Zen Peacemaker Order, which her husband, Roshi Bernie, founded. Humility means that we keep our own projections and interpretations out of the picture, to the extent that we are able, and we remain open and respectful of the other's experience, while being honest about our own strengths and limitations.

III. EMPATHY AND THE OTHER EDGE STATES

EMPATHY IS CLOSELY WOVEN TOGETHER with the other Edge States. When we are experiencing empathic distress, we may attempt to relieve others' suffering through heroic caregiving attempts that smack of pathological altruism that can easily lead to burnout. Our actions may harm not only us but also those whom we serve by enabling their dysfunctions or depriving others of agency. Another Edge State we are prone to is moral suffering; in situations involving injustice or systemic violence, we can easily feel moral distress and outrage by overempathizing with others—which in turn can spiral into avoidance, numbing, and burnout. And Leslie Jameson wrote about empathy potentially being invasive, a powerful example of disrespect.

I remember sitting across from a Japanese teacher in Kyoto. He was attending a training I was giving on compassion. He wept as he told me how overwhelmed he was by the suffering of his students. He was burned out and seemed to have fallen over the edge of empathic distress and moral suffering. Trapped in a highly competitive educational system, he told me that his students were always apprehensive and stressed, and at this point he could hardly distinguish his distress from theirs.

He believed that the educational system was forcing many of his students into becoming *hikikomori*, people who completely withdraw from society. He said there are probably a million young Japanese people, mostly male, who live as recluses in their family homes, and he maintained that one reason for this phenomenon was Japan's educational culture. The teacher worried that he was contributing to the increasing emotional and social isolation of his students through the strict teaching methods that his school required him to employ. Emotionally stressed, worn out, and demoralized, he was unable to separate himself from his students' suffering, and he felt that he could not continue to teach. Like his students, he was breaking down and seeking isolation.

He begged me to teach him how to deal with his empathic distress and his moral conflicts around administering competitive tests and meeting other demands of the Japanese educational system. We spent time exploring grounding exercises and ways to reappraise the situation, as well as approaches to compassion (such as GRACE, outlined in chapter 6). I made sure he understood that these reflective practices were not meant to help people adapt to an untenable situation. I shared that I felt that his distress reflected appropriate concerns about real harm, and I encouraged him to understand his sense of overwhelm as a realistic response to harm. What was important for him to do was to gain his balance and then take action from a place of strength rather than fragility.

IV. PRACTICES THAT SUPPORT EMPATHY

THERE ARE FOUR KEY PRACTICES that can support the development of empathy. The first and easiest is focusing our attention on the body, for grounding and to enhance our capacity to attune to physical sensations. The second practice is deep listening. The third practice is learning to steward our empathic response. And the fourth practice is using the imagination as a way to cultivate empathy and rehumanize those whom we might have objectified.

The research on the relationship between empathy and our ability to attune to our own visceral processes changed my approach to how I train others in empathy and compassion. A meditative exercise, such as a body scan, can increase our attunement to our own physical experience, and it might also extend our capacity for sensing into the experiences of others and make empathy more accessible. The body scan is a simple exercise that involves giving attention to different parts of the body. We can do it sitting or supine, slowly or more rapidly; we can focus on each part of the body in succession, or sweep the whole body with our attention.

Begin by bringing attention to the breath and letting the body settle. Then move your awareness up the body, starting with your feet, then through the legs, pelvic area, stomach, and chest. Next, move your awareness to your arms and fingers, to the neck and head, up to the scalp. Then slowly guide your awareness down through the body back to the feet. To conclude the practice, return your awareness to the breath and take a few moments to relax with an open and quiet mind and heart.

The body scan is a grounding practice that can get us out of the busy mind and into the body. During the scan, we can begin to let go into a more receptive relationship with the body. The experience of sensing into the body can also give us valuable information about our feelings and intuition. Moreover, we can use the scan to sharpen our ability to sense into the experience of others.

Deep Listening

Another way we can foster empathy is through the experience of listening. If we are to truly listen, we step out of self-absorption, self-deception, distractions, away from the trance of our technological devices, and rest with openness and curiosity in the present moment. Opening our experience to include another person is a powerful experiment in inclusion. Really hearing another person requires us to listen with body, heart, and mind and, as well, to listen past the filters of our personal history and our memories.

As a practice, you can choose someone whom you know well or a stranger. Let your awareness gently expand to include them. At the same time, stay grounded. Note what physical sensations and emotions arise within you as you open to their experience. Then see if you can drop beneath any judgments or biases and into a mind that is characterized by curiosity rather than by preferences for or against.

See if hearing this person's voice supports you in opening your awareness more vividly to their experience. What does their voice communicate— what do you hear behind the words? Does listening and being in their presence bring you deeper into their life? Can you sense into what might be going on beneath their skin, in their heart, in their mind? Do you have the feeling that they are "inhabiting" you in some way?

Then release him or her. Touch back into whatever is arising in you at this very moment, and let yourself relax into openness.

Stewarding Empathy

Empathy is often an important feature of compassion, and we need to steward it by remembering the difference between self and other. This may sound like odd advice from a Buddhist, since Buddhism emphasizes that, from one point of view, self and other are not separate. I think we have to hold both truths at once—that we are interconnected with one another and that we are also distinct from each other. We have to walk the delicate balance between opening our experience endlessly and accepting the uniqueness of who we are.

When we are on the verge of losing this balance, we can repeat guiding words to remind us that we care about the other person, but we are not them. I often use the following words as a support when I am sitting with the suffering of others:

> "May I offer my care and presence unconditionally, knowing that it may be met by gratitude, indifference, anger, or anguish."
>
> "May I offer love, knowing that I cannot control the course of life, suffering, or death."
>
> "May I find the inner resources to truly be able to give."
>
> "May I be peaceful and let go of expectations."
>
> "May I accept things as they are."
>
> "May I see my limits compassionately, just as I view the suffering of others."

These phrases, which I learned from Buddhist teacher Sharon Salzberg, can support us "righting" ourselves when we are about to tip over the edge into empathic distress.

The Practice of Rehumanization

The fourth practice I want to offer was developed by John Paul Lederach. John Paul is a sociologist and specialist in conflict transformation and has served as a peacebuilder in Nepal, Somalia, Northern Ireland, Colombia, and Nicaragua around issues related to direct violence and systemic oppression. He has dedicated his life to exploring and implementing alternatives to dehumanization and violence through processes that rekindle empathy, respect, understanding, and mutual identification. He calls this practice *rehumanization*. John Paul explains that rehumanization means fostering our moral imagination in order to see the other as a person first, to see ourselves in others, and to recognize our common humanity. It also involves feeling the suffering of others (empathy) and respecting the basic human dignity of all.

John Paul identifies four kinds of imagination. The first is "the grandchild imagination." By this he means that we should project ourselves into the future and see that our grandchildren and the grandchildren of our adversaries could easily have an intimate and common future. We need to cultivate the ability to imagine ourselves in a relational network that includes our adversaries. Here, empathy is essential in order for us to include our enemies into our experience. This kind of imagination allows us to see beyond our current conflicts and biased ways of thinking. A form of cognitive empathy, it prompts us to work for the common good of all. It also motivates us to understand differences in perspectives, and can be a pathway out of hatred and objectification of others.

The second kind of imagination is making not-knowing, ambiguity, curiosity, inquiry, and humility allies in the process of coming alongside our enemies, those who are suffering, and those who are very different from us. It takes imagination to hold open the heart to inconceivable possibilities, much like Colonel Chris Hughes did in Iraq.

A third kind of imagination is one that allows us to see a different future. John Paul has called this the "creative imagination," the ability to envision the future in a way that rehumanizes all the players and creates the possibility for transformative change, even against all odds. This species of imagination points to resilient purpose and revolutionary patience, the capacity to be not afraid or impatient as we imagine a vaster horizon than we had believed possible.

The fourth kind of imagination is the "imagination of risk"—the risk of not being attached to outcomes, the risk of sitting with the unknown, the risk of reaching out beyond divisions and meeting uncertainty with curiosity and strength. And to have the courage and love to meet the resistance within our own communities and our own minds as we endeavor to end dehumanization, objectification, and suffering.

The power of imagination and healthy empathy can let us see things from a vastly different perspective and can guide and inspire us to resist the normalization of the intolerable. When we dwell in the zone where the two ecologies of empathy and imagination overlap, we can include into our experience the diversity of life and are free to meet the companions of courage and surrender.

V. DISCOVERY AT THE EDGE
OF EMPATHY

A T A MIND AND LIFE Institute conference on neuroscience and compassion in Japan, I shared with His Holiness the Dalai Lama the story of a doctor I knew who was selflessly caring for a woman with breast cancer. His Holiness put his hands together and bowed his head, his eyes wet with tears. But a moment later, his expression changed to one suffused with kindness as he acknowledged the doctor's good work. It was remarkable to see how His Holiness was able to shift from a brief moment of empathy and seeming distress to compassion and happiness.

I had also witnessed his ability to make instantaneous shifts in topic and emotion during my visits to his residence in Dharamsala, where Tibetan pilgrims show up for blessings after their long and dangerous travels into India. We could be in the middle of an intense discussion about science, and when a Tibetan refugee showed up and offered him a ceremonial scarf, His Holiness's eyes would immediately soften as he gazed at the man or woman before him. He would take hold of the refugee's hand, slip into their space, and offer a prayer and words of encouragement. A breath later, he would turn back to his colleagues and resume the technical conversation about neural pathways and the nature of consciousness. It was a powerful display of mental nimbleness.

It's well documented in the neuroscience literature that meditators have more mental plasticity and less stickiness (i.e., when thoughts "stick" or perseverate inside the mind) than non-meditators. Meditation practice, along with an unselfish motivation, can enhance our ability to sense into our own subjective experience and the experiences of others (empathy), yet to let go of thoughts and emotions more easily by automatically down-regulating our emotional response and seeing things afresh. For example, a practitioner may have just as strong or an even stronger response to an emotional stimulus, according to neuroscientist Dr. Antoine Lutz, but is able to recover composure much faster than a novice practitioner. In a paper on attention regulation, Dr. Lutz describes how one outcome of "open monitoring" or open awareness meditation seems to reduce our tendency to get stuck, thus enhancing greater emotional pliancy.

Neuroscientist Gaëlle Desbordes and her colleagues have researched equanimity and meditation. Similar to Antoine Lutz's research outcomes, Dr. Desbordes discovered that one of the benefits of meditation is "a more rapid disengagement from initial emotional response and faster return to baseline." This capacity can facilitate the shift from brief moments of empathic distress into equanimity and compassion.

I remember the moment at another conference when I approached His Holiness with a photo of a young Nepali boy named Tsering who had drowned in the Budhi Gandaki River. An American doctor on our team had been knocked into the river by a huge stone that fell onto the trail from above. The doctor would surely have lost her life had not Tsering jumped into the seething Himalayan waters and grabbed a board for her to hang on to. Though an excellent swimmer, Tsering got caught in a powerful eddy and was swirled around opposite the doctor as they both clung to the board. He saved her life but lost his as he was swept downriver in the relentless monsoon-charged current.

A young Canadian caught the doctor and dragged her onto a boulder. But we never caught sight of Tsering again. A terrible wave of shock passed through all of us as we realized that we had lost a good friend.

Shortly thereafter, I took a *khata* (ceremonial scarf) and Tsering's photo to Dharamsala on behalf of his mother, hoping to ask His Holiness to pray for an auspicious rebirth for her son. As I shared the story with him, time seemed to stop. His Holiness was totally alert, his eyes tender. The space immediately around us was still; the people nearby seemed to be in a kind of slow-motion film. When I finished the story, His Holiness said to me that Tsering would be reborn as a great bodhisattva for his selfless and compassionate act of saving the life of another. These were the words I needed to hear. They were a gift I could carry back to Tsering's mother.

If we can try to emulate His Holiness's ability to quickly shift mental states—a skill we can cultivate through meditation—we will be less prone to falling over the edge into empathic distress. This mental flexibility supports us in making space internally as we encounter the suffering of another and also to stay clear about the distinction between self and other. In our meditation practice, we learn to observe the thoughts, feelings, and sensations gliding and bumping through our subjective experience. The more skilled we are in not identifying with these experiences, but simply observing them, the more we can avoid falling victim to the suffering of others.

If we fall over the edge, and we will sometimes, all is not lost. Empathic distress might serve as an instigating force that pushes us into compassionate action to end the suffering of others and ourselves. We need some degree of arousal, some level of discomfort, in order to mobilize our compassion. We just need to be sure we don't get stuck in the swamp of distress, because it can exhaust us and drive us away from caring for others. If we can learn to distinguish self from other, without creating too much distance between another and us, empathy will be our ally as we serve.

One final intuition: perhaps we don't slip into the skin of others so much as we invite others to inhabit us, to slip into our skin, into our hearts, thus making ourselves bigger, more radically inclusive. Empathy is not only a way to come alongside suffering in our small boat, it is a way to become the ocean. I believe that the gift of empathy makes us larger—if we don't drown in the waters of suffering. And empathy that is alchemized through the medium of our wisdom gives us the energy to act selflessly on behalf of others.

A world without empathy is a world that is dead to others—and if we are dead to others, we are dead to ourselves. The sharing of another's pain can take us past the narrow canyon of selfish disregard, and even cruelty, and into the larger, more expansive landscape of wisdom and compassion.

I also feel that empathy is a human imperative, one that our basic goodness invites us to receive. Remembering the words of the great philosopher Arthur Schopenhauer: "How is it possible that suffering that is neither my own nor of my concern should immediately affect me as though it were my own, and with such force that it moves me to action?" Empathy, when it's healthy, can be a call to action—action that is not about relieving our personal discomfort but about the great blessing of relieving the suffering of the world.

3. INTEGRITY

Without integrity, our freedom is compromised.

Two days before my father died, a flood of stories poured out of him. My sister and I had never heard about his experiences in the Second World War; it was a subject carefully avoided in our family. But suddenly, like some kind of poison he needed to purge, the stories surfaced and our father began to speak.

As commander of the LST naval vessel 393, my father took part in significant WWII events, including the Sicilian occupation and the Salerno landings. He and his 140 men also transported Italian and German POWs across the Mediterranean to prison camps in North Africa. On his deathbed, he recounted how, after landing on Italian soil, his Gurkhas soldiers would drop behind enemy lines, kill Italian soldiers, and cut off their ears. As he told it, the Gurkhas were paid for each ear they brought back to the boat, a grisly currency indeed.

A Christian Southerner, my father had been raised by his family to care about the dignity of life—all of life, including that of his "enemies." But some of what took place under his command violated the basic sense of integrity that was part of his upbringing. A few days before he died, he blurted out the story of an infamous friendly fire incident that happened during the Sicilian operation. A command ship got the word that unidentified aircraft were in the area. Jumpy and exhausted, my father's

men mistook the Allied planes for Axis warplanes. All the Allied naval
vessels in the area started firing on the Allied planes, which apparently
didn't have the code to identify themselves as friends. My father, not
convinced that the planes were enemy aircraft, tried to hold back his
trigger-happy crew, but to no avail. A total of 164 Allied men were killed
and 383 injured.

As our father spoke, I realized that he had experienced great moral
suffering during the war and for decades afterward. Moral suffering is an
emotional complex that my friend and colleague Dr. Cynda Rushton,
endowed professor of clinical ethics and nursing at Johns Hopkins
University, defines as "the distress or anguish experienced in response to
moral harms, wrongs or failures." We suffer morally because we have
integrity and a conscience; it hurts when integrity and conscience are
violated by others or ourselves.

Sadly, my father had never addressed this suffering during the course
of his life. He had served nobly, endeavoring to live by his values under
difficult circumstances. Only as he was actively dying did he express the
anguish and shame that had lain hidden in his heart, a terrible fuel that
had secretly fed his depression and despair as a middle-aged man.

Integrity was a value that my father held dear, one that encompasses
honesty and adherence to moral and ethical principles. The Oxford
English Dictionary defines it as "the state of being whole and undivided."
When our integrity is compromised, we feel divided inside and separated
from our values, as I'm sure my father did.

If we can stand on the high ridge of integrity, keeping our words and
actions in alignment with our values, we can escape harm. But when we
are not able to act in a way that is congruent with our deepest values, we
fall over the edge into moral suffering. There, the feelings of futility, dread,
anger, and disgust can make us sick—emotionally, physically, and
spiritually.

Listening to our father's deathbed stories, my sister and I gained a
greater understanding of his long and quiet torment. The disinhibition
that dying provides activated deep levels of his psyche, and, even though

his disclosures were emotionally charged, he seemed not to be afraid of his imminent death. Part of completing his life was sharing with us the assault on his conscience experienced during the war. I felt he was trying to teach us something about the human values of courage, dignity, and restraint— restraint of himself and his gunners.

At the conclusion of these episodes of sharing, after a period of physical flailing, our father dropped into a peaceful place. My sister and I had borne witness to his suffering and held his truth so he could let go of it. In the end, he was free to die blameless and without shame, which was a gift to all of us.

I. STANDING AT THE HIGH EDGE
OF INTEGRITY

I AM NOT A MORAL philosopher. Even so, investigating the nature of integrity and morality has been an important part of my practice and my
life. In my work as an anthropologist, I discovered that there are many moral
platforms and that notions of what is right and wrong vary from culture to
culture, even from person to person. Yet Buddhism gave me a new way to
understand integrity—one that looks through the lens of suffering. When
we cause suffering to others or ourselves, our integrity is violated. When we
alleviate the suffering of others, our integrity is affirmed.

To have integrity is to have a conscious commitment to honor strong
moral and ethical principles. The words *morality* and *ethics* have various definitions. Throughout this exploration of integrity, however, *morality* will
refer to our personal values related to dignity, honor, respect, and care. *Ethics* will refer to the codified sets of beneficial and constructive principles that
guide society and institutions and to which we are held accountable.

Our values are reflected in our character and are what affirm or destroy
our integrity. Without integrity, our freedom is compromised. I have seen that
integrity can have a fragile edge—perhaps more fragile than that of the other
Edge States. By this I mean that it often takes an experience of moral anguish,
a push, a slip, or a tumble over the edge into the chasm of suffering, to affirm
or reveal integrity. That's why most of the stories I share about integrity include
a component of suffering. These stories emphasize *moral sensitivity* (our ability

to detect moral conflicts and dilemmas) and *moral discernment* (our ability to assess which actions are morally justifiable). They also include large doses of *moral nerve*, a term used by the author Joan Didion to describe someone who has nonnegotiable virtue when standing above the abyss of harm.

Moral Nerve and Radical Realism

The life of Civil Rights Movement leader Fannie Lou Hamer offers a powerful and poignant illustration of how integrity is an Edge State and how courage, wisdom, and compassion play a role in helping us thrive on the high edge of integrity. I was fortunate to learn about Fannie Lou Hamer during the Mississippi Freedom Summer voting registration initiative in 1964. We were both members of the Student Nonviolent Coordinating Committee (SNCC). In 1965, the physicist David Finkelstein and I organized a fundraiser for SNCC in New York City, and we asked Fannie Lou to keynote this gathering.

That night in Greenwich Village, we all drew close to our honored speaker to hear her vision of racial justice and to listen to her powerful singing voice. She also shared her life story. Born in 1917 as the daughter of sharecroppers and the youngest of twenty kids, she had worked as a cotton picker on a plantation from the time she was six years old. She told us that by age thirteen, she was able to pick two to three hundred pounds of cotton daily. Life was hard—worse than hard for her and her family, who often went hungry. She married, and though she and her husband had no children of their own, they raised two kids from impoverished families. In 1961, when she was forty-four years old, she had a surgical procedure for the removal of a tumor. Her white doctor sterilized her without her consent as part of Mississippi's draconian plan to decrease the number of poor blacks in the state.

In 1962, against the orders of her plantation employer, Fannie Lou registered to vote and lost her sharecropping job as a result. She then began working with SNCC on voter registration and literacy. She famously said: "I guess if I'd had any sense, I'd have been a little scared—but what was the point of being scared? The only thing they could do was kill me, and it kinda seemed like they'd been trying to do that a little bit at a time since I could remember." Jailed on a false charge in 1963, Fannie Lou recounted the story of being beaten, nearly fatally, with a blackjack by inmates and then by police. That injury could have ended her life—but it seemed to have only fueled her determination and primed principled moral outrage.

As I listened to Fannie Lou speak, I was electrified. It was clear that her strong sense of integrity, her moral nerve, and her faith more than kept her going through the challenges she encountered. Her actions were aligned with her convictions. Although she didn't put it this way, I am also sure she experienced no small amount of moral suffering—what person in her situation would not as she watched members of her community being disparaged, beaten, and killed in the rural South?

Although Fannie Lou herself was subjected to horrific abuse, she never gave up. In fact, she used her suffering for the benefit of humanity, working courageously with people from both sides of the racial divide even though her life was threatened. That evening in Greenwich Village, she emphasized that she kept her commitment alive by regarding the Civil Rights Movement as a spiritual path. I heard her loud and clear: Show up . . . this is the practice of radical realism combined with rehumanization and the tireless exercise of moral imagination. Fannie Lou Hamer became a role model for me and one of the most influential people in my life. I often reflect on her enormous courage and integrity.

A compatriot of Fannie Lou's was the social activist, historian, and advisor to SNCC, Dr. Howard Zinn. He had enormous respect for Fannie Lou's moral authority as well as her strength in the midst of so much uncertainty and violence. I am sure he was influenced by her spirit when he wrote:

> *To be hopeful in bad times is not just foolishly romantic. It is based on the fact that human history is a history not only of cruelty but also of compassion, sacrifice, courage, kindness.*
>
> *What we choose to emphasize in this complex history will determine*

our lives. If we see only the worst, it destroys our capacity to do something. If we remember those times and places—and there are so many—where people have behaved magnificently, this gives us the energy to act, and at least the possibility of sending this spinning top of a world in a different direction.

And if we do act, in however small a way, we don't have to wait for some grand utopian future. The future is an infinite succession of presents, and to live now as we think human beings should live, in defiance of all that is bad around us, is itself a marvelous victory.

Fannie Lou's life was a victory indeed, a formidable example of moral nerve, integrity, and radical realism.

Living by Vow

Central to our integrity is "living by vow," our ability to be guided by our deepest values, to be conscientious, and to connect to who we really are. Living by vow also points to our moral sensitivity, our capacity to identify morally relevant features in our interaction with others and in the organizations in which we work, and to have the insight and courage to deal with issues of harm.

Integrity can be lived in big ways, as in Fannie Lou's life, and it also shines through the decisions that we ordinary people make every day. Telling the cashier that she has handed us too much change. Standing up for the woman in hijab who is being bullied. Asking our racist uncle not to air his views in the presence of our children.

We might be afraid to take a stand and choose to ignore these situations. We might be in denial or willfully ignorant over the harm experienced by others when transgressive situations arise. We might be morally apathetic or living in a bubble of privilege. But if we aren't trapped by any of these defenses, we will step forward and meet harm with the determination to end suffering.

What keeps us upright is our moral nerve, the courage to stand in principles of goodness. What keeps our integrity on track is our moral sensitivity. We need both a strong back and a soft front, lived equanimity and compassion, to keep us aligned with our values. We also need to have the kind of heart that is wide enough to accept rejection, criticism, disparagement, anger, and blame if our views are against the mainstream. We might even lose our lives, as we uphold our principles.

Your uncle might never speak to you again. Your house might be tagged because you protected a Muslim woman. Or much worse . . . But this is called "living by vow."

Yet many of us have an aversion toward vows. For us, they feel like rules that constrain us. Some of us are rule breakers by nature. Others feel that vows are too religious, and we are hearty secularists. Others simply don't care. We see no reason to make promises or honor commitments. Yet we live in a time of rapid psychosocial change, a time of the normalization of disrespect, lying, violence, and worse. It is important to remember that our vows help us to stay aligned with our deepest values and remind us of who we really are.

The vows we take are a grammar of values reflected in our attitudes, in our thoughts, and in how we are in the world. Our promises and commitments are fundamentally about how we are with each other and ourselves, how we connect and serve, and how we meet the world. Practicing them, embodying them, they reflect our integrity and help give us ballast and meaning as we confront the inner and outer storms of being human.

Vows can be practiced in a literal way, like following the Ten Commandments or the Buddhist precepts. They can also be compassion based, more fluid, and context sensitive. Or they can be based on a wisdom perspective of non-separateness and non-duality. The bottom line is that our vows are a bigger landscape than most of us realize, and they support integrity in our lives and protect our world.

There are the vows that are personal, the internal promises that we have to keep in order to give our lives strength of character. For example, a powerful influence for me has been my mother's life of service. Since I was very young, my personal vow has been not to abandon those who are vulnerable and to always work to end the suffering of others.

Then there are vows that we receive through our religious training. "Do unto others . . . ," the Golden Rule, or the Three Pure Precepts of Buddhism of not harming, doing good, doing good for others. These are vows that we share with others and which ground us in the sacredness of all of life.

There are also practical precepts that help us to live in our world. These are the customs and norms that nourish civility and social cooperation. Treating others with respect. Speaking kindly to others and about others. Being grateful for the gift of our life.

Special vows are those that can transform our selfishness. These vows require that we are strict with ourselves, because they focus on the ego and are related to our destructive emotions. Ego-taming vows teach us that being selfish is simply not practical. Period! Most of us would agree that it is not in anyone's best interest to be greedy, to hate, or to be deluded. Yet, inevitably, we have times of waywardness. Ego-taming vows help us dissolve our self-centeredness, like harsh salt dissolved into the great ocean.

At Upaya, every morning during our intensive practice periods, we chant the Verse of Atonement, an ego-taming vow that invites us to not separate from the harm we cause others and ourselves. The verse reminds us to atone. It goes: "All my ancient twisted karma, from beginningless greed, hate, and delusion, born of body, speech, and mind, I now fully atone." The word *atone* is a good one. *Atonement* means "at-onement," not separating from the truth of the whole of our lives and bringing the fractured pieces together in an act of brave and honest reconciliation.

The most powerful vows are those that point us toward living a larger identity, of being Buddha. These vows support us in recognizing impermanence, interdependence, unselfishness, and compassion. For a Buddhist, this means taking refuge in the Buddha, who exemplifies wisdom and compassion. Taking refuge means we practice "being Buddha." We also take refuge in the Dharma, the teachings and values that guide us to not harm, to serve unselfishly, and to wake up. This means that we embody the teachings to the best of our ability. And, finally, we take refuge in the Sangha, our companions in awakening, even the ones who give us trouble, like our local politician, our father-in-law, our disrespectful employer. This means that we are able to see that we are not separate from any being or thing, and we live accordingly.

For a Christian, this also might mean taking refuge in the Lord Jesus Christ and bringing forth the beatitudes as a lived experience of love and humility. For an indigenous person, it might mean taking refuge in the great earth and the vast sky above, and respecting and cherishing all living beings. No matter our source of vows, I believe that vows are essential practices that support integrity and the development of moral character. Thus, I often say to my students, "Why not be a Buddha now?"

How do we do this? One way is to turn toward those very places that we most resist. We can go to that place we are most scared of and test the strength of our relationship to our vows and values. Fannie Lou Hamer, Malala Yousafzai, and Jane Goodall have stood on the high edge of integrity and faced the hard reality of systemic suffering caused by racism, sexism, environmental destruction, and the disastrous economic disparities of our world. In the midst of radical uncertainty, these women lived their vows to end suffering: continuous vow, continuous practice! Their moral nerve and moral sensitivity have given them the strong back and soft front to meet suffering with what we call in Zen "an appropriate response," which is courage and integrity mediated by wisdom. This is what I believe to be living by vow.

II. FALLING OVER THE EDGE
OF INTEGRITY: MORAL SUFFERING

M ORAL SUFFERING IS THE HARM we experience in relation to actions that transgress our tenets of basic human goodness. It manifests in at least four main forms. *Moral distress* arises when we are aware of a moral problem and we determine a remedy, but are unable to act on it because of internal or external constraints. *Moral injury* is a psychological wound resulting from witnessing or participating in a morally transgressive act; it's a toxic, festering mix of dread, guilt, and shame.

By contrast, *moral outrage* is an externalized expression of indignation toward others who have violated social norms. A reaction involving both anger and disgust, moral outrage at unethical actions can drive us to take action and demand justice and accountability. *Moral apathy* occurs when we simply don't care to know, or when we are in denial about situations that cause harm.

All four forms of moral suffering are present in the story of Hugh Thompson Jr., who was a helicopter pilot and a soldier from Georgia like my father. In South Vietnam on March 16, 1968, Thompson flew over a horrendous scene of U.S. soldiers wantonly raping, mutilating, and killing Vietnamese men, women, children, and infants in what came to be known as the My Lai Massacre. In an incredible display of integrity and courage, Thompson and his two crew members intervened, blocking the American perpetrators and threatening to turn their weapons on them if they didn't stop. Thompson then personally escorted a number of civilians to safety. His moral outrage upon witnessing this out-of-control violence wreaked upon innocent villagers probably gave Thompson the strength to save the lives of some of these men, women, and children and to hold the perpetrators accountable.

The general commanding U.S. forces in Vietnam was William C. Westmoreland. He congratulated the American perpetrators for their "outstanding action," writing that they had "dealt (the) enemy (a) heavy blow." But years later, in his memoir, Westmoreland described that incident as "the conscious massacre of defenseless babies, children, mothers, and old men in a kind of diabolical slow-motion nightmare that went on for the better part of a day, with a cold-blooded break for lunch."

Soon after the incident, Thompson received the Distinguished Flying Cross, which he threw away. The citation praised his heroism "in the face of hostile enemy fire," omitting the fact that the hostile fire was from the American side. Thompson was convinced that his commanding officers were trying to buy his silence, yet another ethical violation. In 1969, he testified against the officers who had ordered the massacre, all of whom were either eventually pardoned or acquitted.

For years, Thompson was vilified by many in the U.S. military, government, and public for his role in the My Lai investigation and trials. Even though he had acted heroically, his suffering related to the massacre and its subsequent cover-up never left him. Deeply wounded by moral injury, Thompson suffered from PTSD, divorce, severe nightmares, and alcoholism. He was only sixty-two when he died.

Thompson experienced moral distress when he realized he had to defy the orders of his superiors in order to preserve his integrity and save civilian lives. His moral outrage spurred him to do the right thing, even though he suffered moral injury that haunted him for much of his life and probably fed his alcoholism (an illness that involves denial and numbness and therefore some measure of moral apathy).

Yet toward the end of his life, Thompson was finally recognized as a hero. He and his crew were publicly awarded the Soldier's Medal for their courage in doing what few could have under the circumstances.

I learned about Hugh Thompson from a student of mine who had served as a Navy SEAL and had attended a talk Thompson gave about ethics in the military. Thompson told the audience that he had returned to My Lai ten days after receiving the Soldier's Medal, thirty years after the massacre. In My Lai, Thompson met a Vietnamese woman who had survived the massacre. She said she had prayed that the soldiers who had shot at them would return with Thompson so they could be forgiven. This woman had undoubtedly suffered moral injury as well, when she saw her villagers being raped, tortured, and killed—but she was able to transform that injury into forgiveness.

It would be helpful to know how the perpetrators of the massacre have lived with their actions. Unless they are morally apathetic, they must have suffered too. In 2010, a squad leader who was part of the debacle said that he did what he did because he feared execution. "If I go into a combat situation and I tell them, 'No, I'm not going. I'm not going to do that. I'm not going to follow that order,' well, they'd put me up against the wall and shoot me."

The squad leader's fears may have been well-founded, and people caught in these kill-or-be-killed scenarios deserve our compassion. Still, it is Hugh Thompson who stood on the high ground of integrity; his moral injury and outrage gave him the courage and energy to take action when faced with unconscionable acts.

Moral Distress

Throughout my decades of work in end-of-life care, many clinicians have confided in me about the moral dilemmas they have faced when the burden of prolonging a patient's life begins to outweigh its benefit. Some have been required to perform CPR—a painful and often futile procedure—on a patient with only a few days to live. One clinician told me a story about withholding blood products from a patient who needed them only because of insufficient supplies in their institution. Many have shared that they have argued with their teams about what intervention would really serve, and were unable to pursue the best path because of hospital policy or patient expectations. Some have fallen into moral apathy because of burnout and lost their capacity to care.

My experience over decades has focused on working with clinicians, some of whom experience moral distress daily. Years ago, a colleague and I were asked to consult with a team of nurses who served on a cardiac intensive care unit (CICU). The team was demoralized and close to breaking apart. For nine months, they had cared for a cardiac transplant patient. The donor's heart had turned out to be defective, and the health of the patient, Roy, was in steep decline.

Understandably, Roy and his wife were desperate and willing to do anything to prolong his life. His cardiac surgeon had painted an optimistic picture, suggesting that Roy would do well with the interventions he was recommending.

But this was not what happened. Over the months, Roy had endured agonizing amputations from gangrene, bedsores, frequent cleaning and changing of the dressings on his raw wounds, recurrent pneumonia, drug-resistant infections, and dependence on mechanical ventilation. Roy's pain became uncontrollable, and he sank into mute despair.

The nurses shared that they had become increasingly distressed as they tried to tend to Roy's physical and mental wounds. A few told us they couldn't bear going into Roy's room, as they felt their care of him was causing him even more pain. One confided that dealing with Roy's gangrene and its putrid odor had caused her to vomit when she left his room. Others kept performing their duties but felt alarmed at the anguish of their patient. Some shared that they felt numb and just simply went about their tasks as though in a trance. As for Roy, he had lapsed into dark silence. After nine months of agony for Roy and increasing moral distress for the nurses, Roy passed away while still in the CICU.

Listening to the nurses, I recalled that Hippocrates recommended three goals of medicine: "cure, relief of suffering, and refusal to treat those who are overmastered by their diseases." These experienced nurses felt that Roy had indeed been overmastered by his disease, and the care they were being asked to provide was not only futile but also seemed harmful to their patient. To make matters worse, the surgeon seemed to have discounted their concerns, and they felt overmastered by him and by hospital policy.

Some of the nurses felt guilty and ashamed for avoiding their patient. Some were totally shut down and morally apathetic. And some were morally outraged, blaming the surgeon for what they felt was behavior that verged on unethical. All of them suffered from moral distress.

During their meeting with us, the nurses asked what they could have done in a medical system that is dedicated to extending life *at any cost*. They also wanted advice about how, under these conditions, they could shift out of the emotional reactivity of wanting to abandon the patient or of falling into moral apathy or outrage. They felt that their integrity had been seriously compromised in the course of caring for this patient and that they had violated their values and principles of compassionate care. Further, they had lost their moral nerve, and asked us how they could restore self-respect and integrity.

We listened. We supported them listening to each other. We shared with them how they might reframe their experience. We explored alternative scenarios. And then we suggested that they explore forgiveness: self-forgiveness, forgiveness of each other, and forgiveness of the surgeon and the institution.

The story did not end with our consultation. Over a two-year period, my colleague continued to work with this team and assisted them in cultivating moral resilience. The team explored meditation practices to enhance mental flexibility, grounding, and insight while in high-intensity situations. The team also examined their personal values and the principles that guided their institution. They saw that their own principles were not always in alignment with institutional expectations. They also explored the concept of *moral remainder*, the painful emotional residue that lingers following actions that violate one's sense of integrity. They began to realize that moral remainder is to be expected in the aftermath of most ethical dilemmas and that accepting moral remainder was an important part of building resilience.

But for the staff on this team, this process was not just a matter of healing. Learning to be morally resilient led to their empowerment. This team took the initiative to change policy so that cardiac patients who are declining can receive appropriate palliative care. As of this writing, most of the team continue to work together on this cardiac intensive care unit.

The Pain of Moral Injury

Whereas moral distress may be short-lived, moral injury is damage that can take a long time to heal, if it ever does. Moral injury is a complex psychospiritual and social wound resulting from a violation of our integrity when we witness or participate in unconscionable acts. It often affects those in the military, for obvious reasons. Like the My Lai squad leader, many soldiers feel powerless to assert their individual beliefs and values in opposition to institutional imperatives. During such situations, the edifice of our integrity can collapse, and we might follow orders we feel are wrong—or we might fail to intervene in the midst of grave harm, even though our conscience calls us to do otherwise.

The term *moral injury* refers not just to the wound sustained but also to the long-term psychological damage it causes. Sufferers are haunted by feelings of dissonance that may last a lifetime and can include depression, shame, guilt, withdrawal, and self-loathing. The feelings associated with moral injury can also prompt the anger and disgust that prime moral outrage and feed the addictive behaviors that are linked to moral apathy.

Alienation is another hallmark of moral injury. Upon their return to civilian life, those returning from military deployment can feel disconnected from their peers, friends, and family. Because most civilians don't know what it's like to serve in the military, they have a hard time relating to the experience of vets, who can fear being viewed negatively for what they were compelled to do. They also may dread being lauded as a hero if some of their actions were morally ambiguous or transgressive.

Of course, moral injury is experienced not only by military personnel. It is a wound sustained by the politician who lies to gain votes and realizes he is compromising his integrity; by the employee of an oil and gas company who is demoralized by the environmental destruction she is complicit with; by the educator who pushes his students to pass tests at any cost and feels guilty for harming them; and even those who try to prevent this harm, simply by witnessing the harm. I believe we need to recognize the extent to which moral injury is found in our society, so that we can better address it.

I experienced moral injury on the night of November 6, 2001, when Terry Clark was put to death by lethal injection inside the Penitentiary of New Mexico. Capital punishment—killing as punishment for killing—is a practice that causes moral injury to many of those involved, even those who try to prevent it. I got a disturbing view into this practice, which is still retained in thirty-one of our states. It touched my life forever.

Terry Clark had been convicted in early 1986 of kidnapping and raping a six-year-old girl. While out on bond that summer, he raped and murdered a nine-year-old girl, confessing to his crime days later. Although New Mexico had not executed a prisoner since 1960, a jury sentenced Clark to death.

Incarcerated, Clark went through the appeals process until 1999, when he dropped further appeals and began waiting to die. I was part of a team that tried to convince Clark to reverse his decision and reinstate the appeals process so he would not be executed. Obviously, we were unsuccessful.

Clark seemed to be a tormented man. A colleague and I would sit on the concrete floor outside of his cell and converse with him through the small food port in the imposing metal door separating him from us. He barely spoke above a whisper, and his cell was always filled with gray cigarette smoke.

On the evening of his execution, around fifty of my students and friends gathered outside the Pen, located along a rural highway near Santa Fe. In protest, we sat silently on the bare ground in the cold dark night. We were not alone. Near us, the family and neighbors of the murdered girl were chanting, "Kill him! Kill him!" After a while, perhaps influenced by our stillness, they grew calmer and began to sing "Jesus Loves Me, This I Know." We all waited.

At 7:30 P.M., a correctional officer came outside to inform us that Terry Clark had been put to death. Our group fell into even deeper silence. I felt sick. Sicker when I heard the cheers from those who had supported his execution. I knew that Clark had committed these terrible crimes. Still, I could not come close to reconciling using murder as punishment for murder. The Buddha taught nonviolence. He worked to reform killers rather than punish them. Following his teachings, most Buddhists feel that capital punishment is unethical, that killing for killing does not absolve anyone. Most of us also object to the concept of "justifiable homicide" because it serves to normalize non-justifiable homicide (i.e., murder).

As it had not executed a prisoner for more than forty years, the New Mexico Corrections Department was not prepared to carry out the execution. They had to bring in a team from Texas. Many of the Pen staff spoke to me privately about their moral concerns in having this execution take place on their watch.

On the day Clark was put to death, I was told that he was so frightened that he asked to be tranquilized. As the execution was taking place, one of the psychologists in the death house wept as Clark, terrified, gazed into her eyes. My associates who were in the death house with Terry Clark were forever changed and ultimately left the corrections department.

We don't hear their stories often enough, but many team members performing executions suffer long-lasting anguish. "When the switch was thrown that first time, and I realized I had just killed a man, that was pretty traumatic," Dr. Allen Ault told *The Guardian*. In the mid-nineties, as then commissioner of the Georgia Department of Corrections, Ault gave the order for five executions by electric chair. "Then to have to do it again and again and again, it got so that I absolutely could not go through with it," he said.

These premeditated killings made Ault feel degraded to a level "lower than the most despicable person." After the fifth execution, Ault's distress was so strong that he resigned from his post. To this day, he still feels haunted by the men whose lives he ended. "I don't remember their names, but I still see them in my nightmares," he said.

Several of his team members sought therapy for handling their trauma. Ault said he personally knows three people who have participated in executions and who later committed suicide. They were not able to integrate the moral remainder, and moral injury and then death were the outcome.

When moral remainder keeps us awake and populates our nightmares with demons, we suffer. Ault quit; others have taken their own lives. Just as physical pain tells us that something is wrong in our bodies, moral suffering tells us that our integrity is being violated, and this information can help us guide our actions back into alignment with our values. Like Ault and my associates who left, we can remove ourselves from the situation while simultaneously working to change the system's institutional violence.

Moral Outrage and the Stickiness of Anger and Disgust

Then there is moral outrage. One summer evening in the sixties, I stepped out of the building where I lived in New York City and came upon the startling scene of a man yelling at a woman. Suddenly, the man ripped off a radio antenna from the car he was standing next to and began to whip the woman with it. Without thinking, I put my body between them and shouted at him to stop. Morally outraged, I had no thought to my own safety. The scene of a man abusing a woman set me afire, and I reacted accordingly.

Moral outrage has been defined as a response of anger and disgust in relation to a perceived moral violation. In that street scene, I was not only witnessing physical violence but gender violence as well. Fifty years later, the sensation in my body of encountering that violence is still present for me. It was the shock of outrage and revulsion, and nothing could have stopped me from moving between the two of them.

As I stood there, heart pounding, the woman hurriedly thanked me and fled from the scene. The man threw the antenna on the street, snarled at me, and walked away. In retrospect, I am pretty sure I was not acting from egoic motivations when I tried to stop the violence; I wasn't out to gain the approval from others or boost my self-esteem. I had no time for a self-centered thought—I simply could not slip by this horrifying scene without intervening.

What motivated my action was a quick and deep surge of moral outrage combined with compassion.

Over the years, I've witnessed moral outrage manifesting in healthy and unhealthy forms in the worlds of politics, activism, journalism, medicine, and in my own experience. Attempting to dig below the surface, I've seen that moral outrage, like pathological altruism, can sometimes reflect an unacknowledged need to be perceived as a "good" person, and we may believe that our superior moral stance makes us appear more trustworthy and honorable in the eyes of others. Our righteous indignation can give us a lot of ego satisfaction and may relieve us of guilt about our own culpability: "We're right, others are wrong; we are morally superior, others are morally corrupt."

The social critic Rebecca Solnit further unmasks the self-serving dimension of moral outrage in her *Guardian* essay "We Could Be Heroes: An Election-Year Letter." She notes that some on the far left often engage in "recreational bitterness," turning moral outrage into a competitive sport by making the perfect the enemy of the good, finding fault with advances, improvements, and even outright victories. Solnit notes that this stance does not advance any causes, and it actually undermines alliance building. Ultimately, I wonder how much recreational bitterness played into the outcome of the U.S. 2016 election by widening the divide between liberals and the far left.

Recreational bitterness and other forms of moral outrage can be contagious, addictive, and ungrounding, and they can make us sick. A small dose can get us going. Binging on it will do us in, and that's what our adversaries want. When we are angry and emotionally overaroused, we begin to lose our balance and our ability to see things clearly, and we are prone to falling over the edge into moral suffering.

However, many of us feel that we violate our own integrity if we don't hold others accountable for the harm they cause. In the face of moral violations, we cannot be bystanders or protect ourselves through denial. To preserve our integrity, we must speak truth to power. This is what I call *principled moral outrage.*

Principled moral outrage involves elements of the other Edge States: altruism, empathy, integrity, and respect. In 1981, the neuroscientist Francisco Varela, along with Harry Woolf, the director of the Institute for Advanced Study at Princeton, and I visited a primate laboratory. The basement lab housed dozens of small cages with rhesus monkeys inside. Harry and I approached one cage. We saw that the top of the monkey's skull was sawed off and his brain was exposed. Electrodes were making direct contact with this little monkey's brain. The poor monkey was cuffed and held immobile, but his eyes said it all—they were filled with pain and horror. Harry sagged at my side and kneeled on the floor in front of the monkey. He seemed to be asking for forgiveness. Shaken, I stood and gazed into the monkey's eyes. I took in what I felt was his pain, and sent mercy to this little one.

Later, I told Francisco that I thought it was thoroughly immoral to do this kind of research. Animals were often sacrificed in the course of neuroscience research. Facing that monkey, I experienced more than a touch of moral outrage. Something had broken open in me. I decided to use my anger and disgust as a way to drop deeper into my commitment to end suffering. I resolved to never let experiments with animals off my radar. As for Francisco, it was not long thereafter that he gave up animal research as well. I don't know what Harry did; I lost track of him soon after. But I did not lose track of that monkey. He lives inside of me nearly forty years later.

I experienced profound compassion for that monkey. And wrenching disgust was also part of the complex of emotions I felt in that lab—disgust at the cruelty that humans are capable of toward their fellow sentient beings. An important quality of moral outrage is that it involves feelings of revulsion in response to a perceived breach of ethics. Social psychologists have studied the effect of disgust on moral discernment. In one study, when jurors in mock trials were exposed to a disgusting smell, they meted out harsher verdicts against the defendant. Disgust seemed to amplify their experience of moral outrage, leading to stricter judgments. Another study found that people who tend toward stronger feelings of disgust find people in their in-group more attractive and have more negative attitudes toward people in out-groups. This might be a reason why moral outrage can be so polarizing—it widens the divide between self and other.

Internally, we may have conflicting responses to our own moral outrage. Whereas anger can excite aggression, disgust can produce withdrawal—which can mean hiding within our in-group and objectifying and avoiding the out-group. Martha Nussbaum, an ethicist and jurist, uses the phrase "the politics of disgust" to critique laws that discriminate against the LGBT community on the basis of disgust, such as bans on same-sex marriage and anti-transgender "bathroom bills." She notes that such politics support bigotry, intolerance, and oppression.

As the ethicist Dr. Cynda Rushton writes, "Moral outrage can become the glue that holds a group together in a sense of solidarity against those who threaten their personal or professional identities, values, beliefs, or integrity. The sense of moral outrage can become contagious and, if unexamined, can exacerbate differences and fuel separation rather than connection and cooperation."

In working with various social profits over the years, I have learned that our fondnesses and fears can easily predispose us to respond in certain ways to moral dramas. When I felt that I had to disclose my concerns about the mismanagement of an organization I was involved with, I struggled. I was a longtime friend of the CEO, and I cared about him. I had expressed my concerns directly to him, yet the pattern of abuse continued. Finally, I felt morally obligated to report directly to the board of directors my concerns about the CEO mishandling staff, projects, and funds. I knew that my affection for the CEO had delayed me in taking a stand, but finally I felt I had no choice. I felt disgust about the situation and was disappointed with myself in not speaking out.

Rational thinking plays an important role, of course, but often a subordinate one. "What makes moral thinking moral thinking is the function that it plays in society, not the mechanical processes that are taking place in the brain," says Harvard psychology professor Joshua Greene. What finally pushed me to disclose my concerns to the board was my conscience, not my conceptual mind.

A chaplain wrote about problems in his workplace, a prison for young adults. "I found that I was actually embarrassed to say that I hurt as a result of seeing what constituted 'care' in the system. How the system itself was set up to be violent, to provoke violence. To witness such suffering in young people, I was upset, frustrated, outraged, and deeply ashamed." This chaplain was suffering from empathic distress, moral outrage, and guilt.

In some ways, outrage is a justifiable response to an action that is morally transgressive, such as the torture of monkeys in a lab or the neglect of young people in prison. But even less serious moral issues, like mismanagement of an institution, can cause us anger, disgust, and principled moral outrage. When moral outrage is episodic and regulated, it can be a useful instigator of ethical action. There is plenty to be outraged about in the world, and our anger can give us the energy we need to confront injustice. Strong emotions can help us recognize an immoral situation and can motivate us to intervene, take a stand, even risk our lives to benefit others.

However, when moral outrage is self-serving, chronic, or unregulated— when it becomes the very lens through which we view the world—it can be addictive and divisive. Shaming, blaming, and self-righteousness also put us in a superior power position, which can feel satisfying in the short term but which isolates us from others in the long term. And constant overarousal can have serious effects on the body, mind, and spirit—from ulcers to depression and everything in between. It can also have serious effects on how others perceive us. In the final analysis, I have learned that moral outrage can have beneficial or harmful consequences not only for ourselves but for our relationships and even our society. Our discernment, insight into our intentions, and our ability to regulate our emotions are what make the difference in whether moral outrage serves or not.

Moral Apathy and the Death of the Heart

We live in a world with extremes of direct violence and systemic oppression, giving us plenty of opportunities for moral suffering. How do we respond to corporate and political corruption, the abuse of women and children, the refugee crisis, racism, economic injustice, environmental exploitation, homelessness? The list goes on. Part of working with moral violations is to recognize and transform the psychosocial values and behaviors that make avoidance of suffering a norm.

I feel it is essential to not let ourselves be trapped by the need to be perceived as a "decent" person per se. More often than not, we must risk rejection or worse to stay aligned with our deepest values. Author Sarah Schulman notes that instead of confronting the moral transgressions of our society, too many of us have opted for "mental gentrification" by letting our common sense and decency be colonized by privilege. We don't want to be uncomfortable or make others uncomfortable, we are conflict averse, so we avoid the reality of suffering—and systems of violence grow stronger. Many in our world today have opted for mental gentrification instead of dealing with moral transgressions. "The revelation of truth is tremendously dangerous to supremacy," Schulman writes. "We have a society in which the happiness of the privileged is based on never starting the process towards becoming accountable."

This fourth form of moral suffering is *moral apathy*, when our denial, lack of caring, or willful ignorance make it possible for us to ignore or wall ourselves off from the suffering of others. "I'm terrified at the moral apathy," wrote James Baldwin in *Remember This House*, "the death of the heart, which is happening in my country. These people have deluded themselves for so long that they really don't think I'm human."

I grew up in a place nicknamed "White Town," a "restricted" community in southern Florida where neither Jews nor African Americans were allowed to live. Our family and our community lived in a bubble. The counterpart of "White Town" was "Colored Town," literally on the other side of the railroad tracks.

Every workday, my father would get into his Ford Thunderbird or Lincoln Continental and cross the tracks to drive to Colored Town's not-so-Grand Avenue to pick up Lila Robinson. My family had hired Lila in 1946, when I was felled by a serious illness at the age of four. Her roots were Bahamian, and her deep roots were African. She worked for us as a housekeeper and cook, and over the years she became a force of loving influence and strength in our family.

When Lila first came to us, I had no idea that in Coral Gables (White Town's real name) we lived in a community of exclusion. Like fish who are not aware that they are swimming in water, our family swam in waters of racism, classism, privilege, and the belief that our religion was "the" religion. We were ignorant of—or we chose not to look at—the reality of the racism that permeated our lives. We suffered from the worst kind of apathy—the apathy that is born out of objectifying the other and denial born out of living in a bubble of privilege.

When my health began to improve, I would ride with my father into West Coconut Grove (Colored Town's real name) to pick up Lila. I still remember the smell of fried food, the understocked mom-and-pop stores, the tired automobiles, the good music, the warmth of the community. West Coconut Grove was another world from my all-white grammar school and our country club, with its golfing, bridge, and bullbat hour. I could not help but see the stark differences between these worlds, and yet I was not entirely convinced I was living in the "better" one.

I didn't know what Lila was paid, but when I saw where she lived with her three daughters, I knew it must have been a pittance. Her apartment was inside a "concrete monster," the moniker for the wretched semi-high-rises built in West Coconut Grove as some kind of misguided version of urban renewal. These mold-filled, roach-infested concrete boxes baked their residents in the heat, and I was worried for this person who was so kind to me and whom I loved.

When Lila told me that her grandmother had been a slave, I was stunned. Merrick Demonstration School didn't teach us about slavery, but I knew what it was and that it was a really bad thing. Still, we didn't speak about slavery in our household. I heard about golf, Brownie scouts, and business deals.

Lila and I seemed to live in two different universes. Yet our universes intersected. The universe my family occupied exploited Lila's and was substantiated by "othering." Without knowing it, Lila, through her humanity, opened my eyes to the white privilege that had protected our family from the harsh reality of racism. And this made me who I am today, with a deepening awareness of how moral apathy continues to poison our world.

There are other bubbles of apathy. One is the bubble of isolation. Years ago, a student of mine who was in the Special Forces wrote me about choosing isolation to avoid facing his suffering around the moral injury he had sustained as a combatant. In an email communication to me, he wrote that as a veteran of combat he had taken refuge in the bubble of solitude to deal with the trauma of war but his isolation transformed into apathy.

> *I have been ordered into situations created by entitled men who deferred their way out of such experiences. I have seen that war creates nothing but victims. To date, the United States has still not officially recognized the actual number of dead civilians in the Iraqi war, nor will it adequately respond to war's debilitating effects on its own soldiers and their families. In a sense, I, too, was one of the invisible, and to cope I retreated to the mountains in order to be alone. In my isolation, meditation, reading, and reflecting on the dharma helped a great deal, but I was without community or purpose. My isolation eventually moved beyond healing and became a crutch: I became apathetic and safe.*

This man had the courage to step out of his apathy and enter Upaya's Buddhist Chaplaincy Training Program as a way to explore how to serve others. He had a lot of healing to do. When he spoke about the missions he served in, I could see that he was deeply wounded by war. His story gave me a more nuanced understanding about what it was to be morally injured and to take refuge in apathy. Guilt, shame, and self-loathing were part of his experience of moral injury, as was denial. And, in the end, he rediscovered his courage and compassion. I had to admire his will to heal.

James Baldwin identified the antidote to apathy: "Not everything that is faced can be changed. But nothing will change if it is not faced." My Special Forces student came into Upaya's Buddhist Chaplaincy Training Program as a way to abandon his protective isolation and face his suffering.

In my own way, I resisted the lure of moral apathy by participating in the Civil Rights Movement of the sixties, as it compelled me to face the horrors of racial injustice. It also showed me the necessity of entering various charnel grounds of suffering in order to better understand them. My experiences volunteering in a hospital psych ward in New Orleans in my early twenties, protesting the war in Vietnam and later other wars, sitting with dying people, teaching meditation in prison, and bearing witness at Los Alamos and Auschwitz all have probably thinned the skin of the privilege that I was born into.

Roshi Bernie Glassman calls such journeys "taking a plunge." By taking plunges, we can transform ourselves—and, ideally, we can also help to transform the institutions and cultures that engage in harm. But to take a plunge and be in a charnel ground—like Syria, a prison, or illness—we need will, determination, staying power, and finally love and wisdom. These environments are where moral character is shaped and where real integrity can be born.

III. INTEGRITY AND THE
OTHER EDGE STATES

M ORAL SUFFERING IS AN ECOSYSTEM that can feed into the toxic side of all the Edge States: pathological altruism, empathic distress, disrespect, and burnout.

In the summer of 2016, Kosho Durel, a Upaya resident, and Joshin Byrnes, who developed a project on homelessness for Upaya, led a Street Retreat with nine practitioners in San Francisco, a city where about 6,700 people live on the streets. As I have described, Street Retreats were developed by Roshi Bernie as a way for practitioners to take a plunge into the reality of homelessness and better understand the systemic forces that keep people subject to oppression. Retreat participants sleep on the street, beg for money and food, eat at soup kitchens, walk and talk with whomever they meet, bear witness to drug deals and thefts and hunger, and touch into the vulnerability they feel in this situation. Most participants experience moral suffering as they gain an intimate view of our society's classism, racism, and moral apathy. They are compelled to practice Not-Knowing and Bearing Witness and are often inspired toward Compassionate Action.

For the 2016 San Francisco Street Retreat, Kosho and Joshin arrived early to scout out the soup kitchens and safe places on the streets where they could sleep. Kosho wrote that walking through the Tenderloin District, he "was shocked by the number of people living on the street, the drug use, the litter and pollution, the crumbling buildings, the crumbling bodies of people."

Kosho and Joshin decided to visit the soup kitchen run by Glide Memorial Church, a historically progressive Methodist church engaged with race, class, and LGBTQ rights. The soup kitchen was not what they expected. Kosho describes its basement cafeteria as a room with concrete floors, metal furniture, and thirty-foot-high walls "painted a sanitizing yet unclean pale blue like a waterless swimming pool." He wrote that between fifty and one hundred people were eating on their meal ticket shift; they ate silently with their heads down and then were pushed along so that the next shift could eat.

He and Joshin "emerged shaken" from their experience, with probably a significant dose of empathic distress and moral outrage. They then made their way to the United Nations Plaza in the Civic Center area. "There, people smoked crack by the fountain, disabled people moved along in wheelchairs or took rest, and disabled people with mental illnesses wandered aimlessly. Others just sat on the concrete chatting."

Kosho noticed a pillar in the plaza that is engraved with the UN's Preamble to the Universal Declaration of Human Rights: "Whereas recognition of the inherent dignity and of the equal and inalienable rights of all members of the human family is the foundation of freedom, justice and peace in the world, / Whereas disregard and contempt for human rights have resulted in barbarous acts [and so on]."

The contrast of these words with the reality of the San Francisco streets was a big wake-up call for Kosho. "Young professionals, mostly men, walked by with headphones plugged into ears, plugged into smartphones without the slightest recognition of another person, and I thought, 'This is it, we're doomed. This is chaos. This is so, so sad.' The tech firms have headquarters literally right across the railroad tracks from the Tenderloin. . . . I imagine that these young men are making six and seven figures. To the south, block after block is being redeveloped with new glassy, plastic, metal, and blandly modernist apartment buildings to house the privileged. The people on the street in the Tenderloin have witnessed housing costs skyrocket. To have shelter in this unwanted neighborhood, people have to pay $1,500 per month for an efficiency apartment or be fortunate enough to have government assistance." Then Kosho remarked, "Maybe you're feeling a bit of my moral outrage."

He went on to say, "And yet, in the ethical sphere of my spirituality there's a vow not to hold on to resentment or rage. There's a vow to be aware of all the feelings, thoughts, and sensations that come up. There's trust that allowing all experience—the whole plaza—to penetrate me will transform me. This is the work of uncovering and releasing my biases and prejudices."

I think for Kosho, and really for most of us, this is not so easy. His words remind me of the painful issue that finally became visible for me as a teen: that class and race divide us and are the source of deep suffering. Yet the worlds of privilege and poverty inter-are, as those who are privileged directly and indirectly exploit those who are poor; those who have less means often serve those who are privileged. When I saw the truth of this, I felt angry, disgusted, and helpless—but this was also a turning point that woke me up to the necessity of service to those who are subjected to structural and institutional oppression, as well as to transforming the beliefs and the institutions that engender structural violence. It also showed me that we are all accountable to the ugly truth of racism and the harm it begets. Yet I'm not sure we whites can ever escape our privilege, because it's something that society unconsciously gives us whether we want it or not. Rather, we can learn how to leverage it to help others who are less privileged. I also had to be wary of not falling into pathological altruism, which easily could have happened.

I believe that Kosho had a similar experience. "You see, I have this class trigger that gets pulled," he said. "And then I want to keep firing. It's a manifestation of anger reinforced by what I've seen and how I've seen throughout my three decades of life. Maybe it's fear that narrowed my sight. Seeing everything as 'us versus them' can be a way of coping with pain and feeling safe, but it's in the avoiding of feeling the pain of privilege and oppression that grasping (suffering) emerges."

Kosho discovered that transforming moral outrage doesn't mean fixing the situation. "With many people who participate in Street Retreats there is an impulse to help and to fix, to be the savior for the victims." Kosho recognized the temptation to use pathologically altruistic strategies to alleviate the pain of moral outrage and empathic distress. He wrote: "Participants might try to give money that we have begged for to feed ourselves to someone else who is begging, which reifies the identity of the helper and the helped. So, there's suffering. Less often, I see participants with the revolutionary desire to attack the young professionals, a mythic narrative that under certain conditions possesses me. . . . [B]oth the fixing and fighting modes of behavior arose when I made my home on the streets. I can make strangers by means of unreflective, reactive helping just as much as I can from waging war—even when I don't act, divisions are drawn in my mind. My mind and my body can be and have been complicit in setting up boundaries and breaking down neighborhoods. I don't believe it has to be this way." Here, respect becomes an important factor: respect for the principles and vows that are essential guiding forces in this situation; respect for others, whether of poverty or privilege; and self-respect, which could easily crumble in this fraught environment.

Kosho explained, "On Street Retreat we are encouraged to suspend action, to drop our formulaic opinions about right and wrong, and to let the need to know fall away. There's a great opportunity that arises from this process. We see things just as they are without the filters of guilt and blame. And so I've felt that underneath the anger is grief for the pain of sickness, old age, and death, and underneath that is sadness, and encompassing all of these emotions is a deep sense of being connected, of being one body. Then Compassionate Action arises out of the pure motivation to befriend all of my neighbors, whether they experience affluence or poverty, giving and receiving what is needed. This is a deep relationship, action to heal each other and ourselves."

From our reaction of moral suffering, we can so easily harm ourselves and those whom we wish to serve. Kosho learned that moral injury and outrage, which are often sourced in empathic distress, can lead to pathological altruism. Moral injury and outrage can lead to behaviors that are unintentionally disrespectful and destructive. They can also lead to burnout, when we feel we can't help yet one more suffering being. Kosho's wise approach to being with homeless people gives us some sense of how we can nourish healthy Edge States while courageously sitting in the fires of inner and outer charnel grounds.

IV. PRACTICES THAT SUPPORT INTEGRITY

W<small>E FACE MORAL DILEMMAS EVERY</small> day—some truly confounding, some minor. How do we stand grounded on the tenuous edge of integrity without falling off? And when we do slide into the swamp of moral suffering, how do we make our way back to compassion's shore? When your heart breaks and your conscience leaks through the cracks, you'd better look deeply not only into your own heart but also into the hearts of those who suffer, and into the hearts of those who harm. This is how we can acknowledge the truth of suffering and commit to standing on the high edge of integrity, where we can see both difficulty and dignity.

Expanding the Circle of Inquiry

Our meditation practice can help us learn to be alert to transgressions of conscience and to calibrate our moral compass. When we are confronted with a moral issue that threatens our integrity, it's good to ground ourselves by noticing what the body is telling us. We can begin by taking an in-breath and, on the out-breath, allowing our attention to settle into the body. If we feel tightness in our shoulders, chest, or gut, we should pay attention to that information. Often the body knows before the conceptual mind does that we are in the grip of danger.

Next, we shift our attention to the heart, touch into our intention, and be aware of any emotions that are arising in this moment. Our emotions can influence how we perceive moral dilemmas, so we try to notice what we are feeling without being swamped by our emotions. As the poet Rainer Maria Rilke said in his poem "Go to the Limits of Your Longing": *No feeling is final.*

From tuning into our feelings, we turn our attention to whatever thoughts are arising. Being aware of our thoughts in this moment might help us become more consciously aware of how we are conceptualizing our experience. Our views, biases, and opinions often motivate us to act, and action arising from opinions might not serve. (Roshi Bernie always says: It's just my opinion!) So bring awareness to our thoughts—but maybe don't jump to conclusions or move too fast. We can use the process of inquiry to recognize our tendency to react or withdraw, and to regulate our feelings before they spur us to unwise action.

Once we have a sense of our own situation, we can explore expanding our awareness to include the experience of others. What might their perspectives be? Attuning to their bodies and hearts, seeing the situation through their eyes, we can ask: What's at stake for them?

We can then expand our circle of inquiry into the wider context in which a moral conflict is occurring. We must look deeply into the systems that are feeding the conflict. What might the system need of us and others so that a constructive outcome might be possible? And how can we also sit with "not knowing" and learn from uncertainty?

Wisdom tells us that there is no perfect solution and often no easy way through. We probably will have to live with at least a little moral remainder. But we can commit to learn from our experience and develop a more contoured relationship with our own integrity.

Vows to Live By

I took my first Buddhist precepts more than forty years ago, not knowing how much I needed them. As a young person, I was curious about everything.

I was also experimental, pretty fearless, and socially engaged—and I didn't mind taking risks and testing boundaries. Somehow, I knew I needed a set of practices that would support opening my heart, opening my life to others, and expanding my potential to serve. I also needed guidelines on how not to harm. I needed a way to wake up, to love, and to care more bravely for others. In retrospect, I'm sure that following the precepts decreased the harm I might have caused others. They also served as a path for testing and growing my integrity toward another kind of freedom.

We can see vows as promises, guidelines, practices, and values. In Buddhism, they are the pivot that turns us toward stability and wisdom. They also reflect our commitment to live a life of integrity: to treat others and ourselves with consideration, to care for others, to cultivate a steady and inclusive mind and heart, to meet the world with giving hands. They reflect what we care about, what our priorities are, what choices we make, and what we need to let go of.

When I am not clear about what road to take, I might ask myself: What would Buddha do? This is not about asking the impossible of myself. Rather, it is a reminder that the seeds of freedom are already in me. My vows water those seeds, and this seemingly innocent question has helped me avoid quite a bit of harm.

To make it easy to remember the Five Precepts of Buddhism, I crafted this version, which is greatly simplified from the original Five Precepts of Buddhism but still covers a lot of ground.

Knowing how deeply our lives intertwine, I vow:

1. To not harm and to revere all of life
2. To not steal and to practice generosity
3. To avoid sexual misconduct and to practice respect, love, and commitment
4. To avoid harmful speech and to speak truthfully and constructively
5. To avoid intoxicants and to cultivate a sober and clear mind

Those five vows provide enough material to fuel a lifetime of practice. They can serve as a moral compass that shows us the way and tells us when we are going astray. When we follow them, we can usually stand strong at the edge and avoid falling into moral suffering. This isn't a fail-safe formula, of course. We are human and cannot keep the precepts perfectly nor always live by our values. But I have learned over many years that we need to maintain the *intention* to practice them. We must do the best we can, no matter what. When we fall short, we can be strengthened by humility, which helps us be more compassionate toward those who harm others.

No matter what, it's not a bad thing to nourish our humility so that we don't get caught in the trap of judgment and moral outrage toward those whose behavior appears to be less ethical than ours. Living by vow is an invitation for us to take responsibility for our own suffering and our own awakening, and it often entails difficult choices. Sometimes we have to do the thing that is hardest for us to do.

Practicing Gratefulness

There is one more vow that I feel is essential to integrity: the vow to practice gratefulness. We know that integrity is about wholeness of spirit and great kindness to the world. The Buddha also was clear that gratitude is an expression of integrity: "Now what is the level of a person of no integrity? A person of no integrity is ungrateful and unthankful. This ingratitude, this lack of thankfulness, is advocated by rude people. It is entirely on the level of people of no integrity. A person of integrity is grateful and thankful. This gratitude, this thankfulness, is advocated by civil people. It is entirely on the level of people of integrity."

I have come to realize that our capacity to feel grateful does not necessarily depend on our life circumstances. In my work with materially impoverished communities and with dying people, I have seen that gratitude is a state of mind and heart that is fundamentally generous and open and that is not weighed down (at least in the moment) with wishing things were different.

During our Nomads Clinics in Nepal, our Nepali friends and patients express their gratitude so freely, embodying the civility and integrity the Buddha spoke of. Receiving this gratitude is an experience that is rooted in mutual trust and tastes of joy.

I'm also grateful for the gifts I have received from my dying patients. A wedding ring. A Pablo Neruda poem. A red knitted cap. A small statue of the Buddha. A folded napkin in the shape of a crane. A pack of gum. The gentle squeeze of the hand. A soft smile of thanks. I have felt the blessing of each one of these treasures, as they reflected the integrity, humor, generosity, and trust of the giver. They inspire my gratitude as well.

Sometimes, though, our ability to give or receive gratitude is blocked by "the mind of poverty," a state of mind and heart that has nothing to do with material poverty. When we are caught in the mind of poverty, we focus on what we are lacking; we feel we don't deserve love, or feel alienated from love, and we ignore all that we have been given. The conscious practice of gratitude is the way out of the poverty mentality that erodes the heart and with it, our integrity.

In order to counter any discouragement I might feel at the end of a day, I take time to recall with gratitude all that has been given to me. Sometimes I recall the sunset I just witnessed, or an email from a student whom I have not seen in years, or the light in a student's eyes that tells me they are doing well, or even a difficult moment that taught me a good lesson. Gathering up these moments at the end of the day is a practice of gratitude that gives me a sense of the value of life and of relationship. It is a kind of counting of blessings. But I can't hoard those blessings. In my heart or directly, I share them with someone who could use the goodness or learning from my day.

I also try to write at least one person every day to thank them for the good work they are doing, the blessings they have contributed to my life, or the love they have given to others. As the abbot of Upaya Zen Center, some days I have the joy of writing several emails or cards of thanks for the support of our center. I believe that, like compassion, the practice of gratitude benefits both giver and receiver and enriches the experience of connection.

Meditation also nourishes gratitude, as it can make us more aware and appreciative of the present moment. Meditation enhances our ability to view moral dilemmas with greater clarity and gives us a level of emotional equanimity that supports gratefulness. It also offers us the opportunity to recall our values and intentions and to remember our vow to benefit others. And it makes us aware of impermanence, which helps us let go of complaining; if the present moment is not a pleasant one, we remember that it will shift, and we can ask: What can I learn here?

Our vows and commitments, including the practice of gratefulness, are about living a life of conscience, courage, and non-harming. They are a way for us to open our lives to the deeper truth that we are not separate from each other—that we share a common body, a common life, and a common aspiration for well-being for all. As we come to know this, live this, practice this, an alchemy of gratitude ignites our hearts into the warmth and honor of integrity.

V. DISCOVERY AT THE EDGE
OF INTEGRITY

I N THESE COMPLICATED TIMES, WE have plenty of opportunities to transform moral suffering into *moral resilience*, what ethicist Cynda Rushton defines as "the capacity of an individual to sustain or restore their integrity in response to moral complexity, confusion, distress, or setbacks." When we have moral resilience, we are able to stand strong in our integrity, even in the midst of moral adversity.

There is a Japanese practice called *kintsukuroi*, meaning "golden repair." Kintsukuroi is the art of repairing broken pottery with powdered gold or platinum mixed with lacquer, so that the repair reflects the history of breakage. The "repaired" object mirrors the fragility and imperfection of life—and also its beauty and strength. The object returns to wholeness, to integrity.

I am not suggesting that we should seek brokenness as a way of strengthening integrity, although some cultures do pursue crisis in their rites of passage as a way to develop character and open the heart. Rather, I am proposing that the wounds and harms that arise from falling over the edge into moral suffering can have positive value under the right circumstances. Moral distress, the pain of moral injury and outrage, and even the numbness of moral apathy can be the means for the "golden repair," for developing a greater capacity to stand firm in our integrity without being swayed by the wind.

Over my years of traveling to Japan, I have held several of these exquisitely restored vessels in my hands. I have seen that the "golden repair" is not a hidden repair. It shows clearly a vessel's undisguised damage. It combines ordinary stuff and precious metals to repair the crack but not hide it. This, I believe, is how moral transformation happens and integrity opens—not by rejecting suffering but by incorporating the suffering into a stronger material, the material of goodness, so that the broken parts of our nature, our society, and our world can meet in the gold of wholeness.

4. RESPECT

*Respect is one of the great treasures of being human, ennobling us
and opening us to love.*

When I was four years old, I fell seriously ill and lost my eyesight for two
years. After I recovered, I had a hard time keeping up with my age-mates.
I was smaller and skinnier than many of my peers in my first-grade class.
A group of girls made a sport out of ganging up on me and putting me
down. I don't recall their words, but I do remember how it felt to be
disparaged. I also remember creeping into the backseat of our family's
station wagon after school one day and crying. I didn't understand. My
mother comforted me, but her words did little to soothe the sting of scorn.

The lessons I learned from being bullied have stayed with me all these
years. These days, my concern about disrespect is greatly amplified
because incivility is on the rise. I have been sensitized not only by those
childhood episodes but also by my experiences inhabiting a woman's body,
working in academia, and serving on various boards of directors. And
more, I'm alarmed to observe the abuse that people in our nation endure
because of the color of their skin, immigration status, physical abilities, or
sexual orientation. It is especially disturbing to see others who are seen as
threatening being socially marginalized and banned from our country.
I am concerned about what this is doing to the very fabric of our society,
where dignity is not valued, disrespect is becoming normalized, and lack of
civility seems to be eroding our moral sensibilities.

On the other hand, I think that most of us are aware of the importance of respect in our world today. Life might depend on it! To have respect for others means to honor their autonomy and right to privacy, to act with integrity toward them, and to be loyal and truthful to them. It also necessitates that we have enough self-understanding to realize that we share a common destiny with others; we are all human, and we suffer, and will die.

Anthropologist William Ury writes in his book The Third Side: *"Human beings have a host of emotional needs—for love and recognition, for belonging and identity, for purpose and meaning to live. If all these needs had to be subsumed in one word, it might be respect." When we feel respected, we feel valued and "seen." When we respect others, we stay grounded in humility, morality, and care for others and ourselves. Respect builds healthy empathy and integrity (both Edge States); it also lends dignity and depth to our human relationships and our relationship with the planet. It is the basis of love and justice and the path for transforming conflict into reconciliation.*

This is why I see respect as an Edge State. When we stand on the high ridge of respect, we express the best of the human heart. We can free others and ourselves from inner and outer oppression, while nourishing the roots of civility, safety, and sanity. We can look deeply into things and beings as they are, with all their virtues and failings, and hold them with compassion and insight.

But it's all too easy to slide off the precipice into a toxic swamp of disrespect. If our personalities or values clash with another person's, we may express our disrespect through subtle or not-so-subtle disparagement. When we deny the basic humanity of others, we smother our own humanity. And when others deny our humanity through disrespect, we can feel diminished, disempowered, and demoralized.

On the individual level, disrespect escalates conflicts and causes suffering to all involved. On the systemic level, disrespect erodes the very ground of our society and our world. If we recognize respect as an Edge

State, we can keep ourselves from getting sucked into the swamp of disrespect. And if we do get sucked in, perhaps we can find our compassion and courage within that dark pool. Hopefully, we can discover how respect is one of the great treasures of being human, ennobling us and opening us to love.

I. STANDING AT THE HIGH EDGE
OF RESPECT

I N A NEUROSCIENCE MEETING IN Dharamsala, I watched His Holiness the Dalai Lama stop in the middle of a heady science discourse, reach for a note card, and gently move the card against the flesh of his other forearm. He then handed the card to Tsoknyi Rinpoche, who was sitting next to him. His Holiness had noticed a small bug crawling on his arm, scooped it onto the note card, and gave it to Tsoknyi Rinpoche so that it could be freed. As Tsoknyi Rinpoche carefully removed the insect from the room, His Holiness returned to his high-level discussion. I remarked to myself that His Holiness seems to treat all beings with respect, even the smallest among us.

In Upaya's Chaplaincy Program, we explore what respect is and isn't. In order to feel respect, we must be grounded in integrity, understanding, and self-knowledge. To show respect to others, we must communicate truthfully and constructively, keeping our promises, upholding dignity, and honoring choices and boundaries.

Respect for others is a reflection of respect for ourselves, as well as of respect for the ethical principles that inform healthy societies. In addition, I have learned from working with clinicians, educators, and students that respect is *not* about withholding constructive feedback for the purposes of avoiding conflict, or about condoning behaviors of others that violate integrity. Respect and integrity are connected Edge States; they inter-are, and respect often necessitates us "speaking truth to power," or being clear about what one perceives as harm and calling for an end to it.

Respect is also a critical ingredient in relationships of every kind—if respect is damaged, and it's not restored, partnerships are at risk. I have learned over my years as Upaya's abbot that it is essential for community members to treat each other as friends and collaborators, not competitors. We also need to cultivate deep regard for each other's well-being and to trust each other enough that we can respectfully communicate about situations of abuse. This is about creating a culture of both integrity and respect.

Respect for Others, Principles, and Ourselves

There are three aspects to respect: respect for others; respect for principles and values; and self-respect. To have respect for another means to acknowledge their worth and value. We can respect our opponents, and hopefully, we respect our familiars. We may seriously disagree with what they say and do, and we might not fully understand who they are—but at some level, we appreciate them as people and realize that we are all born vulnerable and will probably die vulnerable.

We can even respect those who bring about harm, if we have insight into the nature of their deeper situation. Years ago, I was not an admirer of the vice president of our country. Often I struggled with my aversion toward the man. One day, I decided to focus on him in my meditation practice. I saw him as a baby, then as a young boy. I considered the fact that one day he would die, and that death might not be so easy for him, given all the suffering he had caused others. I recognized that although I might not want to have dinner with him, he was still a human being—and shaming him would do neither of us any good. I also realized that if I were called to sit by his bedside as he was dying, I would be there for him. I was also very clear about the imperative to take a stand against the principles that he represented. I could separate the man from his deeds. I could open my heart to the person while objecting to his actions toward others.

Since that time, I have seen more clearly the truth of suffering in those who abuse others. This view has helped me avoid getting stuck in the swamp of aversion when I encounter a person who is dangerous to others. I'm not apathetic about the harm they are doing—but imagining them as a baby or a dying person puts their lives in perspective for me. If their hostility is aimed at me, this practice helps me take their affronts less personally—their disrespect is probably mostly about them, not me. And just like when I was working in the penitentiary with those who had murdered, I hold the truth of this person's delusion equally with my perception of who they really are beneath the deep layers of their suffering. I also hold them responsible for their deeds and for their own awakening.

Two Hands Together

When we respect someone, we understand our interconnectedness with them. My friends in Nepal ritualize mutual respect and interconnectedness by putting their hands together, bowing to each other while saying "Namaste," which means, "I bow to you" or "To the divine within you." This is an expression of the interconnectedness of self and other and a recognition of who the other really is. I have observed that one of the first things a Nepali child learns is to put their hands together in a gesture of connection and respect, then to offer this gesture to family, friends, and strangers alike.

The first time I met His Holiness the Dalai Lama in the 1980s, I noticed that he bowed very low when approaching others, as though to say, "I respect you." No matter if he were meeting a Tibetan who had just crossed the frontier or a head of state, His Holiness always offers the same deep bow of humility, not holding himself above others. Just this simple stance has endeared him to millions. "My religion is kindness," he says; his deep bow reminds us of exactly this.

The second form of respect is respect for moral principles. This is about connecting to our deepest values and acting from that place, even in difficult circumstances. The writer Joan Didion called this kind of respect *moral nerve*. From a Buddhist perspective, having moral nerve involves standing in our principles and precepts and recognizing the truth of interdependent co-arising: "This is, because that is." Sitting across from a Buddhist teacher who is knifing into a steak, I see the links of cause and effect, whether the suffering of animals or the cattle industry's impact on climate change. I make a conscious choice in that moment to not contribute to more suffering, and order the lentil stew. Later, I share with him my views on eating preferences.

Self-respect, the third form of respect, is about throwing off the chains of shame and self-reproach. Didion writes that the source of self-respect is "character—the willingness to accept responsibility for one's own life." She explains, "Self-respect is a discipline, a habit of mind that can never be faked but can be developed, trained, coaxed forth."

Didion continues, "To have that sense of one's intrinsic worth which, for better or for worse, constitutes self-respect, is potentially to have everything: the ability to discriminate, to love and to remain indifferent. To lack it is to be locked within oneself, paradoxically incapable of either love or indifference." Put another way, when we truly know our basic goodness, we are unlocked from the trap of the small self, one who is isolated from its connections, one who is trapped in apathy. Then we can let go into the embrace of self-respect, thus becoming an inclusive self who is interconnected with all beings.

Washing the Feet of Others

When I was a young person attending an Episcopal girls' school, Bible studies were required. One story about Jesus has always stayed with me: the story of how he washed the feet of his disciples at the Feast of the Passover, the night before he was crucified. This act of respect and humility was a profound lesson to his followers on love and service.

On Maundy Thursday 2016, another man knelt before refugees in a housing facility just outside of Rome. The refugees were from Eritrea, Mali,

Pakistan, and Syria, and their faiths were diverse as well: Muslim, Hindu, Coptic Christian, and Catholic. In the midst of increasing anti-immigrant sentiment in Europe, Pope Francis washed the feet of migrants and asylum seekers on that holy day. He said, "Today, at this time, when I do the same act of Jesus washing the feet of twelve of you, let us all make a gesture of brotherhood, and let us all say, 'We are different, we are different, we have different cultures and religions, but we are brothers and we want to live in peace.'"

Living in peace. Respecting others. Being a servant to the most vulnerable among us. I thought about Pope Francis's selfless act of love and compassion when, in the fall of 2016, our Nomads Clinic team working in Dolpo, Nepal, decided to wash the feet of our patients. I felt this was a way we could give more deeply to the villagers whom we were serving. In Asia, feet are considered impure, and it's an expression of humility and respect to touch the feet of another. Our team washed the feet of not a dozen but hundreds of men and women. At first, we were hesitant. Was this okay to do? Would it embarrass people—or was it a way we might bridge cultural differences and make a loving connection with our patients?

The first to dip into the warm water and soap up the feet of a middle-aged woman from Dolpo was a young lawyer named Pete. He touched this woman's feet so respectfully and tenderly that I think both were surprised. Then a young man from Northern California began to work; Sean brought a lot of joy to his service in washing the worn feet of farmer and herder alike. Tonio the same; joy in his face as he carefully washed the feet of young and old. A well-known writer on conservation, Bill, was on his knees, washing the feet of an elderly man, whose toes were twisted like old rope.

Bowl after bowl of warm water was brought to the foot washers. Soap, scrubbers, and bowls were readied each clinic day. By the end, our team had washed hundreds of feet—old feet, young feet, feet with painful bunions, feet that were bent and arthritic, feet that had maybe never been washed, and feet that had walked many mountains. It felt like an act of love, respect, humility, and atonement.

Later, I asked the spiritual head of the village, Dolpo Rinpoche, for his feedback. He said, "I was told that you did this. This made the people of Dolpo trust you very much. No one ever touches the feet of our villagers. But your people touched not only the feet but also the heart. That was a very Buddhist thing to do. But also it never happened before in Dolpo. Our people will never forget you."

Water Is Life

For Buddhists, water is about clarity, purity, and calmness of mind and heart—qualities that make compassion possible. Water is offered at shrines in many parts of Asia so that we can remind ourselves to nourish these qualities in ourselves. Our foot-washing stations in Dolpo were shrines of sorts, and with water, we were able to make an offering of respect to each person. I also think that this practice was, on an unconscious level, a way for us to ask forgiveness from all indigenous people for generations of disrespect, abuse, exploitation, and genocide at the hands of Westerners. It was an act of atonement.

While we were washing feet in Dolpo, people from all over the world were arriving in Standing Rock, North Dakota, to protest the construction of the Dakota Access Pipeline (DAPL). The pipeline would run under Standing Rock's sources of drinking water, the Missouri River and Lake Oahe, putting them in danger. As I walked through the raw and rough Himalayas, I thought about how both the Lakota community and the indigenous people of Dolpo have long held a great reverence for water: water as a path; water as life-giver and carrier; water as purifier and nourisher. Water symbolizes tears, cleansing, immersion, the feminine, and wisdom. And without water, nothing grows, nothing lives.

Moving through the mountains with our team, observing the dwindling threads of water in the drying Himalayas, I heard inside myself the Lakota words *mni wiconi*—water is life. The Lakota say that the blood of grandmother earth is these waters, the source of all life. I reflected on Flint, Michigan, its water poisoned by lead and racism. I remembered my friend

Wendell Berry telling me about the sick, black rivers and creeks in Kentucky where mountains had been blown apart for their coal.

When I returned from Dolpo, I learned from friends and students that *mni wiconi* echoed throughout the camps in Standing Rock, as water protectors led a return to respect for the sacred, respect for the traditional ways, respect for our earth. I was moved to hear that the Standing Rock movement was started by a group of teenagers as a way to combat an epidemic of drugs and suicide on the nearby Cheyenne River Reservation. Against the strong tide of suffering, these teens decided to take their healing into their own hands by helping young people in their community transform self-destruction into compassionate action. They were consciously exploring how sacred activism could be a powerful countervailing force against not only the "black snake" of the DAPL, which threatened the drinking water of the Standing Rock Reservation but also against the sickness of self-hatred that was afflicting their people. Learning about civil disobedience from environmental activists, they began to realize a deeper kind of obedience to Spirit and to their traditional ways.

One of my chaplaincy students, Karen Goble, introduced me to Sophie Partridge, a mother and writer, who came from London to Standing Rock in the bitter cold of December to support the water protectors. She shared that besides *mni wiconi*, the phrase she heard most often was *mitakuye oyasin*, which means "all my relations." During prayers and meetings, people used this phrase when they wanted to speak and when they had finished speaking. Listeners repeated it back to them to affirm that they had been heard.

Mitakuye oyasin, a sign of respect and love, is an acknowledgment that we are all interconnected, as Sophie wrote, "to everything and everybody else . . . to worms and slugs as well as eagles . . . to brambles and toadstools and nettles as well as to great redwoods and rainbows." We are related not only to people we love but "to those people we would rather separate from ourselves with an ocean."

"What made my experience at Standing Rock so powerful," Sophie wrote in an email that was shared with me, "was that the people I really respected *included* those who oppose them in their prayers—those who hurt them, pepper-sprayed them, hosed them down with water in freezing conditions, those who fired rubber bullets at them, those who put them in cages, treated them like criminals, who lied about them; they genuinely included those people in their prayers. Their prayers are for the water and for the earth. It isn't a war with a good side and a bad side, with an enemy to beat down. We all need water. We are all in this together. What is good for my descendants is good for yours. . . . We are no different in our needs."

The violence faced by the people in the camps at Standing Rock—the mace and tear gas, the attack dogs, the rubber bullets, the weaponizing of water in the freezing nights—could have torn this community apart. As they faced violence, they might have responded with violence. But the community had vowed to respond with nonviolence and respect.

I read later that Eryn Wise, a twenty-six-year-old camp leader, saw on Facebook Live a video feed of her sister being maced. She rushed to where her sister was being attacked by police and jumped into the fray, throwing herself at the police, according to *The New York Times*. Suddenly there were six hands on her shoulders—water protectors pulling her back. Wise caught sight of her brother's face, which she thought was covered in war paint. "He was pointing over my shoulder and shouting, 'We'll pray for you, we'll pray for you!'" His face, she realized, was covered in tear gas, and he was still praying for the attackers. "That brought me back," she said. He was keeping her grounded in respect.

Mitakuye oyasin, all my relations, shares with Buddhism the powerful perspective that all beings, all things are interconnected: waters and mountains, police and water protectors, indigenous peoples and their colonizers. In Dolpo and when I returned to the States, I reflected on a teaching from the founder of the Soto School of Zen, Eihei Dogen. In the thirteenth century, he wrote, "The mind is mountains, rivers, and the earth; the mind is the sun, the moon, and the stars."

This view of an inclusive identity and the truth of interconnectedness in Buddhism is expressed in the practice of *metta* in one particularly interesting form, where we can send lovingkindness to an "enemy." When we feel disrespect, distrust, or even hatred for someone, we can take a leap up to the high ridge of respect and see that we are all interconnected, in one way or another; at the very least, we share suffering. Then we can drop into our hearts, as the water protectors did again and again, and pray that our adversaries may be free of suffering. We may not respect their actions—but we can respect someone's essential humanness and thus their potential for transformation. It's a way to heal our own sense of helplessness, our suffering and anger, and return to standing strong in respect.

II. FALLING OVER THE EDGE OF RESPECT: DISRESPECT

D URING MY FIRST VISIT TO Tibet in 1987, I witnessed Chinese soldiers bullying Tibetans who were doing roadwork in the far west of the country. The soldiers were mocking the workers, insulting them, ridiculing them. I couldn't help but feel anger, as well as fear. After a few minutes, my heart tightened even more as an elderly man who was hauling rocks turned a kind smile toward his tormentor. I thought, *How can he do that? Where is his outrage? Is he not humiliated? Does he not feel victimized?*

Later, I realized that in all likelihood, this old Tibetan roadworker had seen the truth of his tormentor's suffering, the truth of his shame, and was responding with compassion. It was a strong lesson for me, and a reminder that respect can take many forms, including as an expression of deep wisdom.

This old man seemed to have a view of non-separation that most in our culture do not. We tend to see self and other as not connected. We too easily objectify the other as persecutor or victim, objectify ourselves as a victim, or let others objectify us as a victim, persecutor, or rescuer. This attitude of separation was probably at the root of the Chinese worker's bullying behavior, and it forms the foundation of what I see as our current global deficit of respect.

We kill insects and eat animal meat without thinking. We mindlessly regard the homeless person with disgust and disdain. We share a meal with our partner, our attention co-opted by our digital device. We speak sharply to the child crying out for attention in the classroom as the recess bell rings. In the face of our work demands, we rudely push aside the complaint of the employee or constituent. And we can so easily disparage and bully others who are different from ourselves.

Sometimes there might seem like there are justifiable reasons for our disrespect. When our values conflict with those of another, when we disagree with their decisions, or we are offended by their words or actions, we may lose respect for them. When others are aggressive or threatening in their interactions, our respect can be undermined. If someone disrespects us, it's hard not to respond in kind. And though disrespect can take many different forms, it is never justifiable.

Bullying

Bullying is one of the most common ways that disrespect is acted out. Bullying is the use of force, threats, or ridicule to dominate and diminish others. Many of us can relate to this experience; whether on the playground, in the halls of academia, in the boardroom, in a patient's room, around the watercooler, or in our nation's capital, we have experienced or witnessed the suffering caused by ridicule. Maybe we have bullied others . . . or disparaged ourselves. And perhaps we have been belittled by those who feel they are in a less fortunate position than us. Most of us have also been bullied by those in positions of power—our parents, teachers, or bosses.

Bullying can be intense or subtle, aggressive or passive-aggressive. We can bully by being dismissive, as though the person beside us is not worthy of our attention; or we can be just plain rude and unkind. Less subtle forms of bullying include shaming, ridiculing, and humiliating others. Bullying can come at us from our peers, from our superiors, or from those below us in a social hierarchy. It occurs on the individual and the societal level, and it can even originate from the media.

My interest in bullying as a form of disrespect became more focused when I met Jan Jahner, a seasoned nurse who studied in Upaya's Buddhist Chaplaincy Training Program. Jan remarked to me that nurses "eat their young and each other," a phrase coined by researcher Kathleen Bartholomew. I found this a rather alarming way to describe professionals who are known for their compassion. I urged Jan to tell me more about how this works in nursing.

Jan told me that *horizontal hostility* is disrespectful behavior between people who share the same general rank in an organizational or social hierarchy. Also known as *peer aggression*, horizontal hostility is found in many settings. Corporate managers undermine each other, peers shun and exclude each other, and politicians ridicule each other; even spiritual teachers can disparage each other. Feminist writer Denise Thompson defines horizontal hostility as a "scapegoating of those who are accessible because they are not so very different in power and privilege."

Bullying happens not only among peers. People of unequal rank in a hierarchy can disparage each other even more, in a phenomenon known as *vertical violence*. In the workplace, most bullies are bosses and others in positions of power and privilege. Beyond the workplace, teachers can humiliate students, military officers often taunt new recruits, parents might belittle their children, physicians can be rude to nurses, and heads of state insult minority groups.

I have also learned from personal experience and the stories of others that vertical violence can also move from the bottom up, when people lower in a hierarchy attempt to grab power from those nearer the top—or when the disenfranchised fight back in response to abuse from above.

Horizontal Hostility

Every year, in Upaya's training programs for clinicians, I meet nurses who have been wounded by their peers and are considering leaving their profession. Jan told me that some 20 percent of nurses leave nursing not because of difficulty with patients or doctors but because of harassment and rudeness from their peers. The cost of horizontal hostility to the profession of nursing, as well as the cost to patients and health care institutions, is staggering to consider.

In her chaplaincy thesis, Jan told the story of her own experience with horizontal hostility in the workplace. She was working as an ER nurse when she lost her brother to cancer. Her performance at work suffered due to her deep and distracting grief. She wrote:

> *What followed, within a team that had held me in very high regard for a very long time, felt like a snowball. Mistakes that were minor or average in the fast-paced setting became major events; emotions became the subject of gossip and innuendo. As attention on my performance increased, so did anxiety, a sense of being overwhelmed, and a sense of dread. I didn't realize that my vulnerability made most of my comrades uncomfortable, or that the subtle attacks and sabotage were a form of self-protection. I knew that walking around the corner to nurses in a cluster that were suddenly silent meant I was a topic, just [as] I had seen happen to other nurses or EMTs that were being edged out of the team. I felt observed, watched.*

Jan took a six-week leave and returned feeling much more stable and ready to work. However, her team was not ready to let her back in.

> *A myriad of subtle, overt and covert attacks and cold shoulders made it very clear I should seek a position in another department. . . . A setting in which I had thrived had become hostile, and I learned that "my story," whatever that now was, was all over the hospital. I ran into it in the strangest places. It felt like some of the nurses in my smallish hospital were actually feeding off of my former distress, trying to keep their version of my crisis alive. It felt like vultures, looking for something juicy to suck on, were lurking in the vicinity of my efforts to normalize my work life.*

Eventually, Jan moved to a new position in hospice care in a building across the street. Her new colleagues recognized her grief as normal, and she thrived in her role. Still, her sense of self-worth had been damaged by her experience of peer aggression and rejection, and for years she had to brace herself whenever she entered the hospital. "Somehow, these colleagues had gotten to something very central and deeply sensitive during a time of profound vulnerability and challenge," she wrote.

Why is peer aggression so prevalent in nursing, a profession known for its caring? An exploration of oppressed-group behavior gives us insight into its presence in nursing and in society at large.

I learned a lot about peer aggression in the early 1970s, when feminism was taking hold in the United States. Many of us in the movement soon became aware of disrespect arising among our women colleagues. In fact, the term *horizontal hostility* grew out of the feminist movement; the renowned feminist, Civil Rights activist, and lawyer Florynce Kennedy coined the term. She wrote, "Horizontal hostility may be expressed in sibling rivalry or in competitive dueling which wrecks not only office tranquility or suburban domesticity but also some radical political groups and, it must be sadly said, some women's liberation groups. . . . [It is] misdirected anger that rightly should be focused on the external causes of oppression."

Kennedy was active in the Civil Rights Movement in New York at the same time I was working as a researcher at Columbia. I met her at movement events over the years. She was tough and well-spoken, and she took disrespect from no one. The daughter of a Pullman porter, Kennedy grew up black in a mostly white neighborhood of Kansas City. When the KKK tried to drive her family out, her father warded them off with a shotgun. She fought for her rightful place as a student at Columbia Law School, where she was the only black person and one of eight women in her class. In 1965, she was arrested trying to reach her home on East Forty-eighth Street because police refused to believe she lived in that neighborhood. This experience turned her into an activist, and she later founded the Feminist Party.

Internalized Oppression

About horizontal hostility, Kennedy wrote, "We criticize each other instead of the oppressor because it's less dangerous." The oppressor is also sometimes more nebulous, even invisible.

But the more insidious reason for horizontal hostility, Kennedy noted, is that oppressed people can be complicit in their own oppression. She wrote, "There can be no really pervasive system of oppression, such as that in the United States, without the consent of the oppressed." When oppression is the status quo, even those in the oppressed group tend to fall into roles that reinforce the power-over pattern. For example, women may internalize the message that they are weaker than men, and then unconsciously behave submissively around men. This phenomenon is known as *internalized oppression*. Marginalized people are, by definition, more bullied than those in power—and they often take that bullying deep inside, where it manifests as the inner bullying of shame and a lack of self-respect.

Internalized oppression, systemic violence, and various forms of hierarchical abuse create marginalization and the perfect conditions for horizontal hostility. "Divide and conquer—that's what they try to do to any group trying to make social change," wrote Kennedy. "Black people are supposed to turn against Puerto Ricans. Women are supposed to turn against their mothers and mothers-in-law. We're all supposed to compete with each other for the favors of the ruling class."

I learned at a young age that when men bully women to maintain their dominance, it's typically through direct, top-down abuse—from condescending, patronizing, sexualizing, or shaming behaviors like "mansplaining" to actual physical and sexual abuse. Conversely, I saw in the feminist movement that women use peer aggression and bottom-up vertical violence from a position of vulnerability, attempting to equalize an experienced imbalance of power. I observed that women who felt less empowered often tried to bring down women whom they regarded as more powerful. We see this all too often with women politicians, academicians, business leaders, and religious leaders. I have received this treatment myself, and it is tough. Women who display strength can become targets—not only for men and the media, but for other women as well. However, we should not lose sight of the fact that it is more common for men to be bullies than women. Two-thirds of all bullies are men, according to the Workplace Bullying Institute's *2014 U.S. Workplace Bullying Survey*.

Jan explained how self-respect plays into the phenomenon of marginalization in her experience as a nurse:

> *Historically, nursing recruited young women who valued patient care, service, and self-sacrifice. Nurses were confronted with the common perception of being somehow less than (in maturity, critical thinking and skill capability) their medical counterparts within a health care system composed primarily of (older) male physicians. These nurses, lacking power, autonomy, and self-esteem, at times took on the behaviors of the* marginalized, *looking to the powerful for approval and demeaning their own power.*

The stress of being marginalized is a factor leading to peer aggression among nurses, on top of the stress of facing medical emergencies with physical and emotional risks. For Jan, the horizontal hostility began during her mentoring process. She writes that while some of her nurse mentors listened and guided, "others watched and waited for opportunities to humiliate, under the guise of 'weeding out the weak,' possibly stemming from their own socialization into the nursing profession."

Vertical Violence

Top-down bullying, or vertical violence, is prevalent on both the individual and societal level. People with more privilege often put down those who have less, through comments, behaviors, and policies that reinforce sexist, racist, classist, ageist, and heterosexist structures. The Workplace Bullying Institute has found that nonwhites are targets of workplace bullying at significantly higher rates than whites.

Top-down bullying was a central feature of the 2016 U.S. presidential campaign. The Republican nominee openly mocked and disparaged "others" of all stripes: women, blacks, Muslims, people with disabilities, Mexican immigrants, and certainly the other candidate. Some of his supporters have taken his high-profile example as permission to bully and threaten people in these groups, both during the campaign and in its aftermath. In a high school in western Oregon, white students began chanting, "Build a wall! Build a wall!" in the middle of physics class. Soon afterward, a student hung a homemade banner in the school reading "Build a Wall," prompting Latino students in the area to stage a walkout. Elsewhere, Muslim children were called "terrorist," "ISIS," and "bomber." The Southern Poverty Law Center published a report concluding that "the campaign is producing an alarming level of fear and anxiety among children of color and inflaming racial and ethnic tensions in the classroom. Many students worry about being deported."

As Karen Stohr writes in *The New York Times*, top-down bullying has greater consequences than other forms of bullying. "Contempt expressed by the socially powerful toward the socially vulnerable is a much greater moral danger than contempt that flows in the opposite direction," she writes. "As president, Trump occupies a position of exceptional social power. Contempt bolstered by such power becomes far more effective and hence, far more threatening to our grounding democratic values."

My chaplaincy student Michele Rudy worked in Arizona with DREAMers, undocumented children given protection under Obama. She told me that DREAMers were hiding in fear of U.S. Immigration and Customs Enforcement (ICE) raids on their homes, schools, and workplaces. "Children do not want to go to school," Michele wrote. "One mother told us that her son would not leave the bedroom for three days. People have legitimate fear that they will be persecuted and that their lives will be shattered."

Michele was part of a team formed to respond to this moment. "To begin, the DREAMers will go with their families into the white Evangelical churches to expose their humanity and what this means to them. This is very painful for them because they have to show their pain in front of others, even others who may oppose them, in order for this to wake people up from their delusion. We will ask the churches to stand with the most vulnerable if they are persecuted."

Bullying can come from the bottom-up direction too. I often think about what President Barack Obama faced every day of his eight years in office, with racially motivated disrespect from people attempting to undermine his position. Obama always spoke, at least publicly, with respect for and toward all. As First Lady Michelle Obama famously said, "When they go low, we go high."

Like most people in positions of responsibility and authority, I have had my own experiences with being the object of bottom-up bullying over the years; most teachers will relate to this. The first time this happened to me was in 1976, when I taught anthropology at the New School for Social Research. I had 150 students in my class. In the back of the room were three older women who made disparaging remarks about me throughout the class. After tolerating this treatment for too long, and on the advice of the head of my department, I cordially and firmly invited the women to move to the front of the class.

At first they resisted. This was New York in the seventies, and bullying authority figures was "in." But I kindly insisted, and finally they complied. By the second day with them in the front row, we seemed to have made some peace.

Probably I had earned a point or two of respect from them by not putting up with their insults any longer. But I also was to learn that these women came from backgrounds of abuse; being at the New School was a safe place for them, and putting me down to them was a way to raise themselves up. Yet, in the end, we connected, and I think this is what they really wanted. Sometimes, one has to risk getting into more trouble with people in order to open up the possibility for connection to happen. These women taught me that bottom-up bullying usually stems from the helplessness and anger that people feel toward those in power, and sometimes equalizing power can happen in surprising ways.

Power With and Power Over

Respect and disrespect are closely linked with power dynamics: power *with* and power *over*. Respect can be a form of healthy power, of power *with*. Respect for our parents, teachers, our peers, or those who are vulnerable and unsheltered. When we use our power to advance those in a more fragile position, we are acting from respect and from power *with*. When we use our power to advance our own interests at the expense of others, we are acting from disrespect and power *over*.

Power has many pitfalls. Power can make people more self-absorbed, prioritizing their own needs over those of others. Power can disinhibit people to the point where they disregard the social norms of respect, kindness, consideration, and conscientiousness. And power can blunt, and it intoxicates. I believe that bullies are often drunk on power and addicted to exploiting power differences to their advantage so they can control the environment and manipulate others.

Even in groups where peers share the same general social status, subtle power differences can develop based on factors like charisma, leadership qualities, height, age, attractiveness, and physical strength. Bullies know how to leverage these slight imbalances in power into bigger disparities, taking advantage of vulnerability.

On the macro level, power *over* manifests as racism, sexism, and the other "isms." When disrespect is institutionalized into social systems and structures, it is *systemic oppression*. Systemic oppression is what led politicians in Flint, Michigan, to decide that it was okay to risk the drinking water of a majority black population for the purposes of saving money; for years, neurotoxic lead flowed through the pipes of families with children. Systemic oppression was apparently behind the decision to reroute DAPL away from majority-white Bismarck and underneath the Missouri River, the source of water for the Standing Rock Sioux. In 2016, it undoubtedly played a role in why a woman was not finally able to shatter the glass ceiling in the United States and become president. It is at the root of "religious freedom" laws, "bathroom bills," and other policies that legalize discrimination against LGBTQ people. It also manifests in subtler ways that reveal the mind-sets that suffuse the depths of the iceberg, such as microaggressions like "I don't see you as black."

Systemic oppression and disrespect are primed by "othering." East Indian scholar and feminist critic Gayatri Chakravorty Spivak defines *othering* as "a process by which the empire can define itself against those it colonizes, excludes and marginalizes." In the United States, this colonizing has manifested literally as the takeover of indigenous land and the "othering" of Native Americans—and figuratively as the marginalization of people of color, people with disabilities, LGBTQ people, and even those in our correctional system. It has also fed sexual harassment and gender violence. When we are marginalized, shamed, and subjected to "othering," it can be difficult to maintain our self-respect. Our low self-esteem may not be because of personality deficits but because we have internalized society's oppressive attitudes.

Stripped of Dignity

Then there is our prison-industrial system, a place where disrespect and humiliation are normalized. When I was volunteering in the New Mexico prison system, I developed a twenty-week program for prisoners that included various forms of meditation, including *metta* (lovingkindness) practice. The program also emphasized ethics and communication.

On the morning I was to teach *metta* practice, a new prisoner was escorted in handcuffs into the chapel where class was held. He was a huge, rough-looking man with a pockmarked face, and the words ARYAN BROTH-ERHOOD were tattooed across the back of his shaved head. I took one look at him and thought briefly that it might be better to change the lesson for the day. I remember his name—it was John; he was also known as "the Nazi Biker." The guard uncuffed John, left the chapel, and soon appeared in the glass guard box that could be entered only from outside our meeting room.

We began with a check-in. John said nothing, just glowered from the sidelines. As we did some stretching exercises, he remained shut down and motionless, like cold iron. Then I began the mental training portion of the class, suggesting that the students could close their eyes or leave them open, depending on what they felt comfortable with. My eyes were wide open, and so were the eyes of this new prisoner.

I began the guided meditation, asking the "students" to settle into the body and recall someone they knew who had really suffered. I then slowly recited *metta* phrases. "May you be safe; may you be peaceful . . ." Not a minute into this part of the program, John jumped up to his full height and shouted, "You f—— b——! You don't know what you're f—— talking about!" His red-faced rant, and the expletives, continued.

I had no time to think about how to shift the situation. I caught John's bloodshot eye and said with a kind of firm, humorous humility, "I agree with what you're saying. I just don't like how you're saying it!"

The room immediately melted into raucous laughter. Just then the guard burst in, probably expecting to find me cowering in the corner or taken hostage. But I was all right. I believe that my years of practice had helped me be alert and responsive to the near catastrophe I had helped create. My words seemed, at least this time, to hit the mark.

I was grateful to finish the session in one piece and with laughter all around. But the fact is that this was a tough situation for both John and me.

I saw John only one more time—more than a year later. In the meantime, he had killed another inmate. John, who was up for a capital crime and considered very dangerous, was being prepared to be strip-searched before he was escorted into the pod where his cell was. Our eyes connected for a moment, and I could sense his cold rage as the guards readied him for this ritual of humiliation. I reflected on our brief and complicated exchange the year before, and it occurred to me that he had surely been subjected to much degradation since I had seen him and had meted out large amounts of anger himself.

In our previous meeting, he had objectified me; and I had also objectified him with my defensive and humorous remark, which had probably shamed him in front of his peers. I hadn't considered this until the brief moment in the prison hallway, when I glanced at his naked, scarred, and tattooed torso full of electric tension. There seemed to be no interest in the fact that a woman was anywhere near. I noticed a sharp tightening of my chest as I hurried past this humiliating scene. And I felt that any chance for redemption of this gigantic man was probably lost.

John was being stripped of his dignity along with everything else. As much of a bully as he was, the correctional officers handling him were even more powerful as oppressors, asserting their disrespect and dominance with a sense of utter indifference, as though they were handling an inanimate object.

I felt sick to my stomach as I moved down the hall. I was witnessing both vertical violence and systemic oppression in that moment—dynamics that might also be found in our military, hospitals, schools, religious institutions, and government. I could feel into the rage generated by John's helplessness; I also could sense into the cold, domineering meanness of the guards, and I felt I gained some insight into how bullies are made.

Angulimala

Internalized oppression is an element found in vertical violence as well as horizontal hostility. Those who feel internalized oppression may seek to subjugate or harm those whom they perceive to be of lower rank through top-down bullying. Or they may become bottom-up bullies, challenging those whom they perceive to be of higher rank, as John did. Bullies and tyrants also might be unconsciously modeling learned behavior, or trying to equalize perceived unfairness.

I learned from working within the prison system that people don't tyrannize because they feel stronger than others—they do it because they feel *weaker*, and often because they suffer from unacknowledged shame. They fear their own vulnerability, and attacking others becomes a method of self-preservation.

While working "inside," I often reflected on the Buddhist story of the serial killer Angulimala, which demonstrates how hate can be transformed in the right circumstances. During the Buddha's lifetime, just the name *Angulimala* sent chills down many a spine, for the word meant "a necklace of fingers"—the fingers of the people Angulimala had murdered. As the *Anguli-mala Sutra* tells it, Angulimala was "brutal, bloody-handed, devoted to kill-ing and slaying, showing no mercy to living beings." He was laying waste to whole villages, whole regions, with his penchant for murder.

As the Buddha was making his alms rounds one day, villagers, cowherds, and farmers warned him that Angulimala was nearby, and he should keep safe. The Buddha did not heed their advice; rather, he continued calmly on his alms round. Soon, he heard the sound of running footsteps, then an angry shout from behind him ordering him to stop. The Buddha continued to walk on slowly, without concern, exercising a mysterious power that kept Anguli-mala at a distance, no matter how hard he ran. Angry and frustrated, the killer shouted at the Blessed One, "Stop, contemplative! Stop!"

The Buddha replied, "I have stopped, Angulimala, once and for all. It is you who has not stopped."

Startled, Angulimala finally was able to step into the Buddha's path. The Buddha gazed at him with eyes that were peaceful and clear. Now even more surprised, Angulimala asked the Buddha why he was not afraid. The Bud-dha looked at him as though he were an old friend.

Angulimala said, "Monk, you said that you stopped a long time ago, but you are still walking. You said that I have not stopped. What do you mean?"

The Buddha replied that he had stopped harming others, and had learned to cherish the lives of others.

Angulimala said that since human beings do not care for each other, why should he care for them? He would not rest until all were killed.

The Buddha calmly replied that he knew Angulimala had suffered at the hands of others—he had been harmed by his teacher and disparaged by his fellow students. "Humans can be cruel out of their ignorance," the Buddha explained, "but humans can also be understanding."

The Buddha then looked deeply into Angulimala's eyes and said that his monks had vowed to practice compassion and to protect the lives of others. "The way to transform hatred and aggression into kindness is the path of the Dharma."

The Buddha told Angulimala that he was on the path of hatred, and urged him to choose forgiveness and love. Hearing this, Angulimala was shaken to his core. He realized that he had gone too far down the path of harm, and worried that it was too late to turn back.

The Buddha replied that it is never too late, and he urged Angulimala to turn toward the shore of understanding. He vowed that he would take care of Angulimala if he devoted himself to a life of kindness and compassion. Angulimala sobbed and laid down his weapons, promising to abandon hatred and aggression and to become a disciple of the Buddha.

When I first read this sutra, I sensed that for Angulimala, hurting others was probably a reaction to having been tyrannized by his peers and his teacher when he was a child. The story was familiar to me. I had met many men like Angulimala in the maximum-security prison. Wounded. Shut down. Angry. But Angulimala experienced the blessing of transformation because he was perceived deeply by the Buddha. Yes, Angulimala was a serial killer. But he also had the power of good within him, and Buddha saw who he really was, and called that forward.

In thinking about the story of Angulimala, I realized that I had missed my chance with John. John had murdered three men. He was tough, but in looking more deeply, I could feel he was broken. There was no way to turn back time, and I was never to see him again. But he has stayed with me, as a lesson in failure.

On another day at the prison, an incarcerated man said to me, "This is the first time in my life that anyone has ever treated me with respect and kindness." My throat tightened as I met his eyes. Words would not suffice. But the gaze he returned to me was unguarded. Over time, this man became a model inmate—one who made his way to inner freedom, and eventually to outer freedom as well.

Causes and Effects

Through the lens of interdependent co-arising, we can see that disrespect for others arises due to multiple causes and conditions. On the level of personality, bullies feel a false sense of superiority that is sourced in feelings of inferiority, unacknowledged shame, a lack of self-awareness, emotional blunting and blindness, and the defense mechanism of objectifying others. On the level of motive, there may be a seemingly justifiable reason for disrespect, such as when others do things that violate our sense of morality and integrity. On the external level, competitive organizational cultures and institutionalized oppression feed disrespect.

We also have to keep in mind that the emotional, physical, and spiritual effects of disrespect can be deadly serious. In one study on rudeness in the medical profession, five reasons were given: workload, lack of support, patient safety, hierarchy, and culture. Still, if we are targets of disrespect, hostility, bullying, and rudeness, we may feel anger, shame, humiliation, cynicism, and futility—a spiral of emotions that can lead to self-hatred and self-harm. Physically, we can experience insomnia, fatigue, and the threat-related stress responses of fight, flight, or freeze. We may also develop illnesses according to our particular vulnerabilities.

There are interpersonal consequences as well. If we are subjected to disrespect, we might attack the persecutor or punish them. We might withdraw from the situation to the point of leaving our job or the community. Or we might try to get revenge by finding targets to bully, as Angulimala did, thus feeding the cycle of toxic power. And our coping mechanisms, such as substance abuse, might lead to social isolation, mental health issues, and even criminal behavior. Bullies may also experience some of these mental, physical, and interpersonal consequences as their toxic emotions catch up with them.

If we find ourselves stuck in the swamp of disrespect, we need to try to extract ourselves as quickly as possible. For Angulimala, this was the crisis he needed to connect more deeply with who he really was. Just as causes can push us down the path of disrespect, so also can effects drive us back onto the path of respect, civility, and regard. So it was for Angulimala; so it can be for us.

III. RESPECT AND THE OTHER
EDGE STATES

B Y CONVENTIONAL DEFINITIONS, *RESPECT* means "an attitude of consideration or high regard." Respect is an offspring of integrity and empathy. It is sourced in our views, values, and emotions. The etymology of *respect* is interesting. The Latin *respectus* means "to look back and to consider." By contrast, *disrespect* would suggest "to look down upon" and not consider deeply. When we consciously respect another person, a principle, or even ourselves, we experience a natural pause, a turning back to more deeply reflect. From this point of view, respect is not only a noun but also a verb—a process.

In thinking about the process of respect and how it touches the other Edge States, I recall the experience of Susan, a military medic who asked me for advice on how to maintain her self-respect and respect for her values and principles while anticipating service under a new political administration, which she felt exemplified the toxic side of our political system. She confided in me that she had often felt conflicted about participating in the military because of the suffering caused by war. At the same time, she also sensed she had a deeper mission. She said, "I am concerned that I am an integral part of a harmful system, but I also feel that my proximity creates an opportunity to change the system from within in a way that is more efficient and more potent than working for change from outside the military."

During her most recent deployment in Afghanistan, Susan had felt that her role as medic was Right Livelihood, a Buddhist term meaning work that is ethical, providing her with the opportunity to "bring light into a dark place" and to offer respectful care to those who had sustained the wounds and trauma of war. But she shared with me that as someone with the bones of a do-gooder, she sometimes found herself under the sway of pathological altruism. She was also at times overwhelmed by the suffering she encountered (empathic distress) and the intensity of the work demands (burnout), and she felt conflicted about working for an institution whose ethos, in her view, was in a way rooted in violence (moral suffering).

In her communications to me, she acknowledged that to preserve her self-respect, she needed to consider noncompliance if she were asked to carry out unlawful orders. Even with this commitment, she struggled. "I could continue to train the next generation of medics to provide more than just medical care—to soften and meet the pain and rage they witness with deeper compassion. I could continue to be the voice of dissent and questioning inside of a system that self-perpetuates. But will this be enough? Is my presence an implicit consent? Is it a tacit approval of the status quo?"

I sat with Susan's words. I could feel her conflict around providing much-needed care to the injured and dying, while at the same time, she felt she was violating her integrity and her self-respect. My way is not to advise but to inquire. I thought about my father and what his moral injury and resulting loss of self-respect had taught me. I also thought about students of mine who had suffered from the trauma of combat. And I recalled my experience of volunteering within the prison-industrial complex, an institution where disrespect, bullying, and violence are the status quo.

I wrote Susan:

I have asked myself similar questions about your situation, and also about mine, when I worked as a volunteer in the prison system. How are we contributing to structural violence by being inside institutions that cause harm? I think one has to dig deep. Our motivations (like retirement plans or status) might compromise us, so we end up becoming degraded psychologically because we are complicit in harming others in some way and thus harming ourselves. On the other hand, is there a

way we can be inside the system, and exemplify and uphold the values
that inform our lives? Go deep into the questions you are having, and as
well, look at your life in five years, ten years. . . . What do you see there?
Who do you want to be? Who are you now? And if you were given a
year to live, what might you want to do with your life?

Over the days following this exchange, my thoughts often turned to Susan. Self-respect and respect for our principles can be compromised by so
many factors, including our own idealism, our unconscious response to social
expectations, our desires for material security, commitments we have
made and are afraid to break, our lack of awareness of the depth of harm in
a system we are part of, and misplaced altruism.

Susan soon connected with me again. She had been following the events in
Standing Rock and was inspired by the actions of the clergy and people of faith
in their courageous efforts to protect the land. She was clear that she would
refuse to participate in any military intervention against the Standing Rock
water protectors. She deeply respected the water protectors for taking a stand of
nonviolence, and she found the violence toward the water protectors alarming.

At this point, Susan intended to continue in her role as a medic "alongside the ones who are put most directly in the depth of suffering created by
war." But she had a new level of commitment to dissent—one that involved
proactively speaking out. She wrote:

> *I am setting aside the duty of holding my tongue to remain in alignment*
> *with the rule of military law. I accept the risk of being disciplined,*
> *court-martialed, or discharged for doing so. There are moments in which*
> *I will have to speak the truth regardless of the mandate on me to not*
> *engage in political discussion due to my status. Admittedly this feels like*
> *an enormous risk and one that provokes unease in me, but I also feel*
> *confident that it will manifest new ways of being in this difficult time.*

When I saw Susan some weeks later, she had come to a new decision—
she had taken the first steps toward filing for official military status as a

conscientious objector (CO). She told me that the military was subtly bullying her to abandon her CO status claim, implying that she had psychological problems. She looked at me, and we both smiled. I knew that not only was she perfectly sane—she had made her decision using self-respect and respect for principles, with integrity as her guide.

While exploring her dilemma, Susan had gone through a careful process of discernment. She had respected her own deliberation process and refrained from jumping to a quick conclusion. At a certain point, she realized that she was willing to incur the risk of violating military law, and endure the disparagement of her colleagues, in order to stay aligned with her values. Finally, she felt the only option was to apply for CO status. I knew the decision did not come lightly.

I learned from Susan and from others that respect and disrespect exist in a complex ecosystem with the other Edge States. Disrespect of others often reveals a lack of healthy altruism, empathy, and integrity. Consciously activating these qualities can help us shift disrespect back into respect. Disrespect also causes moral suffering, which, like Susan, we experience as a violation of integrity. The places where we work and serve can be fertile ground for bullying, and if we are subject to harassment, we will burn out faster. Burned-out humanitarian workers, military personnel, and caregivers are also prone to taking out their frustrations on their peers, superiors, or even those whom they serve by treating them with disrespect.

Conversely, respect infuses the other four Edge States with strength. Altruism is a powerful expression of respect. Empathy can be a gateway to unconditional regard for others. The moral and ethical principles that make for healthy individuals, organizations, and societies have respect woven throughout them. And engagement can be enhanced by respect. I often think about the great Golden Rule that is shared in different forms by so many cultures: Do unto others as you would have others do unto you. This maxim embodies respect for others, respect for principles, and self-respect.

IV. PRACTICES THAT SUPPORT RESPECT

H OW DO WE HANDLE DISRESPECT in a skillful way—whether we feel it arise within us, or we are on the receiving end of it? What practices might support us, practices that are grounded in respect and that help us cultivate more respect?

The Drama Triangle

In Upaya's Buddhist Chaplaincy Training Program, we teach our students about Stephen Karpman's Drama Triangle, which we use as a social model for analyzing and processing interpersonal dynamics around disrespect, fear, and disempowerment. Whether at work, in family life, or in our friendships, most of us get caught in the Drama Triangle sooner or later. Although not Buddhist per se, the model has a Buddhist bent. It helps us become aware of our habitual, fear-based responses to toxic interactions. The model also provides a perspective that supports us in seeing more deeply into who we really are.

The Drama Triangle maps the roles people become caught in as persecutor, victim, and rescuer. Typically, the drama begins when a persecutor antagonizes a victim—or when a victim perceives or even seeks out an attack by a persecutor. Feeling threatened and disrespected, the victim solicits help from a rescuer, or a rescuer volunteers to fix the situation. Rescuers usually believe they are acting from a place of altruism, but often it's a pathological form of altruism that is an ego enhancement for the rescuer and keeps the victim dependent.

As the players enact their roles, the triangle loses stability; sooner or later the dynamic shifts, and with it, so do the roles. For example, when the rescuer comes to resent the victim's needs, he might shift into the victim role, with the victim becoming the new persecutor. Or the rescuer may lash out in anger, becoming a persecutor. The persecutor may claim to be persecuted, assuming the victim role. In fact, a player in any role can shift to any other role.

The connection between the Drama Triangle and bullying is obvious. Persecutors and victims are necessary ingredients in creating horizontal or vertical hostility, conditions that attract rescuers. As well, a person who feels tyrannized or bullied can easily move into a persecutor role, shaming and blaming the original persecutor. Or, a rescuer may use simulated respect as an excuse for assuming the persecutor's role.

Underpinning the Drama Triangle is the connection between personal responsibility and power. The victim takes no responsibility for their own power, but instead tries to get a rescuer to save them. The rescuer takes responsibility not for themselves, but for the identified victim. The persecutor also refuses to take responsibility for their own actions, denying their contribution to the suffering.

To break this dysfunctional dynamic, we need to look at the situation from a wider point of view, and then take responsibility for our part in the difficulties. Fleet Maull, during Upaya's Buddhist Chaplaincy Training Program, gives good guidelines for how to step out of the Drama Triangle: Be mindful of those situations that trigger us and stay grounded. Don't take things personally. Don't make assumptions. Maintain good internal and external boundaries. Make and keep clear agreements. Renegotiate agreements, if necessary. Keep things in perspective. And work with the following qualities: vulnerability, accountability, self-responsibility, trust, connectedness, and fearlessness.

The Five Gatekeepers of Speech

A powerful asset for working with the Drama Triangle is Right Speech, a Buddhist practice that is one of the bases for connection and care. When Zen teachers in the United States began to deeply explore the role of speech in the systems we inhabit, we realized how often disrespect and disparagement are found in family structures, the workplace, and our religious communities. We began to use the Five Gatekeepers of Speech, questions sourced in the Buddha's teachings, as a tool for appropriate communication. Practicing them means that before we open our mouths, we consider:

1. Is it true?
2. Is it kind?
3. Is it beneficial?
4. Is it necessary?
5. Is it the right time?

These questions are a way of looking deeply into whether what we want to say is necessary at this time and whether it will really serve. Is this the moment when our words are needed to turn a situation around for the better? Or might our feedback be received as bullying, disrespectful, or disempowering?

Yet when answering these questions, I have had to remember an important element of Right Speech that Thích Nhất Hạnh emphasized over the years. In cases of injustice, of disrespect, of harm, of abuse, of harassment, of violence, it's our responsibility to call out the harm in the name of compassion. Nhất Hạnh interprets the Buddhist precept of Right Speech with these words: "Do not say untruthful things for the sake of personal interest or to impress people. Do not utter words that can cause division or hatred. Do not spread news that you do not know to be certain. Do not criticize or condemn things that you are not sure of. Always speak truthfully and constructively. Have the courage to speak out about situations of injustice even when doing so may threaten your own safety." Right Speech is courageous speech. Speech that is compassionate and fearless is grounded in authentic respect. It is also one of the ways that we can step out of the Drama Triangle.

Exchanging Self with Other

Empathy, kindness, insight, and compassion are powerful antidotes to disrespect. Aware of this, I have found the practice of "exchanging self with other" to be of great support in deepening respect, and of nurturing wisdom and strengthening resilience when subjected to disrespect.

This practice was outlined by Shantideva, the eighth-century Indian Buddhist monk, who wrote *A Guide to the Bodhisattva's Way of Life*.

We begin by first recalling our aspiration to be of benefit to others, and that every single being wants to be free of suffering.

Then we honestly consider how our own selfishness and self-cherishing have not brought us real happiness. What has nourished our well-being has been respecting, loving, and caring for others.

Looking deeply, we should also see that everything that benefits us comes from others, whether our bodies, the food we eat, the clothing we wear, the house we live in, even the air we breathe.

Then it is important to understand that from one point of view, there is no difference between self and other and that all beings and things are totally interdependent and worthy of respect and care.

Although for most of us it is usually ourselves that we are focusing on, now we focus our attention and love on another.

For this part of the practice of exchanging our self-cherishing to cherishing others, bring to mind the presence of someone who is suffering. Imagine that you are this person, living their life, enduring their difficulties.

Imagine their suffering as dark smoke and breathe it in. On the out-breath, send all of your good qualities to this one.

After some time has passed doing this practice, return to your own vast heart and let yourself rest in unconditioned presence.

End the practice by dedicating the merit to the well-being of others.

This practice is a powerful way for us to cultivate love and respect for others.

V. DISCOVERY AT THE EDGE OF RESPECT

IN BUDDHISM, WE TRY TO look deeply into the roots of each person's suffering. We can recognize the Angulimala in the bully, in the tyrant, the abuser—the one who needs the right circumstances to rediscover who they really are.

And then there is Mara, the "devil," who showed up again and again in the Buddha's life, trying to intimidate him. As Thích Nhất Hạnh writes, the Buddha would respond: "Hello, old friend. I know you"—and Mara would flee. In another version of the story, the Buddha enumerated to Mara the personal strengths he would use to vanquish him: "For I have faith and energy / And I have wisdom too. . . . Your serried squadrons, which the world / With all its gods cannot defeat, I shall now break with wisdom / As with a stone a clay pot." After vanquishing Mara, Buddha was called "the Victorious One," meaning that he had overcome all obstacles. He had the power to transform the afflictions of his own mind.

Mara is an archetype that represents our anguish, our hatred, our grasping, our confusion, our delusions, our fear. Perhaps when we meet our own Mara, we can say, with a measure of compassion, "Hello, old friend, I know you." We resist the impulse to tyrannize, remaining grounded in understanding and respect. We can also use the Buddha's formula of faith, energy, and wisdom to overcome our personal Mara to find freedom.

In the *Padhana Sutta*, Mara complains: "For seven years I pursued the

Buddha at every step / Yet with the wakeful Buddha I got no chance. / As a crow that hopped around a fat-coloured stone / Thinking 'we may find a tender delicacy' / Flies away in disappointment / In disgust I give up Gotama."

Don't give the tyrant any delicacy to delight on! Be a fat-coloured stone! Whether the tyrant is inside us or an external aggressor, we must first look deeply into ourselves. We can try to cultivate fearless compassion for the tyrant's suffering and delusion. We can thus gain the insight we need to avoid feeding our own oppressive states of mind. We can also cultivate compassion for ourselves and appreciation of our strengths. When our self-respect is strong, we don't need to denigrate others.

When we are standing at the edge tilting toward the abyss of disrespect, our feelings of discomfort can be enough to make us turn inward, toward discovering our compassion for others; toward discovering how we can transform difficult relationships and institutions through the force of respect and love. These experiences can be a doorway to shifting our habitual responses, to learning skillful and compassionate communication, and to realizing the healing power of interconnectedness with our fellow humans and all beings. As we learn to elevate others, we also elevate ourselves.

5. ENGAGEMENT

You cannot become enlightened by being busy.

Years ago at Upaya, I noticed a young Mexican worker who was slowly and carefully stacking adobe blocks to be used in remodeling one of our buildings. During the course of the project, he continued to work with this same quality of mindfulness, and there was often a slight smile on his face, whether he was laying pipe or plastering a wall. At the end of the project, I invited José to stay on at Upaya as our go-to handyman.

José slipped into the stream of Upaya's everyday life, inspiring some of our residents and guests. One day, while working alongside José on a garden project, I thought about an exchange between the seventeenth-century Japanese Zen master Bashō and one of his monks. "What is the essence of your practice?" the monk asked Bashō. The master responded, "Whatever is needed." Like Bashō, José seemed to be engaged in whatever was needed, not just functionally but also existentially, as if his work were a spiritual practice. Whether he was dealing with plumbing issues, electrical failures, or doing flood prevention, José appeared to work with total connection and no stress.

Of course, José was not working in a classroom full of rebellious adolescents. Nor was he dealing with the intractable pain of a dying person or the emotional demands of an unemployed constituent. Those who work in environments where suffering is the daily fare are at risk for *feeling worn out and disheartened. Still, I believe that healthy engagement can cut across all professions.*

I have a colleague who teaches elementary school in a low-income neighborhood. She begins her classes with meditation. Kids' paintings hang on the walls. The windowsills are lined with thriving plants. Her students are at the top of their age group in math, and she attributes that to how they start their day; she tells me her days are good too. I am close to a politician from the Rust Belt who never seems to turn away from his constituents' needs. I hear he almost always has a smile on his face, even as he deals with the complexities of Washington. He is a long-term meditation practitioner.

Then there is the CEO who has shifted her company's priorities toward profit sharing, as well as vision sharing. She has raised four healthy kids at the same time and is flourishing. And the Kentucky poet-farmer who stands by his principles of environmental responsibility, even as nearby mountaintops are being blown off. His humor, dislike of technology, love of the land, and poetry keep him balanced, sane, and prolific.

I have learned from all of them, but perhaps especially from José. Through my friendship with him, I came to see that our deeper identity lies less in what we do and more in how we hold what we do—how we engage with our work, whether laying bricks, making laws, or sitting with dying people.

The term "engagement" is how psychologist Dr. Christina Maslach describes a healthy relationship to our work and service to others, while burnout is the fatigue and discouragement resulting from an unhealthy relationship to our vocation. When I began to examine engagement and burnout, I realized that engagement is an Edge State.

When we stand on the solid ground of engagement, we find strength in our work. Our service to others may have its challenging moments, but in general we are absorbed in and gratified by what we do. Our livelihood enhances the quality of our lives while ideally enhancing the quality of others' lives as well. But when we work too many hours, under untenable circumstances, for too little emotional reward—or when we feel our efforts aren't making a positive difference to others—these factors can push us to the limit of what we can sustain. From there, it's easy to fall over the edge and into the bleak landscape of burnout, where we feel jaded and demoralized, where we lose our heart and taste for work, where we lose our desire to serve.

The violence of overwork can become habitual and lead us to burnout, a swamp that can be difficult to crawl out of. Some stay stuck there for years, unable to reignite their passion. But when we do find our way out of burnout and back to a livelihood that nourishes others and ourselves, we also find resilience, and perhaps even wisdom.

I. AT THE HIGH EDGE OF ENGAGEMENT

I N BUDDHISM, THERE IS A well-known story about the Zen master Pai-chang Huai-hai, who lived during China's Tang Dynasty. Like a good Chinese citizen, he worked every day of his life—except for the day when his monks hid his tools. By then Pai-chang was well advanced in years, and his monks thought he should take it easy for a while. But Pai-chang did not appreciate this prank. He protested that without work, he had no virtue. "A day of no work is a day of no eating," he proclaimed, and he commenced a hunger strike until his monks relented and let him go back to work. Pai-chang's aphorism became a guiding principle of Zen for over 1,200 years: a Zen work ethic, an ethic of engagement, an ethic of *being* "whatever will serve."

Energy, Involvement, Efficacy

Engagement in our work is characterized by energy, involvement, and efficacy, according to Dr. Maslach, who is a renowned expert on burnout. When we are engaged, we feel nourished by our work. We have personal agency and the means to effect outcomes. We have the sense that our work makes a difference to others, ourselves, and perhaps even the world. While it is normal to experience our fair share of frustration and resistance, our commitment to our work—and, hopefully, our love for our work—gives us the strength and wisdom to ride the waves through less fulfilling times.

During a program that I taught with the Benedictine monk Brother David Steindl-Rast, he shared with us that the antidote to burnout wasn't necessarily taking a vacation. "It is wholeheartedness!" he exclaimed, beaming joyfully. I like the word *wholeheartedness*, because it implies that the whole of our heart is engaged. It points to a sense of genuine connectedness to and love for the work we do. In a subsequent talk, Brother David shared that engagement was his own personal strategy for avoiding burnout.

The poet David Whyte recounts a pivotal conversation he had with Brother David, who counseled him,

> *You are so tired through and through because a good half of what you do here in this organization has nothing to do with your true powers, or the place you have reached in your life. You are only half here, and half here will kill you after a while. You need something to which you can give your full powers. . . . [T]he swan doesn't cure his awkwardness by beating himself on the back, by moving faster, or by trying to organize himself better. He does it by moving toward the elemental water where he belongs. It is the simple contact with the water that gives him grace and presence. You only have to touch the elemental waters in your own life, and it will transform everything. But you have to let yourself down into those waters from the ground on which you stand, and that can be hard. Particularly if you think you might drown.*

Brother David continued,

> *This nervously letting yourself down . . . takes courage, and the word* courage *in English comes from the old French word* coeur, *heart. You must do something heartfelt, and you must do it soon. Let go of all this effort, and let yourself down, however awkwardly, into the waters of the work you want for yourself. It's all right, you know, to support*

yourself with something secondary until your work has ripened, but once it has ripened to a transparent fullness, it has to be gathered in. You have ripened already, and you are waiting to be brought in. Your exhaustion is a form of inner fermentation. You are beginning, ever so slowly, to rot on the vine.

Rotting on the vine, indeed! To avoid that unpleasant fate, we must lower ourselves into the waters of the work we want for ourselves and for the world and bring ourselves to the place of fullness, of wholeheartedness in how we serve.

According to Dr. Maslach, those who have an engaged relationship with their work, and who find in it a sense of purpose and agency, are less prone to burnout. They have let themselves down into the waters of life. Researcher Ayala Pines studied insurance agents, workers whose jobs may appear tedious to the average observer. She found that agents who have survived a traumatic experience related to insurance, such as a fire or flood, can work for a long time without burning out because they feel a deep calling to the profession and believe that their work is truly serving people.

How is it that the same work will burn out some people and not others? I was inspired by the story of a family who seems only heartened by a vocation that few of us could handle. In 2012, Cori Salchert and her husband, Mark, began adopting what they call "hospice babies," babies with life-limiting conditions. The Salcherts already had eight biological children of their own, but they felt called to take in these babies whose parents had given them up, unable to cope with their complex care or with witnessing the end of their child's life.

A former perinatal bereavement nurse based in Sheboygan, Wisconsin, Cori Salchert had the expertise to take this on. She also had the heart. The first hospice baby her family adopted was a nameless two-week-old girl who was born with severe brain abnormalities. They named her Emmalynn; she lived for fifty days before she died in Cori's arms. "Emmalynn lived more in fifty days than a number of folks do in a lifetime," Cori said.

Next, the family adopted Charlie, an eighteen-month-old on life support. Despite all of his equipment, the family took him on excursions whenever they could. "He will die; there's no changing that," Cori told *Sheboygan Press*. "But, we can make a difference in how he lives, and the difference for Charlie is that he will be loved before he dies."

Theirs is a story of altruism and also of courageous, selfless engagement. The Salchert family truly swims in the waters of life, even as they bear witness to dying and death. How does this remarkable family manage without burning out? Cori speaks of her family's strong sense of purpose and the power of Christian faith. They also have each other: The whole family has opened to this practice of unconditional love and connection, factors that keep burnout at bay.

I recall often these words of the great Sufi poet Jalāl ad-Dīn Muhammad Rūmī: "Let the beauty we love be what we do. There are hundreds of ways to kneel and kiss the ground." What this family has done for these dying children is beautiful. And this kind of beauty is not separate from wholeheartedness.

The Gift of Busyness

I have no doubt that the Salcherts are incredibly busy. It requires a lot of time and countless small tasks to care for dying children. However, in our culture, busyness is a phenomenon that cuts both ways: It can be a manifestation of healthy engagement, a way to serve deeply, and a result of inspiration and faith. Or it can turn into an addiction, with ever-expanding to-do lists, appointments, distractions. Or it can even be both at once.

Busyness, from one point of view, is a form of seeking behavior that is abetted by the neurochemical dopamine. Dopamine drives us to be motivated, to want and to pursue. It amplifies our arousal levels and makes us more curious. We could call it the juice that fuels our brain's search engine. It can also improve our thought processes and bring energy into our emotional lives. Neuroscience shows that even more than achieving goals, the act of seeking can enhance human satisfaction through the production of this neurochemical.

Recent research on middle-aged and older Americans suggests that being busy and engaged can have beneficial effects on mental functioning. In one study, people over fifty who led busy lives tested better across a range of cognitive functions, including brain processing speeds, memory for specific events, reasoning abilities, and vocabulary.

That study reminds me of the philanthropist Laurance Rockefeller, who worked most of the days of his life and also had a long-term meditation practice. Even into his early nineties, he was actively engaged in areas spanning from conservation to venture capitalism, from business to Buddhism. One day, when he was ninety-four years old, he went as usual to Room 5600 at Rockefeller Center. In the late morning, he didn't feel well and returned home to rest. Shortly thereafter, he died peacefully. He was sharp, motivated, curious, and humor-filled until the end.

I was fortunate to know Mr. Rockefeller in his later years. When I founded Upaya Zen Center, he guided me in how to structure what was to become a very robust and thriving institution. I learned from Laurance that, to avoid burnout, it is important to foster the qualities of appreciation, gratefulness, humor, and curiosity, as well as openness to whatever happens and the willingness to take risks. He also taught me that it is important not to have heavy expectations of ourselves or others, and to not be attached to outcomes, but simply to do our best to benefit others. His lessons have proved invaluable to me and informed my leadership as Upaya grew into a large organization.

Over many years, I have been thoroughly engaged in taking care of this place and her people and maintaining a committed meditation practice, plus teaching all over the world and doing service projects. It has been good for my health. I love my work. I cherish my students, my studies, my practice. It is a full and real life for a person of any age. According to research, even the stress we feel when we give a talk or meet a project deadline has similar beneficial effects on the body as the stress of exercise—it mobilizes immune cells and can enhance memory and learning. So far, so good.

I believe that when we are able to infuse our work with a sense of connection and purpose, dedication and wholeheartedness, faith and joy, we can stand at the edge in healthy engagement. However, when our work takes on a compulsive and addictive quality and we become caught in the dopamine loop, combined with the dry rust taste of fear in the mouth, Dr. Maslach tells us that cynicism and burnout usually follow.

Work is about our energy. Even the word *work* has the same root as the word *energy*. Through our work, we give energy to the world, to others, and to ourselves.

I say to my students, *Take yourself to the powerful edge of meaningful work and give your best. Use your days well to truly benefit others and bring joy to yourself.* In my view, there is little more rewarding in life than healthy and dedicated work for the love of others and the world.

So, whether you're a clinician, teacher, CEO, human rights worker, bricklayer, artist, mother, or Zen practitioner sitting on a cushion, I say, go for it! Be nothing less than wholehearted—and let "the beauty we love be what we do."

II. FALLING OVER THE EDGE
OF ENGAGEMENT: BURNOUT

WHEN OUR ENGAGEMENT GETS OFF-balance and our work seems driven by fear, escapism, or compulsion, we are vulnerable to burnout—that bleak experience of fatigue, pessimism, cynicism, and even physical illness, accompanied by the sense that our work is of little or no benefit to anyone, including ourselves.

In trying to understand the experience of burnout, I read about the life of the man who made the term famous. As I contemplated the details of his personal history, maybe Dr. Freudenberger did not suffer from burnout, per se, but he was certainly engaged to the point of obsession in research and mapping out the process.

Herbert Freudenberger was born in Germany to a Jewish family just seven years before Hitler came to power. After his family's factory was seized and his grandmother was beaten by Nazis, Freudenberger left Germany alone at age twelve, using his father's passport. He sailed to New York and went to live with a step-aunt, who kept him in an attic and made him sleep in an upright chair once she realized that his father could not pay her for the boy's care as promised. Freudenberger escaped this untenable situation at age fourteen and lived on the streets of Manhattan until he was taken in by a cousin.

When his parents finally made it to the United States, Freudenberger took a factory job to support them. Meanwhile, he attended night school at Brooklyn College, where he met Abraham Maslow, the eminent psychologist.

Maslow encouraged him to study psychology and became his mentor. Freudenberger went on to earn his master's and doctorate degrees while continuing to work at the factory.

With all this, Freudenberger launched a successful psychoanalytic practice in 1958. In the 1970s, he started working with a free clinic for substance abusers in East Harlem, where he volunteered after a full day at the office. At the free clinic and in other therapeutic communities, Freudenberger observed what happened to mental health and substance abuse counselors when they felt demoralized by patient outcomes. In 1974, probably inspired by Graham Greene's novel *A Burnt-Out Case*, he introduced the term *burnout*. This work launched him to his status as one of the nation's foremost psychologists.

Freudenberger was a driven man, working fourteen or fifteen hours a day, six days a week, until three weeks before his death at age seventy-three. As his son, Mark Freud, told *The New York Times*, "His early years, unfortunately, never really left him. He was a very complicated man, and deeply conflicted because of his upbringing. He had very little childhood. He was a survivor." We have to wonder whether his real subject in the study of burnout might have been himself—or whether he was able to stay within the healthy realm of engagement. Regardless, burnout became his cause and his professional identity.

Freudenberger defined burnout variously as "a state of mental and physical exhaustion caused by one's professional life" and "the extinction of motivation or incentive, especially where one's devotion to a cause or relationship fails to produce the desired results." According to Freudenberger and his colleague Gail North, burnout tends to follow a certain story line: We feel compelled to prove our value by giving our work 100 percent. We work so hard that conflicts develop with family members and colleagues. We make mistakes due to lack of sleep. Hard work becomes our new value system. As our perspective narrows, we deny our emerging problems. Others see our situation, but we don't. We withdraw from our loved ones and become more and more socially isolated. We feel apathetic and increasingly depersonalized. To fill our emptiness inside, we may turn to addictive behaviors. We feel depressed, may experience mental and physical collapse, and in the extreme, might even consider suicide.

Who Burns Out?

In 1981, Dr. Maslach codeveloped a detailed survey known as the Maslach Burnout Inventory (MBI). Considered psychology's standard for measuring burnout, the MBI asks questions about the sufferer's sense of three main factors: emotional exhaustion, cynicism, and inefficacy. (These factors are the opposites of those she uses to define engagement: energy, involvement, and efficacy.)

These factors correlate with profession and lifestyle to some extent. The first factor, emotional exhaustion, tends to claim people in professions with high emotional demands, such as health care, social work, activism, and education. It also affects people who have less social support, including single people, as well as those with underlying depression and anxiety.

The second factor, cynicism, tends to claim the more idealistic among us, including younger people, who are prone to disillusionment when reality doesn't live up to their expectations. Any of us can be prone to feeling the third factor, a pervasive feeling of ineffectiveness—like we're failing at what we set out to achieve, despite our best efforts. From there, it's a quick downward slide into believing that our work is just plain meaningless, period. And these are the makings of a crisis, especially when our self-esteem and identity are tied up in our work. If our work means nothing, what does our life mean?

I don't know what it's like to feel powerless, frustrated, and cynical as a result of work, but I have heard the stories of hundreds who have been caught in the terrible grip of these symptoms—social workers, prison guards, teachers, EMTs, doctors, and nurses. Burnout is an occupational hazard in any profession and in any country. Statistics on NYC public school teachers show that 45 percent have left their jobs within five years probably due to burnout. The prevalence of burnout in medicine has led to an alarmingly high suicide rate: male physicians are 1.4 times more likely to take their own lives than men in the general population; female doctors, 2.3 times more likely.

Burnout also claims people in high-stress corporate jobs, such as CEOs, lawyers, high-tech workers, and Wall Street bankers—those who take work home every night and feel great pressure to perform. With smartphones so ubiquitous, many people feel they cannot escape work even for a good night's sleep. Research shows that when we are in it just for the money, and not for a higher set of values, such as helping others or creative satisfaction, we tend to burn out faster.

Burnout is so common that it has become its own industry; in the United States, a whole industry of coaches, therapists, counselors, and doctors has arisen around treating burnout and work trauma.

Addicted to Busyness

Busyness has been considered a virtue at least since the days of the Catholic saint Jerome, who coined the phrase, "Idle hands are the devil's workshop." Protestantism also views work as inherently virtuous. Its famous work ethic emphasizes productivity as a way to keep the devil at bay. Through these and other influences, work has become a core aspect of our cultural and individual identities in modern-day America. What we do for work, how many hours we take to do it, and what we accomplish on the job are all essential to how many see themselves. Our egos and sense of self-worth are caught up in it. "What do you do?" is typically the first question we ask a new acquaintance, and we tend to form opinions of them based on their answer.

Work is so important to us that workaholism has become a status symbol in the workplace, with coworkers often competing with each other over how late they stayed at the office last night or how many hours they worked over the weekend. Workaholism is actually expected in many work and service environments in the West as well as the East. It's a form of addiction that is particularly insidious because it's socially condoned—it's productive, after all, and many believe that work has inherent moral value. Addiction to work and to busyness has become for many a guiding principle, a kind of religion—but one that is more or less devoid of real spirituality.

Thomas Merton wrote,

> *There is a pervasive form of contemporary violence to which the idealist most easily succumbs: activism and overwork. The rush and pressure of modern life are a form, perhaps the most common form, of its innate violence. To allow oneself to be carried away by a multitude of conflicting concerns, to surrender to too many demands, to commit oneself to too many projects, to want to help everyone in everything, is to succumb to violence. The frenzy of our activism neutralizes our work for peace. It destroys our own inner capacity for peace. It destroys the fruitfulness of our own work, because it kills the root of inner wisdom which makes work fruitful.*

I also appreciate the words of professor and writer Omid Safi: "We live in a culture that celebrates activity. We collapse our sense of who we are into what we do for a living. The public performance of busyness is how we demonstrate to one another that we are important. The more people see us as tired, exhausted, over-stretched, the more they think we must be somehow . . . indispensable. That we matter."

Years ago, I had an office at the Library of Congress next to the office of Dr. George Chrousos, an endocrinologist specializing in stress. I asked him whether people could become addicted to their own neurotransmitters. He replied with an emphatic "Yes." He said that our biochemical soup of neurotransmitters easily primes our compulsive anticipation and pursuit of rewards in the dopamine loop and can seriously stress us out.

A few years later, I met Dr. Kent Berridge at a Mind and Life meeting in Dharamsala. He showed us a video of rats in his experiments who were stimulated to crave saline water, although they did not naturally like it. The rats had gotten stuck in the addiction cycle. Dr. Berridge commented that consumption makes for more consumption, even when it is not pleasant.

Similarly, our busyness stokes our appetite for more busyness, even though our compulsive activity becomes less satisfying and more stressful with time. More is never enough, and as we run on this hedonic treadmill, our attention can become completely co-opted by our endless quest for stimulation (even stimulation that is unpleasant or harmful), and we may withdraw from intimacy and connection.

When work takes over our lives and psyches, we become like the hungry ghost, an archetype in traditional Buddhism for a person who is on the hedonic treadmill of craving and addiction. It's a ravenous creature with skinny limbs, a hair-thin neck, a bulging stomach, a tiny mouth, and an appetite that can never be satisfied. Even more disturbing, whatever the hungry ghost puts in its mouth turns to poison. Workaholism takes us into the malignant territory of the hungry ghost. It's like we keep shoving more and more hours of work and relentless activity into our tiny mouths, bloating our stomachs with the poisonous chemicals of burnout.

Drinking the Poison of Work Stress

A 2015 Gallup poll found that 48 percent of Americans feel they don't have enough time to do what they really want to do. This rate has held more or less steady for the past fifteen years. And 90 percent of working mothers say they are rushed some or all of the time, according to a Pew Research Center survey that same year.

For some of us, this internalized pressure to perform starts in college or even high school. We seem to cherish what Hermann Hesse called "aggressive haste." We take a heavy course load, pull all-nighters to write papers and study for exams. This pattern continues into our training years, such as medical residencies with their night shifts and double shifts. During our professional or service life, the hours typically get longer. Many of us actually relish this at first. Focused immersion, coupled with sleep deprivation, can put us in an altered state that energizes us. The stress releases dopamine—and when the high wears off, we need another hit. So it's easy to see why, in the United States, ten million people work more than sixty hours per week, and 34 percent of workers don't take even a single day of their allotted vacation time.

In the era of Old English, *bisig* meant "careful, anxious." The word *busy* evolved in a different direction, but I think that more than a whiff of anxiousness persists. We feel pressured for time, and this time scarcity puts us in a chronic state of hurry that ultimately, and ironically, makes us less efficient with our time. The human brain has a certain response to poverty: the perception that we have too little of something makes us obsess about it to the point where other abilities and skills suffer. Time scarcity causes the release of cortisol, a fight-or-flight hormone that has deleterious effects on the body over time, including weakening the immune system. Like dopamine, cortisol is energizing at first, and speedy, but it leads more quickly to exhaustion. Again, in the short term, our bodies respond pretty well to stress, but when stress is chronic, it can cause a whole array of health problems.

Chronic work stress will probably push us over the edge into burnout and its cousin *vital exhaustion*, a constellation of physical and emotional symptoms that includes physical exhaustion and feelings of hopelessness. Vital exhaustion often precedes heart disease, possibly as a causal factor. It is also linked to autoimmune disorders, depression, and cognitive impairment.

Burnout is also frequently closely linked to conditions in the workplace. According to Maslach, these include working with little social support, autonomy, or control; working in an unjust environment or in the service of values we don't respect; and working for too little financial, social, or emotional reward. Maslach called for a study of workplace environments and how they relate to burnout. As she wrote in 1982, "Imagine investigating the personality of cucumbers to discover why they had turned into sour pickles, without analyzing the vinegar barrels in which they'd been submerged!" However, Maslach emphasized that burnout is usually not only the "fault" of the institution but also of the fit between the institution and the individual.

It can be almost beneficial for workplaces to burn us out—to keep us so numb that we don't have the motivation to change the conditions and policies that foster burnout. Or they may reward us for drinking the very poison of work stress and speediness through paying us for overwork, optimization, or setting high production goals, including patient quotas. This is a form of systemic oppression, which includes the harm that institutions and their policies inflict on the people who work for them.

III. ENGAGEMENT AND THE OTHER EDGE STATES

A LL OF THE EDGE STATES can fuel burnout. Pathological altruism and empathic distress can exhaust us, as can moral suffering and being exposed to disrespect. When we overidentify with suffering (empathic distress) and overwork to end suffering (pathological altruism), burnout usually follows. When our integrity is compromised (moral suffering) or we encounter disrespect toward others or ourselves, burnout is common. Or if we are subjected to systemic oppression, or structural violence based on privilege and power, then anger, futility, and burnout can be an outcome.

Every year, I travel to Japan and teach clinicians compassion-building practices. Typically, before me is a room full of very hardworking doctors and nurses. They tell me they are always on call, they work at least sixty hours per week, and they feel they can never do enough for their patients or the institutions where they work. These clinicians face tough inner and outer expectations, not unlike their Korean and Chinese counterparts; in all three of these countries, death by overwork is well known.

Some of the Japanese clinicians have shared with me that they identify too strongly with patients who are suffering. This takes them down the slippery slope of empathic distress, where they experience emotional exhaustion, depersonalization, and meaninglessness that are hallmarks of burnout. Not a few have told stories about feeling moral distress about the values of their institution, the actions of coworkers, or the medical interventions they are compelled to perform. Disillusionment, cynicism, and futility frequently follow, leading to burnout. Nurses especially are vulnerable to bullying by doctors, their nurse peers, and even their patients. Of course, being the target of disrespect and hostility in the workplace can lead to the physical and psychological symptoms of burnout.

Several years ago, I sat with Japanese nurses who were bullied by a male patient suffering from cancer. The nurses looked shell-shocked. This had been going on for too long, and they were totally exhausted from facing this patient's aggression, day after day. They shared openly about their despair in not being able to cope and being constantly abused by someone they were trying to help. They were cooked, done, finished.

Japanese nurses are a dedicated lot. They will go to the end of their resources to take care of their patients. But these nurses had no resources left, and they looked like they were sitting in a graveyard. Pathological altruism, empathic distress, moral suffering, and disrespect had crushed them, and every single one of them was demoralized and burned out. They also felt guilty and ashamed that they could not handle this situation. They told me they felt like they had failed their patient, the hospital, each other, and themselves.

I only had a short time with them. After listening to each one of them speak openly of their exhaustion and despair, I reviewed GRACE, the practice of cultivating compassion as we interact with others. I suggested that before seeing the patient, they get grounded, pausing at the door of the patient's room and taking a mindful breath. They also could recall why they had chosen to care for dying people, and take a moment to remember to be aware of their potential for reactivity and, as well, their patient's mental and physical suffering; this might put things into perspective. Recognizing that their fear of him was understandable, they could consider that bullying is also suffering. He was dying of cancer and was terrified. He was in pain and could not deal with it. He had lost agency, the ability to control the course of his life and the way he was dying.

Toward the end of the encounter with these nurses, I also suggested to them that they visualize him as a baby, helpless and afraid. He had been there once a long time ago, and maybe was there again as a result of being so sick.

In addition, they might consider not personalizing his attacks and see that acting defensively probably made matters worse. And it was important to practice deep listening with him and each other. Maybe this could help give them insights into how to set boundaries and take care of themselves and each other in the storms of disrespect they were being subjected to.

I was to learn later that our time together seemed to have served the group. When the next patient with similar behavior came into the palliative care unit, they were able to allay their feelings of fear and futility, and approach this second patient with more balance and with compassion.

Another story about burnout comes from my associate Maia Duerr, who worked in the U.S. mental health system for ten years and eventually burned out, not because of the relationships with her clients or coworkers or her work schedule—but because of her understandable response to the fraught mental health system. "I witnessed the revolving door of patients going out of the hospital and into the community only to be readmitted a short time later," she wrote. "It seemed to me that we were missing an essential piece. My work required me to come up with treatment plans for the 'rehabilitation' of my clients, but I kept wondering how being avoided, feared, pitied, locked up, and medicated to the point of oblivion affects a person's mental health, beyond any psychiatric challenge he or she faced."

Maia's integrity was being violated by the values and conditions of her workplace. She suffered from justifiable moral distress. Her clients were being disrespected and, from her point of view, seriously maltreated. Moreover, she was not able to change the system that she was serving in. The toxic work conditions were unsustainable for her, and burnout was the outcome. She left her job, but not until she paid a stiff personal price.

Power, ambition, competition, addiction to work, resentment, and fear also feed burnout. These driving forces are ego poisons that can show up in Edge States; power, ambition, and resentment in disrespect, as well as moral outrage and moral apathy; addiction in pathological altruism and moral suffering; and fear in pathological altruism, empathic distress, moral suffering, and disrespect.

The "culture of emergency" that produces burnout has many contributing factors, yet there are ways to recover trust and your humanity. Coming to know work as mindfulness practice. Keeping our lives open not only to the outer world but to our inner world. Making sure our values are aligned with our work, and also humor, play, and no work! Ovid, the Roman poet, wrote in his *Ar Amatoria,* II. 351: "Take rest; a field that has rested gives a bountiful crop."

And one more suggestion: I once heard Harvard Business School professor Bill George offer an important and often neglected approach to transforming burnout related to a lack of meaning in our work. He said that when we see the positive impact we have in our work, cynicism, fatigue, and feelings of inefficacy can dissolve and we can be inspired to work in a way that is more open, dedicated, balanced, and mutually serves. This can be the medicine that modulates the fire of burnout and turns it into the passion to engage with our whole heart.

IV. PRACTICES THAT SUPPORT ENGAGEMENT

IN MY TWENTIES, I WORKED in a research environment at Columbia University. There was no small amount of stress in that office. It was common for me to work fourteen-hour days, seven days a week, and I could run chi-squares (a statistics test) by hand at lightning speed. I was fascinated by what I was doing, but how I was doing it was not entirely sustainable!

During my stint at Columbia, I began practicing Zen as a way to deal with stress, and I hoped to combine contemplative practice with social action. All Zen students get assigned to kitchen duty sooner or later. When I first began working in a Zen kitchen, I assumed that the point of cutting up the carrots was to get the work done as quickly and efficiently as possible, like doing a chi-square at warp speed. I gradually realized that this was not exactly the point. From a Zen perspective, cutting up the carrots is about just cutting up the carrots. After I cut up a few thousand carrots, I discovered that the practice of "just cutting up the carrots" has a lot to offer.

Work Practice

I can easily understand how, from the outside, cutting up the carrots can seem like a boring task. But my Zen colleague Roshi Zoketsu Norman Fischer describes such common work as a vehicle for meditation and as an offering to others. When we treat our work as an offering, we give it freely for the benefit of others, says Norman. He writes that "work as offering is a kind of burning up of the self in the activity of work . . . just doing it completely without holding anything back. There's no sense of an observer or of any practice at all. There's just doing what you do completely with a good spirit." I think this is what Brother David means when he uses the word *wholeheartedness*—truly not holding back. Being one with whatever we are doing. Burning up the self. Letting go of the self. In this way, we work for life instead of working for a living.

The Japanese expression *mujodo no taigen*, which means "actualizing the Way in our everyday life," gives us some sense of this. We Zen people learn that work is a medium for doing ordinary tasks in an attentive and unitive way. One day, kitchen duty becomes not a duty but a practice, a way to cultivate the heart and mind while serving others. The carrot, the knife, and I are one thing; we are fully connected, and this connection includes those who eat the food, the farmer who grew the carrot, the trucker who brought the carrot to market, and the sun, rain, soil, and really everything.

A bit of Asian history might give more context for understanding work as a medium of practice. At the time of the Buddha, the Sanskrit word *bhavana* meant cultivation, related to farming—tilling the soil, sowing seeds, watering, weeding, harvesting—so the family and village could be fed. The Buddha expanded the use of *bhavana* to include cultivating the field of the mind through meditation. This metaphor even shows up in the robe that monastics wear, which is in the design of a rice field.

When Buddhist monks first made their way from India to China two thousand years ago, the Indian monks did not work. Instead, they wandered from village to village begging for alms. This was not acceptable in China, where the Confucian work ethic valued common labor. The Buddha's agrarian metaphors caught on in China, as they fit with the work ethic of the Chinese: "cultivating the mind," "sowing the seeds of the Buddha's teachings," and "the field of liberation."

Buddhist contemplative practice combined with the Chinese work ethic into what we now know as *work practice*, or using work as a medium for cultivating wisdom and compassion. Monastics in the larger Chinese monasteries farmed to feed themselves. They called their daily activity "farming meditation." Farming was virtuous, slow, good work, like the virtuous, slow, good work of cultivating the mind.

And what about our lives today? I like what Buddhist teacher Clark Strand says about "meditating inside the life you have." He does not separate out meditation as something apart from our life and livelihood. "Where you meditate has everything to do with how useful your meditation will be. But by where, I don't necessarily mean in which room of the house, or whether you live in a quiet spot or not. I simply mean that you should meditate inside the life you have. If you are an accountant, meditate inside an accountant's life. If you are a policeman, meditate inside of that. Wherever you want to illuminate your life, meditate precisely in that spot."

So, to avoid or transform burnout, perhaps the first thing we do is to meditate inside the life we have. . . .

Practicing Right Livelihood

What kind of life do we have? Of the factors in the Noble Eightfold Path of the Buddha (Right View, Aspiration, Speech, Action, Livelihood, Effort, Mindfulness, and Concentration), Right Livelihood is the one that is most directly connected with engagement and burnout. At its core are several questions. How can we do work that is good for ourselves, our family, our community, our earth, and future generations? And how can our work become a path for awakening out of our suffering and delusions?

The Buddha defined Right Livelihood by what we should *not* do for work. "A lay follower should not engage in five types of business," he wrote in the *Vanijja Sutta*. "Business in weapons, business in human beings, business in meat, business in intoxicants, and business in poison." I also like the way Thích Nhất Hạnh explains how to practice Right Livelihood: "You have to find a way to earn your living without transgressing your ideals of love and compassion. The way you support yourself can be an expression of your deepest self, or it can be a source of suffering for you and others."

Thích Nhất Hạnh is saying that we should choose work aligned with our values, whether it is the work of teaching children, caring for the dying, or managing a business in a compassionate and generous way. Aligning with our values includes not only *what* we do and *why* we do it, but *how* we do it. We have to make sure we do our work with integrity. Even if we choose a profession that helps to end others' suffering, we might still end up doing that work from a place of pathological altruism or empathic distress, moral suffering or disrespect—and these toxic expressions of Edge States can easily lead us into burnout.

Whatever our role, whether as a nurse, doctor, teacher, therapist, or CEO, we sometimes don't realize that we are suffering, and that we aren't giving ourselves enough time to recover from the harmful effects of our work. When we find ourselves falling over that edge, we need to take a step backward and look deeply at how we might be feeding our own suffering and the suffering of others by losing our balance and losing our love for what we do.

No Work Practice

During my years of work with those who were dying, I could often meditate inside the life I had. I walked down the hospital hall, giving attention to my breath and each step. I sat at the bedside, resting in my breath and in the presence of the dying person. I sat in team meetings, internally touching into why I was doing this work, grounding myself through attention on the breath and the body. Then I could offer more attention and care to those in the meeting.

And sometimes, I could not find my composure; it got away from me, like a tide quickly receding from the shore of the present moment, and I found myself worn out and discouraged. Not exactly burned out, but getting close. During those times, I had to take care of myself. I would nap, walk in the mountains, read a book, meditate, or perhaps best of all, just be lazy and aimless. Essentially, I had to press the Restart button, which meant turning off the machine!

There were also times when the cascade of events became too much for me to handle. When my father died, and shortly thereafter a close friend died, and I was also working with a number of dying people, I had to step away from my work for a while. I was not burned out, but I had become very sensitive to sickness, dying, and death, and I needed time to grieve the losses I had experienced. I was grateful that I had the opportunity to take time off, unlike many clinicians who are often told to "get over it" and get back to work.

The kind of pause I gave myself after my father's death is essential for most of us, if we are to make a sustainable commitment to engage with the suffering of others. We must know loss in our own life so that we may know loss in the lives of others. We need time to learn from our own difficulties, and time to renew our energy, our motivation, our perspective. We also must take time to be goalless and let things cook on their own.

Sometimes long pauses, like the one I took after my father's death, are essential, while at other times, micropauses are enough to help us regain the balance we need to stay on the solid ground of engagement. Too often, we don't even realize that we are losing our footing and are sliding over the edge.

To take a micropause, we can begin by noticing sensations in the body. If we interrupt our speediness to shift our attention to the in-breath and the out-breath, we can attune to the body's signals that something is off. Just by shifting our attention to the breath, we have already changed the neurochemical context of our experience, and some of the anxiety that primes the unhealthy aspects of our drive can begin to drop away. Then, we can recall, however briefly, our intention to serve without harming. This intention also applies to not harming ourselves.

We can learn a lot through inquiry. We can be curious. Why am I pushing myself so hard? Why am I staying in this toxic workplace? Is there anything I can do to shift my internal experience or workplace conditions in the direction of less harm? How can I build resilience in these challenging circumstances?

We can seek to understand and investigate. We want to note our biases and exercise discernment without judging. We can be radically honest about our motivations, while avoiding self-obsession or criticism. We can also be aware that our curiosity is about nourishing the conditions for wisdom and compassion to arise.

And even when overwork might stem from an addiction to the neuro-chemicals related to seeking and pleasure, this seeking behavior can lead us toward investigating our physical experience, an exploration that may give us valuable insight about our body and mind and about why we push ourselves so hard.

We must also give ourselves time to stop and to rest. Not just because we need time to grieve or to heal—but just because aimlessness is a natural part of life, and many of us have forgotten how to be without a goal and let go and wander. In a society that is so utterly goal-driven, it can be pretty challenging to slack off. But in fact, "wasting" our time might be just what we need. Maybe we are not wasting time, but *being* it.

A well-known adage in Zen is, "Nowhere to go, nothing to do." This is an invitation to stop running after anything, including enlightenment. So, I invite myself to let go . . . and whether I let go by sitting in Upaya's *zendo*, or I wander out of my little writing space and go out for a stroll in the meadow next to my hermitage, this is time well given, not well spent! When we look at time as a resource to be "spent," the beauty, surprise, and nourishment from being aimless is not so very accessible.

Being aimless, ignoring the god of efficiency, and getting lost for a while—these are lessons that Thoreau and my mother taught me. "Not till we are lost," said Thoreau, "in other words, not till we have lost the world, do we begin to find ourselves, and realize where we are and the infinite extent of our relations." Or, as my mother used to say, "Joanie, we don't have to go anywhere. We are already here." The beach near our Florida home never looked more beautiful in those moments. Nowhere to go, nothing to do . . . Lost and found in the moment . . . Just practice this . . . Maybe here is where we find wholeheartedness and our true freedom.

V. DISCOVERY AT THE EDGE
OF ENGAGEMENT

Astudent recently said to me, "Roshi, you seemed to have done so much in your life. How did you manage that?"

I paused, smiled, and then replied, "On a good day, I rest a lot."

I didn't mean that I take naps every day, though at my age, this is happening every so often. I am also not talking about the kind of rest that a good vacation provides you. Nor the kind of rest that is escapist. Rather, it is the kind of rest found in the experience of being relatively at ease in the midst of things, even quite difficult situations; ease that is about having a lack of resistance to what is before me, and being present and steady. This mix of no-resistance and steadiness is something we cultivate in Buddhist meditation. In my own meditation practice, I learned that giving full attention to an object (such as the breath) engenders steadiness and ease, as well as power and rest. When we strengthen these qualities, we can usually meet life with Brother David's "wholeheartedness."

In Buddhism, being occupied and preoccupied is not a source of merit. You cannot become enlightened by being busy. In fact, busyness distracts us from what is happening in the present moment, which we need stillness to perceive. This perspective is reflected in a wonderful exchange between two Zen teachers during China's Tang Dynasty, Yunyan and Daowu.

Yunyan is sweeping the ground. Daowu, who is older, says, "Too busy!"

Yunyan replies, "You should know there is one who is not busy."

Daowu asks, "Then are there two moons?"

Yunyan then holds up the broom and says, "Which moon is this?"

This story first appears in a thirteenth-century compilation of koans. The younger Yunyan is sweeping the ground. Maybe there is a taste of busyness and self-importance in how he is sweeping.

When Daowu calls him out for being too busy, Yunyan probably stops sweeping. But he then gives Daowu a clichéd Zen answer: "There is one who is not busy." This is the kind of answer a new Zen student might give—right out of a bad Zen book.

Daowu sees that this answer is a Zen dodge, and he doesn't let Yunyan off the hook. Yunyan, the sweeper, has split the world into two. "You mean there are two moons?" challenges Daowu. There is the doer and the non-doer? There is the busy person and the still person?

Yunyan sees his mistake. He lifts the broom off the floor, stopping his busyness, and holds it in front of Daowu. "Which moon is this?" he asks.

At that moment, Yunyan has been lifted above differences, duality, and self/other. He understands that reality is not divided into doer and non-doer, doing and non-doing. Reality is just this moment, with no broom on the ground, no doer, no deed, no one being busy, nothing to be busy about. And he awakens.

I found Zen relatively early in life. I was also raised Protestant. So, I've been immersed for a long time in the notion of work as virtue. It has been important to me to see work as a spiritual practice—a place where doer, doing, and deed are not separate; a place where I am not busy; a place where I can wake up.

The late Zen teacher Katagiri Roshi writes in *Each Moment Is the Universe*: "We tend to see practice in terms of time—as if we were climbing a ladder step-by-step. This is not the Buddhist idea of practice. When you climb a ladder, you do so with your eye on the future. With this approach to practice, there is no peace, no spiritual security—only a hope for the future. . . . Refined action is not like this. From the start, it lies in peace and harmony."

Katagiri Roshi explains that Zen master Dōgen (founder of the Sōtō school of Zen) used a peculiar term related to the concept of sanctuary.

"*Sanctuary* here means the universe," Roshi continues. "Wherever you may be, your life is sustained and supported by the whole universe. The main purpose of human life is to maintain this sanctuary. It is not to climb a ladder to develop your own personal life."

Katagiri Roshi is describing the unity of heart, mind, body, the world, and this moment as a sanctuary, a place of no resistance, a place of refuge. It is that moment when Yunyan holds up the broom in front of Daowu. This very moment is that place. Not seeking, not fleeing. But resting in the midst . . . this is why we practice, so we can actualize awakening inside the life that we have.

Play

Perhaps we can learn the most about burnout from those who have gone over the edge but found a way back to health. Like Shonda Rhimes, the creator and executive producer of the TV show *Grey's Anatomy*, who gave a TED talk in 2016 about her flow addiction and burnout. To produce seventy hours of TV per season, she was working fifteen hours a day, seven days a week—and she was loving every minute of it. She calls the space she got into "the hum." "That hum sounds like the open road, and I could drive it forever," she said. "The hum is music and light and air. The hum is God's whisper, right in my ear."

But one day, the hum stopped. "What do you do when the thing you do, the work you love, starts to taste like dust? . . . When the hum stops, who are you? What are you? What am I? . . . If the song in my heart ceases to play, can I survive in the silence?"

During this gray, silent period, she started accepting her daughter's invitations to play. And something important happened—the more she played with her kids, the more the hum came back. What Rhimes needed was play, the opposite of her high-stress work. And she needed more time with her kids, whose growing-up process she was missing while she was working so much.

She realized that the hum was not just about work—it was also about joy and love. She said, "Now, I'm not that hum, and that hum is not me—not anymore. I am bubbles and sticky fingers and dinners with friends. I am that hum. Life's hum. Love's hum. Work's hum is still a piece of me, but it is not all of me. And I am so grateful."

Today, whenever her children ask her to play, she says yes. Typically, their attention span is only fifteen minutes, so that's easy enough to spare, even while managing four TV shows. "My tiny humans show me how to live," she says. She credits play as saving her career.

Connection

As with all the Edge States, getting stuck in the swamp of burnout can also serve us. A crisis in values can make us reflect on the course our life has taken. Burnout is an affliction that can point us back toward our inner life and encourage us to work with the mental patterns that have compelled us to engage in self-harm and disconnection from others. It can show us what has gone awry, and if we listen more closely to the needs of the heart and body, our loved ones, and the world, something new and beautiful can grow from the mud. And we can come to joy through the power of engagement, through the healing of rest, play, and connection.

Omid Safi, director of Duke University's Islamic Studies Center, brings to light a dimension of engagement that opens toward the human heart. He writes,

> In many Muslim cultures, when you want to ask them how they're doing, you ask: In Arabic, Kayf haal-ik? or, in Persian, Haal-e shomaa chetoreh? How is your haal?
>
> What is this haal that you inquire about? It is the transient state of one's heart. In reality, we ask, "How is your heart doing at this very moment, at this breath?" When I ask, "How are you?" that is really what I want to know.

I am not asking how many items are on your to-do list, nor asking how many items are in your inbox. I want to know how your heart is doing, at this very moment. Tell me. Tell me your heart is joyous, tell me your heart is aching, tell me your heart is sad, tell me your heart craves a human touch. Examine your own heart, explore your soul, and then tell me something about your heart and your soul.

Tell me you remember you are still a human being, not just a human doing. Tell me you're more than just a machine, checking off items from your to-do list. Have that conversation, that glance, that touch. Be a healing conversation, one filled with grace and presence.

Put your hand on my arm, look me in the eye, and connect with me for one second. Tell me something about your heart, and awaken my heart. Help me remember that I too am a full and complete human being, a human being who also craves a human touch.

One day in southern France, I stopped by a garden that Thích Nhất Hạnh was tending. He was gardening very, very slowly. As I approached him, he looked up from his weeding, smiled, and said, "I couldn't write poetry or teach without tending to mustard greens." He was connecting to the earth as a way to connect to life and this moment, as well as to writing and teaching. And in that moment, he was also connecting to me. He was showing me his *haal*. It occurred to me that though Thầy had written more than one hundred books, he never seemed busy.

Busyness can take us close to the edge. But even when our lives are quite full of activity, it's possible to stand in engagement without falling off the edge into burnout. We must stay mindful not to push ourselves too far, and to back off when necessary in order to regain our balance. This can be as simple as an inhale and a long exhale between patients or meetings. State shifting. Or as simple as tending mustard greens or plastering an adobe wall.

Maybe it's not entirely bad that burnout can cause vital exhaustion and collapse—because chronic busyness and workaholism are not a healthy way to spend our days. All that activity diverts us from what is real and can even be a way to avoid choosing a livelihood that is aligned with our values. And often our obsession with work and service is a way to avoid real intimacy with our loved ones and with the true needs of the present moment and the wider world. Burnout and vital exhaustion become an emergency brake, so we are forced to shift gears, slow down, even stop. It requires us to renew our deepest spiritual aspirations and to look deeply at what we stand for, what we care about, what our values are, and what is our true calling. To find joy and beauty on the path of service. This is what I believe Dōgen meant by the words "giving life to life."

6. COMPASSION AT THE EDGE

*As long as space remains / And as long as living beings remain, /
May I too remain / To dispel the misery of the world.*
—Shantideva, Chapter 3, verses 21–22 (adapted from Stephen Batchelor)

When we're at the edge, in danger of falling over the precipice into suffering, compassion is the most powerful means I know for keeping our feet firmly planted on the earth and our hearts wide open. When I heard the little Nepalese girl's cries as her burns were being cleaned, compassion helped me stay grounded in empathy and navigate away from empathic distress. When I have confronted the systemic violence of war, racism, sexism, and environmental degradation, compassion has reminded me of my values, helping me to act from a place of integrity rather than getting mired in chronic moral outrage. During my years of sitting with dying people and volunteering in a maximum-security prison, compassion kept me from burning out. Compassion has been my greatest ally in the hardest of times. Not only has my life been strengthened by compassion, but those whom I have served may have benefited as well.

I have also been the recipient of compassion; my life has been profoundly affected by times when others have shown me great kindness. Many years *ago, I was lying on a hospital bed, waiting for surgery, shivering with fear. A Buddhist friend sat with me. As the team arrived to take me into the operating room, my friend squeezed my hand and with a steady gaze said, "Remember who you really are." His touch, his words sent a wave of relief through me, and I dropped into a place that was larger than my dread of surgery, vaster than my fear of death. As I was wheeled down the hall, words spoken by the late Roshi Hakuun Yasutani flashed across my mind: "The compassion of the undifferentiated body of no-cause comes burning forth."*

When, like my friend, we offer compassion, it burns forth from our hearts like a comet. This is the spirit of Avalokiteśvara, the bodhisattva of compassion, who hears the cries of the world and responds with a boundless heart—one that does not sink like a heavy stone in the waters of suffering but is broken open like a geode to the rare space within, glittering with light for those who are struggling in darkness.

For decades, I have traveled the geographies of compassion, exploring its structure and the deeper processes at play in this powerful landscape. I have examined scientific studies on compassion, received teachings from Buddhist adepts, shared stories with caregivers, sat with prisoners and dying people, trained educators and business people in approaches to compassion, and used my meditation practice as a medium of investigation. And then there are the challenges that life has given me—the perils that have also been ripe with possibility.

Compassion is defined as feeling genuine concern about the suffering of another and desiring to improve that one's welfare. Compassion also helps us meet our own suffering, and that of others, with an appropriate response. And, remarkably, compassion is the path out of the toxic aspects of the Edge States: pathological altruism, empathic distress, moral suffering, disrespect, and burnout. Why? Because compassion calls forth our best human capacities—attentional balance and caring, unselfish intention and insight, and ethical action—in a way that no other response does.

I. SURVIVAL OF THE KINDEST

S PEAKING AT A CONFERENCE I attended in Dharamsala, India, His Holiness the Dalai Lama said, "Compassion is not religious business; it is human business. It is not luxury . . . it is essential for human survival." I truly subscribe to His Holiness's words—that compassion is a necessity for human survival. And I want to take his words one step further: I am convinced that compassion supports the survival of *all* species on our planet.

His Holiness later wrote, "However capable and skillful an individual may be, left alone, he or she will not survive. However vigorous and independent one may feel during the most prosperous periods of life, when one is sick or very young or very old, one must depend on the support of others. . . . I believe that at every level of society—familial, tribal, national and international—the key to a happier and more successful world is the growth of compassion."

The English naturalist Charles Darwin would agree. Darwin wrote in *The Descent of Man* about the importance of "sympathy" (what today we would call compassion), exploring the tendency of humans and animals to help those in distress. He shared the story of a zookeeper who was attacked by an aggressive baboon. "Several years ago a keeper at the Zoological Gardens showed me some deep and scarcely healed wounds on the nape of his own neck, inflicted on him whilst kneeling on the floor, by a fierce baboon. The little American monkey, who was a warm friend of this keeper, lived in the same compartment, and was dreadfully afraid of the great baboon. Nevertheless, as soon as he saw his friend in peril, he rushed to the rescue, and by screams and bites so distracted the baboon that the man was able to escape."

Darwin recognized that such heroics are more likely when the rescuer and rescuee are part of the same in-group. That little monkey was good friends with the zookeeper and so was probably motivated to risk his life to save the zookeeper from death at the hands of the baboon. Darwin wrote, "It is evident in the first place that with mankind the instinctive impulses have different degrees of strength; a savage will risk his own life to save that of a member of the same community, but will be wholly indifferent about a stranger; a young and timid mother urged by the maternal instinct will, without a moment's hesitation, run the greatest danger for her own infant, but not for a mere fellow-creature."

But Darwin also recognized that extraordinary circumstances will inspire some people (and beings) to great compassion toward strangers. "Nevertheless many a civilized man . . . who never before risked his life for another, but full of courage and sympathy, has disregarded the instinct of self-preservation, and plunged at once into a torrent to save a drowning man, though a stranger. In this case man is impelled by the same instinctive motive, which made the heroic little American monkey, formerly described, save his keeper by attacking the great and dreadful baboon."

Darwin hypothesized that evolution selects for these traits, perpetuating them in descendants. "In however complex a manner [sympathy] may have originated, as it is one of high importance to all those animals which aid and defend one another, it will have been increased through natural selection; for those communities, which included the greatest number of the most sympathetic members, would flourish best, and rear the greatest number of offspring."

Darwin could have called this phenomenon "survival of the kindest." It's a theory that runs contrary to the cutthroat "survival of the fittest" paradigm commonly attributed to him (which is actually Herbert Spencer's over-simplification of natural selection). Darwin concluded his exploration with the idea that "sympathy" is not only essential for our survival—it also forms the foundation of our sense of personal morality and the ethical systems that inform social well-being.

More recently, Dutch ethologist and primatologist Frans de Waal has suggested that the roots of compassion can be found deep in our evolutionary history. De Waal has documented numerous acts of kindness and moral behavior among nonhumans, including apes, dogs, birds, and even mice. We can ask, if mice do it, why not us?

Science and Compassion

Whether compassion is rooted deep in our biology or springs from our conscience; whether it is instinctual, intentional, or socially prescribed, we know from scientific research that compassion enhances the welfare of those who receive compassion and also benefits those who are compassionate. It even benefits those who simply observe an act of compassion. Compassion is one of those experiences that deeply affects the human heart, whether we give it, receive it, or observe it.

Compassion also appears to enhance physical health. The strong social connections associated with compassion seem to reduce inflammation, support immune function, speed recovery from illness, and lead to increased longevity, according to a meta-analysis of numerous studies by researcher Julianne Holt-Lunstad and colleagues. In a study conducted by Dr. Sara Konrath, volunteers lived longer than non-volunteering peers if the reasons for volunteering were altruistic rather than self-serving.

In another study, the nonverbal communication of compassion calmed patients' autonomic nervous systems and regulated breathing and heart rate variation. Research also suggests that receiving compassion reduces post-surgical pain and decreases surgical recovery time, improves trauma outcomes, prolongs the survival of terminally ill patients, improves glucose control, reduces mortality at better rates than smoking cessation, and boosts immune function. By creating all these health benefits, compassionate interactions with patients might even reduce systemic health care costs and the costs of stress on clinicians.

What happens to long-term meditation practitioners when they are exposed to pain and suffering? Neuroscientists Richard Davidson, Antoine Lutz, and colleagues at the University of Wisconsin discovered that open awareness meditation appears to reduce negative anticipation to pain. In the same study, these long-term practitioners also experienced pain less adversely and recovered more rapidly from being unpleasantly stimulated. In another study, Dr. Davidson and his colleagues learned that expert practitioners, while generating compassion, responded more strongly to emotion-laden human vocalizations than to novice meditators. They also saw that the expert practitioners' capacity for cognitive and affective empathy was greater than novice practitioners. These are important discoveries on how mind training might enhance resilience in relation to being subjected to an unpleasant stimulus, as well as to be more attuned to the suffering of others.

In a study led by neuroscientist Dr. Helen Weng, also in the laboratory of Dr. Davidson, young adults trained to increase their experience of compassion behaved more altruistically when playing an economic game in the experiment. When they evoked feelings of compassion while viewing images of people who were suffering, they also showed increased activity in brain areas associated with empathy and understanding of others, as well as in emotion regulation and positive emotions.

Over my years of sitting with dying people, I saw that compassionate presence reduces the fear that dying people experience and supports them as they approach death; it also has a profoundly positive effect on those who serve the dying, particularly if a caregiver has a contemplative practice.

Years ago, Dr. Gary Pasternak, the medical director of Mission Hospice in San Mateo, California, and a long-term meditator, sent me an email I've never forgotten. He wrote,

> I'm up late admitting patients to the inpatient hospice unit. Just
> when I think I'm too old for these late nights without sleep, a person in
> all their rawness, vulnerability and pain lays before me and as my

hands explore the deep wounds in her chest and my ears open to her
words, my heart cracks open once again. . . . And this night a sweet
36-year-old woman with her wildly catastrophic breast cancer speaks of
her acceptance and her hope for her children, and she speaks with such
authenticity and authority. And her acceptance comes to me as the
deepest humility a person can experience and then again, once again, I
remember why I stay up these late nights and put myself in the company
of the dying.

Gary's words reflect respect and a quietness of heart, as well as humility and courage. He was able, in the medical world of distractions, time pressure, and sleep deprivation, to slow down and open to life and death, to listening and love. And, in the midst of his patient's pain and his own, he remembered who he really was. This is compassion—the ability to turn toward the truth of suffering with the wish to relieve that suffering. And then awakening with humility to the precious gift of serving others selflessly.

Experiencing compassion also seems to diminish depression and anxiety because it opens our horizon beyond the narrowness of the small self. As researcher Dr. Emma Seppälä, wrote, "Research shows that depression and anxiety are linked to a state of self-focus, a preoccupation with 'me, myself, and I.' When you do something for someone else, however, that state of self-focus shifts to a state of other-focus."

Filmmaker George Lucas, though not a scientist, has a similar take on compassion. When asked what his film *Star Wars* is really about, he said, "There are two kinds of people in the world—compassionate people and selfish people. Selfish people live on the dark side. The compassionate people live on the light side. If you go to the side of the light, you will be happy because compassion, helping other people, not thinking about yourself, thinking about others, that gives you a joy that you can't get any other way."

Looking at the faces of our Upaya residents as they serve food to homeless people, I see respect and caring in their eyes, and an absence of pity, self-importance, and fear. Watching clinicians work in Upaya's Nomads Clinic, I see the same. I also recently heard one of my chaplaincy students, Cathy, a nurse who serves dying people in the LGBTQ community, speak to the profound benefit she herself experiences in opening a door of safety and support for this community.

Another powerful aspect of compassion is related to moral character. Albert Schweitzer understood this when he wrote: "I can do no other than be reverent before everything that is called life. I can do no other than to have compassion for all that is called life. That is the beginning and the foundation of all ethics." He affirmed Arthur Schopenhauer's perspective that "compassion is the basis of morality." Research has found that being compassionate upholds our moral principles and gives meaning to our lives. According to the psychology researchers Daryl Cameron and Keith Payne, when we restrain compassion we will feel that our moral identity is compromised.

Psychologist and specialist in ethical leadership Jonathan Haidt has conducted studies on morality, culture, and emotion that suggest that when we see someone help another, it creates a state of "moral elevation" that inspires us to do the same. University of California–San Diego professor James Fowler, who studies contagion mechanisms, also confirms that helping is contagious. An article appears in *The New Yorker* about Upaya's Nomads Clinic in Dolpo, Nepal. The article, by Rebecca Solnit, has inspired clinicians from all over the world to serve in our medical clinics in Nepal, and more and more Nepali doctors and nurses join our clinics, moved by service to others. An American man, a young lawyer, washes the feet of a Nepali patient. Others in the team are moved and ask to join in; love and respect become contagious in a matter of moments. Goodness is inspiring, elevating, and, fortunately, catching.

I have long felt that compassion is central to being fully human. It is a key to reducing systemic oppression and nurturing a culture of respect, civility, and belonging. It is also an element in what makes cultures, organizations, and humans successful. To help us understand the necessity of compassion, science is making a strong case for its benefits and validating the importance of compassion for our survival and fundamental health—an insight that Jesus, Buddha, and Mohammed had thousands of years ago, and my grandmother had a century ago. Maybe for some of us, science can point us back to who we really are.

II. THREE FACES OF COMPASSION

FOR MANY YEARS, I WONDERED if compassion could be seen from perspectives other than what most of us are familiar with: the kind of compassion that is focused on another's suffering, particularly those in our in-group. I had a breakthrough in my quest to understand this when I read the fourteenth-century Zen master Muso Soseki's *Dialogues in a Dream*. Soseki discusses the kind of compassion that is most familiar to us, where we direct our compassion toward others. Social psychologists call this "referential compassion." He also notes two other faces of compassion: compassion that is based on insight, and compassion that has no object, but is nonreferential and universal.

Referential Compassion

Most of us experience compassion toward those with whom we share close connections—our parents, children, spouses, siblings, and our pets. We also tend to feel compassion more readily for our friends, colleagues, neighbors, and members of our own culture or ethnic group. We may feel a stronger connection with those who have suffered in ways that we ourselves have experienced. Because I was blind as a child, I long ago noticed that I feel a vivid identification with and compassion for blind people.

Referential compassion may also extend beyond the circle of our familiars to include those whom we don't know, such as victims of sexual harassment or police violence, or the unsheltered and refugees. It can also extend to creatures and places.

This kind of compassion is embodied in the story of the women from La Patrona, a small village not far from the city of Veracruz. One day more than twenty years ago, two sisters, Bernarda and Rosa Romero Vázquez, were returning from purchasing milk and bread for breakfast. They stood at a train crossing while a freight train approached. They were surprised to see train hoppers clinging to the tops and sides of boxcars and young people riding the rods beneath.

A man hanging on to one of the first boxcars called to them, "Madre, we are hungry!" As car after car passed, more shouts filled their ears: "Madre, we are hungry!" Before the last train car, Bernarda and Rosa tossed their newly purchased food to those who could catch it.

When Bernarda and Rosa returned to their family home that morning, they were afraid they would be punished for giving away their family's breakfast. But, no matter, they had to share what had happened with their mother, Leonila Vázquez Alvizar. Instead of punishing the sisters, the family gathered together to see what could be done, and a plan emerged.

Since 1995, when the sisters tossed the first food to transiting migrants, nearly every day these sisters and other villagers of La Patrona have stood beside the railroad tracks with food for those riding the rails to a hoped-for freedom.

"La Bestia," the Beast, is a moniker for the trains that have carried thousands north through Mexico to our borders. When La Bestia passed on its route through Veracruz and neared La Patrona, the village women, or as they are called, "Las Patronas," dash to the railroad tracks with bulging plastic bags of freshly cooked beans, rice, and tortillas. As the train hurtles by, they toss their offerings to the hungry migrant train hoppers.

I was told that sometimes the train slows at night so Las Patronas can more easily give away their food bags. But by day trains whiz through the village, and women of all ages stand strong in the violent currents of wind generated by the speeding train, reaching out to the desperate and hungry. It is an act of pure compassion.

Over the years, tens of thousands of meals have been offered. So far, the flow of migrants north continues in spite of violence, border walls, detention centers, and drug lords. La Bestia has carried its human cargo north, day after day, and Las Patronas have met them with food in hand.

Las Patronas have built a clinic and small rest house for weary train-hopping migrants. The kitchen has expanded, and those who cook and toss food bags include more people, including village men. They are also working with organizations across Mexico, lobbying the government for more protection for migrants. Patrona Norma Romero said, "While God gives me life, and migration continues to exist, I believe I will be here helping."

And as Guadalupe Gonzalez told the BBC, "We never expected it to turn into something so big. I think it's because it came out of nowhere, it came from just the little that one can give." Her words strike deeply.

That same BBC report on Las Patronas made a poignant observation. "Las Patronas took their name from their village. But it has a wider religious connotation too, *patrona* meaning "patron saint" in Spanish. For the migrants, who grab a potentially life-saving donation from a woman they may never see again, the name could not be more apt."

Hearing about Las Patronas from my Mexican friends in Santa Fe, and following their miraculous and humble work through media reports, I am moved by the great compassion and bold determination of these women who show up day after day, cooking and delivering beans, rice, and tortillas for those traveling north. They represent to me the best in the human heart. Compassion, altruism, grit, dedication, and engagement—and the power to transform suffering, against all odds.

Insight-Based Compassion

Referential compassion is deeply valued in our society, and that is a good thing. Yet there are forms of compassion that are less familiar to most of us. Soseki writes about insight-based compassion, a concept that also exists within Tibetan Buddhism. This kind of compassion is more conceptual.

Soseki's discussion focuses on impermanence and dependent co-arising. From my perspective, as a contemplative and caregiver, insight-based compassion also encompasses the understanding that compassion is a moral imperative—and we can deduce that ignoring suffering can have serious consequences for self, other, and society.

When we see someone in need, ideally, we feel morally compelled to act. We don't just walk by. We don't feel indifference or moral apathy. Responding to suffering with compassion is the "right" thing to do, an affirmation of respect and human dignity. When we experience the suffering of others from this perspective, and when this understanding is supported by our natural kindness and our aspiration to relieve suffering, then our heart will be filled with wise compassion.

Not so long ago, I was sitting at the bedside of a woman who was dying of liver cancer. Her legs were so swollen with edema that the skin over her shins was splitting open. This was the day before she would take her last breath, although I didn't know it at the time. She had been a close friend and had fought cancer for years. I experienced great compassion for her, referential compassion, as she was being tossed about by confusion and pain; when I took her hand into mine and spoke softly to her, I felt the overwhelming wish to relieve her suffering. By the same token, through the lens of insight-based compassion, I was able to see her situation in terms of the truth of impermanence, that her suffering was a discrete moment in time and was made up of non-suffering elements. I also felt deep in my heart that responding to her suffering was a moral necessity. These perspectives kept me from succumbing to empathic distress and helped me hold the space for her in a less reactive way—and finally, to be with her with greater love.

Non-Referential Compassion

Soseki also suggests that there is a third form of compassion that is unbiased. We can call this *non-referential compassion*—that is, compassion without an object. This third form is true compassion, Soseki says.

I experienced this form myself once. I was teaching in Toronto and staying in a private home. Getting out of the shower, I slipped on the wet floor and fell, shattering my thighbone and trochanter. I knew a really bad thing had happened when I looked at the angle of my leg. A few heartbeats later, I was seized in the grip of excruciating pain. Being a good Southerner, I politely called out, "Help! Can someone help me?" My voice was thin as a reed, and I could barely breathe. Within minutes my host, Andrew, arrived, gently braced my back where I was sitting on the floor, and shouted to his wife to call an ambulance. I could not move and could hardly speak, but Andrew knew what to do. Like a tree, he supported my spine and remained perfectly still, so I could let go into the spaces between the wrenching pulses of pain.

When the first responders arrived, a young medic came into the bathroom and announced that they were going to move me onto a gurney. My mind and body balked at his words—I was already on the edge of blacking out, and I could feel my blood pressure dropping from the intensity of the pain. I looked the young medic straight in the eyes and said, "Before you move me, I need something to control the pain." The medic told me in a flat voice that he was not licensed to administer morphine. "Get someone who is," I said. I wasn't kidding. He dialed his phone to bring in a licensed provider.

Ten long minutes later, an older medic arrived. He kneeled beside me and took my blood pressure, which was ocean-bottom low. He nodded and with a syringe pulled clear liquid from a small bottle. He stretched out my arm, but my veins had collapsed from shock and the needle poke yielded nothing.

He tried the other arm, then each of my wrists, then I don't remember where; I only recall noticing the sweat drip down his face as he tried to help me, his mouth drawn and the skin taut around his eyes.

The young medic was standing beside the bathroom wall, looking pale; his eyes rolled up as though he was going to faint. He seemed distressed watching me get stuck with the needle six times. My heart opened to him, and at that moment my veins opened too, flushing my body with blood. The needle slipped in, and I felt enough relief that I could be moved.

As the first responders carried the gurney down the long staircase, my body, pitched at a dangerously steep angle, slid inches down and froze up again. Finally, I was in the ambulance and we were racing through Toronto's streets toward the hospital, siren screaming. It was Friday the thirteenth and a full moon in June.

The older medic leaned close to me, and I sensed that something was weighing him down. Without thinking, I touched his knee and asked if he was all right. It was a strange question for me to be asking under the circumstances, but it arose out of nowhere, the kind of nowhere that is there during deep meditation, the nowhere that is present when pain has eclipsed the self.

His eyes wet, he said in a barely audible voice, "My wife is dying of breast cancer." In that moment, nothing existed but this suffering human beside me and the inexplicable warmth I felt in my body, in my heart, in the atmosphere between us. In that moment, my pain vanished completely. I looked into his eyes, and they were wet and unguarded.

Writing this, I recall the words of songwriter Lucinda Williams: "Have compassion for everyone you meet for you do not know what wars are going on down there, where the spirit meets the bone." In the ambulance, I had no idea, and that is the point. . . .

In the ER, I was put on a morphine drip, cathed, given a cool cloth for my head, and left in an outer hall. My new friend sat silently beside the gurney for some hours, until I got rolled away to x-ray. I saw him once more after my surgery. I don't know his name, never asked for it, didn't think to ask; but there we were. He had come alongside my boat, and I had come alongside his.

In retrospect, I realized that, in the midst of my own critical state, I had opened into an experience of universal compassion. The experience was not about him, nor about me. The upwelling of boundless concern and love for another had dissolved my sense of self, and with that, my pain had melted away. "The compassion of the undifferentiated body of no-cause comes burn-ing forth."

Over the years, when I've shared the story of the fall I took in that To-ronto bathroom, dozens of people have responded with similar stories in which their own suffering ended spontaneously when they felt unbidden compassion for another. What kind of compassion was this? It wasn't pre-meditated or even intentional. It arose from my bones, broken though they were—and it gave me relief, surprising relief. I believe it touched the medic as well.

During a recent visit with my old friend Ram Dass, we were talking about compassion. He reminded me of these words from the *Ramayana*, the Indian epic. Ram, who is God, asks Hanuman, the Monkey God, who embodies selfless service: "Who are you, Monkey?" Hanuman replies: "When I don't know who I am, I serve you. When I know who I am, I *am* you." My old friend and I smiled at each other. Is this not the deepest ex-pression of compassion?

Asanga and the Red Dog

I asked myself some months later what had made this experience possible. A story from Tibetan Buddhism gives me a hint as to how we can nourish universal compassion. The fourth-century yogi Asanga spent many years meditating in a cave. He meditated on Maitreya, the Buddha of loving-kindness, hoping to receive a vision and teaching from him. Even though Asanga practiced year after year, Maitreya never showed up.

One day, after twelve years of sitting in his cave practicing and waiting for Maitreya to appear, Asanga decided that he'd had enough of cave time. With his staff in hand, he left his hermit's fastness and began to make his way down the mountain path. As he proceeded along the narrow way, he caught a glimpse of something ahead that seemed to be lying across the nar-row mountain path. Drawing closer, he saw a red dog lying still in the pale dust. Looking more closely, he found that the dog's hindquarters were covered with raw, ugly sores. On closer examination, he discovered that the sores were filled with wriggling maggots.

Asanga immediately wanted to help the dog, but he did not want to harm the maggots. His compassion was so overpowering that he dropped to his knees and stuck out his tongue in order to gently remove the maggots without harming them. Before his tongue touched the mass of squirming larvae, the red dog transformed into the compassionate Maitreya.

Why didn't Maitreya show up for Asanga in his cave?

I think that Maitreya would only come when Asanga was called into action in the service of another. And I am also sure that Asanga's twelve years of cave practice were not wasted, even though Maitreya did not show up for him there, at least not in a form he could recognize. For Asanga's openness and compassion had grown deep and wondrous through his years of commitment and dedicated practice. Practice here yielded the golden fruit of undivided, non-referential compassion. Still, his compassion needed a reason to be activated, and the red dog gave Asanga the opportunity to practice compassion both with and without an object.

This speaks to the profound value of our relationships and that our own liberation is bound up with the liberation of others. This story also points to the value of making our aspiration to benefit others an integral part of our practice, even if we are far from those who need help. And it reminds us that being with suffering is a path of practice that is energized by this deep aspiration.

Like Asanga's awakening, our own awakening from delusion happens when we are bigger than our small self and when we are in some way drawn through the knot of suffering into the wider world around us. Thus, the wounded dog and squirming maggots gave the yogi the precious chance to embody (not merely to contemplate) his wish to benefit others. To have non-referential compassion is to have a heart and mind that are open to the suffering of all beings and ready to serve in an instant. It is universal, boundless, pervasive, and without bias. As the illusion of the small self falls away, we remember who we really are.

This kind of compassion is the essence of our character; it permeates our whole being. We can feel it for anyone and everyone at once—the person suffering from excruciating sorrow, the bloodied child in Aleppo, the elephant in a moldy zoo, the woman on methamphetamine—even the drug dealer, the abusive parent, and the warmongering politician. When we recognize that there is no separate self, and that all beings and things are interconnected, we are ripe for universal compassion. This is the experience of a person who has a deep practice or who is naturally predisposed toward great kindness and concern for the well-being of others.

Like compassionate Avalokiteśvara, when we experience non-referential compassion, we respond to any need. It is like salt in the water of the great ocean, like the air we breathe, like the blood in the body; it is the very medium of our lives and our minds. "Throughout the body, hands and eyes."

III. THE SIX PERFECTIONS

THE SIX PARAMITAS, OR PERFECTIONS, of Buddhism are the compassionate qualities that bodhisattvas like Avalokiteśvara embody: generosity, virtue, patience, wholeheartedness, concentration, and wisdom, giving us strength and balance as we stand on the edge. The word *paramita* can be translated as "perfection" or "crossing over to the other shore," meaning the shore that is free of suffering. The Perfections are both the path to becoming a bodhisattva and the realizations of the path. As a path, the Perfections are the practice of enlightened qualities of our character. As realizations, they are the gift of practice. Each Perfection is an expression of our boundless heart and a special kind of medicine that cures afflictions of every kind. Each, in a sense, is a different facet of compassion.

The first Perfection, *Generosity*, is giving compassionate support, protection, teachings, and attention to those who need it. As philosopher Simone Weil said: "Attention is the rarest and purest form of generosity." Then there is serving food to the homeless person in the shelter; sitting with a dying person who has been abandoned by her family; protecting the victim of spousal abuse; inviting into our home the refugee looking for a place to land. Generosity is giving our patients and our students the attention and space to make their own decisions. Standing tall at Standing Rock to protect a river and a people; speaking truth to power to safeguard the rights of women, children, and our future.

Generosity is also expressed in sharing the treasure of spiritual teachings with others. My teacher Roshi Bernie Glassman, in spite of a recent stroke that had left half of his body paralyzed, flew to Poland to the Auschwitz Bearing Witness Retreat in 2016. Roshi Bernie brings others to bear witness in Auschwitz as part of his compassionate commitment to transforming alienation and hatred so that another holocaust does not consume our planet. He believes that by bearing witness in Auschwitz and other places of unspeakable horror, we can remember who we really are, and remember to love.

Along with love, there is another expression of the Perfection of Generosity, though it does not appear in the traditional texts. This came to me many years ago, when I was first doing service work in Nepal. Being at altitude and in the wilds of the Himalayas, I felt very vulnerable. As I sat with patients from the remote villages we were serving, I realized I had better get grounded. The notion of "giving no fear" came up for me. This was the practice I needed to engage when serving our patients in the high mountains.

Give no fear . . . It's a place from which we can bear witness to the pain and suffering of this world and connect with others without attachment to self, other, or outcome. It's a way of perceiving who we really are—of knowing that we are made of love, courage, and great compassion. It's a way of seeing past fear into the vast landscape of the human heart.

The Second Perfection is the Perfection of *Virtue*, or living by vow. The Perfection of Virtue is about directing principled compassion toward all beings, even those who harm others. When compassion is absent, then suffering ensues. To avoid harming others or ourselves—to be courageous, caring, and trusting—we live by vow. This is compassion and actualizing the spirit of the bodhisattvas.

Over the years, I have learned a lot from my students that compassion and vows inter-are. They live within each other. The vows we receive in Buddhism are about doing good, not harming, and caring for others. Daily, most of us are faced with moral challenges. Yet, most of us have learned how important it is to not violate our integrity. There is the clinician who daily makes life-and-death decisions that prioritize her patients' well-being over institutional expectations. The managing director who does what she can to protect her employees from harmful company policies. The whistle-blower who protects our rights of privacy at great risk to himself. All of these people have been guided by their integrity. This is the Perfection of living by vow.

The third Perfection is *Patience*—revolutionary patience with others and with ourselves. Patience means being fully in the present moment and letting go of the aggression we might experience when we realize that we cannot control outcomes. The flight is canceled—and we blame the reservation clerk. Our close friend is dying, and the nurse is slow in checking her vitals; we blow up at this harried clinician who is caring for too many patients. We want things to go our way. We want a timely outcome; we want closure. We can't bear to wait, to pause, to trust . . . to just let go.

When I think about patience, I think about A. T. Ariyaratne, who leads the Sarvodaya Shramadana Movement in Sri Lanka. I spent time with Ari (as his friends call him) in Japan years ago at a meeting of Buddhists from all over the world. The largest NGO in Sri Lanka, Sarvodaya uses the teachings of the Buddha as a powerful means for compassionate social change. Sarvodaya is a way for people to express their natural compassion by working together to improve the conditions of their local communities, so that economic and social healing from war can happen.

Ari told me that his country has seen five hundred years of conflict among Hindus, Muslims, and Buddhists. Four hundred of those years were also spent under colonial oppression. I was staggered by these numbers. Then Ari looked at me with eyes gleaming and said, "It will take five hundred years to transform these conditions—and I have a plan!" A five-hundred-year plan. Ari is a patient man indeed.

Ari explained that his 500-Year Peace Plan includes peace activities around the country, followed by economic development projects in the poorest areas of Sri Lanka. He added that every one hundred years, a council of elders will need to assess how things are going.

Ari is not young. He is in his eighties. He is healthy, but reality will prevail. Yet all the Perfections are his allies, especially patience and also *Whole-*

heartedness, the Fourth Perfection. Ari knows what it is to live life as a compassionate imperative with no holds barred.

In my own life, I try to practice wholeheartedness as an antidote to the subtle discouragement that occasionally arises. It takes energy and determination to keep showing up, whether in the hospital, classroom or boardroom, the refugee camp or war zone. It also takes zeal, will, and concentration to live the wisdom of no escape, no hiding out, no denial.

The Fifth Perfection is *Concentration*, or attentiveness, which, along with patience, is a way to prevent escape from the present moment. The Buddha used a wonderful metaphor for our lack of attentiveness. Just "as a monkey swinging through the trees grabs one branch and lets it go only to seize another, so too, that which is called thought, mind or consciousness arises and disappears continually both day and night."

The Buddha used another animal metaphor to exemplify concentration: Be like a deer in the forest: one who is alert, gentle, and present to whatever arises. A forest deer also symbolizes nonaggression and serenity. By emulating the deer, we can transform the monkey mind into the mind of a bodhisattva and gain access to compassion and wisdom.

The Sixth Perfection is *Wisdom*, which is about directly experiencing the nature of reality. This is another reason why the Perfection of Concentration is so important—wisdom is not accessible if we are not totally open, unbiased, and attentive.

But what is wisdom?

Being smart is not necessarily about being wise. We can sense this distinction by exploring how we see the difference between a smart person and a wise person. A smart person might have knowledge and is usually beholden to facts. A wise person, on the other hand, has the power of discernment and the presence of compassion.

From a Buddhist perspective, wisdom can be seen through two lenses: wisdom that is relative and wisdom that is ultimate. Relative wisdom is seeing and understanding the interconnectedness of all beings and things, the truth of impermanence, the causes of suffering, the way to freedom from suffering, and living the imperative to free others from suffering.

Even though he was not a Buddhist, the physicist Albert Einstein had a deep understanding of "relative wisdom." He wrote:

A human being is part of a whole, called by us the "universe," a part limited in time and space. He experiences himself, his thoughts and feelings, as something separate from the rest—a kind of optical delusion of his consciousness. This delusion is a kind of prison for us, restricting us to our personal desires and to affection for a few people near us. Our task must be to free ourselves from this prison by widening our circles of compassion to embrace all living creatures and the whole of nature in its beauty.

From a Buddhist perspective, "ultimate wisdom" is based on our direct experience of letting go of how we view so-called reality; any description we contrive about reality separates us from the direct experience of "things as they are." Reality isn't a state; it happens, it emerges moment after moment. In this, I have always liked what Huang Po says about the trap of conceptualization: "Here it is—right now. Start thinking about it and you miss it!"

Wisdom and compassion are facets of each other. Shunryū Suzuki Roshi, the beloved Sōtō Zen monk and founder of San Francisco Zen Center, shared his great wisdom and compassion in his last moments of life. Just before he died at the San Francisco Zen Center in 1971, a close student went into his room. The old Zen master's skin was stained dark by his illness; he was thin and small in his narrow bed, his hands just over the covers. His student looked at him and asked, "Roshi, where shall we meet?" as though there was a particular destination where the two would encounter one another after death. There was a pause, and then the dying man raised one hand and made a circle, inviting his student to meet him in that very moment. This is the Perfection of Wisdom; and this is also compassion, great compassion.

The Perfections are powerful guidelines for developing a loving, courageous, and wise heart and for creating a compassionate society. They are a path to freedom.

I often use phrases that reflect the Perfections as a way to call them forth. Each Perfection contains all others. That's why I usually practice with just one phrase, letting it soak into my marrow.

We begin by gathering our attention on the inhale and dropping into the body on the exhale. Next, we recall our intention to end the suffering of others. We then might let the heart and mind rest on a single phrase, or, if we wish, we can slowly proceed through all the phrases:

MAY I BE GENEROUS.

MAY I CULTIVATE INTEGRITY AND RESPECT.

MAY I BE PATIENT AND SEE CLEARLY THE SUFFERING OF OTHERS.

MAY I BE ENERGETIC, STEADFAST, AND WHOLEHEARTED.

MAY I CULTIVATE A CALM AND INCLUSIVE MIND AND HEART SO I CAN COMPASSIONATELY SERVE ALL BEINGS.

MAY I NURTURE WISDOM AND IMPART THE BENEFIT OF ANY INSIGHTS I MAY HAVE TO OTHERS.

And we can ask, *Why not embody the spirit of bodhisattvas, who have realized a mind and heart of fearlessness, wisdom, and compassion? Why not stand at the edge and take in the view? Why not do it now?*

IV. COMPASSION'S ENEMIES

DESPITE THE OBVIOUS VALUE AND benefits of compassion, our world today seems to have a deficit of it. This deficit is fed by a number of factors, including our ideas about what it means to care and the disconnection that results from our ever-greater reliance on technology. Too often today, connectivity is emphasized at the cost of connection, fast thinking is more valued than slow thinking, growth comes at the expense of depth, building a portfolio is valued more than building an ethical culture, and perceptions of time poverty distract us from the present moment. I believe that the antidote to all these ills is to make compassion a primary value that we bring to life within the microcommunity of our one-to-one interactions, and within the macrocommunity of the planet.

In Buddhism, beneficial qualities of the mind have far enemies and near enemies. *Far enemies* are opposites; compassion's far enemy is cruelty. *Near enemies* are harder to detect; they are unhelpful qualities that masquerade as helpful ones. For example, pity is a near enemy of compassion, because it involves a sense of regret, plus deceptive concern for those who are suffering. William Blake, for example, called pity a distraction, and wrote that it divides the soul!

Other near enemies of compassion include fear and even outrage. Near enemies easily disguise themselves as allies or analogues of compassion. But these emotions can drain us so much that we can't respond in healthy ways to the suffering of others, and we actually may end up doing harm.

There are other obstacles and challenges to compassion. We tend to oversimplify compassion, and if we don't understand how compassion functions in our lives and in societies, we may have an aversion toward it or even fear it.

We might feel that compassion is fatiguing, that it can make us sick, and that we can lose our boundaries and be judged as weak or unprofessional. We may believe that compassion prioritizes sympathy over justice—that it can be meted out indiscriminately and sometimes irrationally. For some clinicians, whether or not to cultivate compassion may be a dilemma in itself. Medical school students are taught to be *dis*passionate in order to maintain their objectivity and make decisions based on facts rather than feelings. Many doctors also believe that suffering can be emotionally contagious and could overwhelm them if they let it in. They are also socialized to view compassion as religious, unscientific, and a possible indication of weakness.

In contrast, nurses, hospice workers, and family caregivers are expected to act from compassion. Yet they, too, may fear getting emotionally involved due to the risk of losing their boundaries and experiencing empathic distress or burnout.

Wanting to be perceived as compassionate is another trap. We might feel our worth is measured by how compassionate we are or appear to be, and thus present ourselves in the world as a "compassionate person," while needing approval, validation, admiration, and even authorization. So we should beware of people who advertise themselves as compassionate. Not everyone walks their talk.

Another obstacle to compassion is distraction. We can place some of the blame for this on our digital devices and our addictive behaviors around them. "Finding moments to engage in contemplative thinking has always been a challenge, since we're distractible," Nicholas Carr, author of *The Shallows*, told *The New York Times*. "But now that we're carrying these powerful media devices around with us all day long, those opportunities become even less frequent, for the simple reason that we have this ability to distract ourselves constantly."

One study, which measured smartphone use among participants ages eighteen to thirty-three, found that participants used their phones an average of eighty-five times per day! This convenient diversion fills moments when we might otherwise have greater awareness of our surroundings, including noticing the suffering of others. And frequent use of digital devices, according to Carr, has detrimental effects on cognition, concentration, and our ability to be healthily introspective.

Another major challenge to compassion is time stress. As we saw in the section on engagement and burnout, it seems normal to be caught in busyness and "aggressive haste," which Hermann Hesse called "the enemy of joy."

Our busyness and speediness distorts our attempts at compassionate engagement with others, and, in the end, can cause moral distress. Even forty years ago, time pressure was shown to inhibit compassion in the Good Samaritan study, a famous experiment by Princeton researchers John Darley and Daniel Batson. In this study, the researchers met seminary students in one building and instructed them to walk across campus to another building. Some students were told they were already late and needed to hurry, while others were told they had plenty of time to get there. En route, both groups passed a person slumped in an alley, moaning and coughing, who seemed to be drunk or hurt. This person was an actor placed there by the researchers. In the group that had time, 63 percent stopped to help. In the group that was already late, only 10 percent stopped. Ethical action, it seems, may be inversely correlated with the speed of one's life. When they arrived at the lecture hall, many students who hadn't stopped appeared anxious—more anxious than those who had stopped. It seemed they felt moral distress over the choice they'd made to meet researchers' expectations rather than to help the victim. Beyond this experiment, distractions and time pressure influence the decisions we make when facing moral dilemmas, including whether we extend help to others.

The Arithmetic of Compassion

Another factor that can challenge compassion is overwhelm. When we hear about large-scale problems like the global refugee crisis, species extinctions, and climate change, our brains can shut down in a kind of psychic numbing. It's not that we don't care—it's that the problem is too large to even really conceive of, so we put it aside and don't take action.

It's a well-documented phenomenon that our desire to help declines exponentially as the size of the suffering group grows—even from one to two. The Polish poet Zbigniew Herbert called this phenomenon "the arithmetic of compassion." In an experiment on charitable giving, psychologist Paul Slovic, Ph.D., and his colleagues studied the arithmetic of compassion. Slovic writes, "We found that people might be inclined to send money to an individual person in need, but that if they heard that a second person also required aid but could not be helped, they were less inclined to donate to the first person. Meeting that need no longer felt as satisfying. Similarly, when the need for assistance was described as part of a large-scale relief effort, potential donors would experience a demotivating sense of inefficacy arising from the thought that the help they could provide was but 'a drop in the bucket.'"

This phenomenon is known as *pseudo-inefficacy*—"pseudo" because our sense of inefficacy is a perception, not a reality. But it's a perception that serves as a powerful de-motivator when we know that there are some we cannot help.

This mental shutdown is not only metaphorical but literal. Neuroscientists have found that the anterior cingulate cortex (ACC), which they believe controls our attention to emotionally arousing stimuli, becomes quickly habituated to disturbing stimuli and stops responding. This may be a kind of defense mechanism so we don't get too overwhelmed by negative input. I have little doubt that our constant access to bad news today, via social media and online news sites, contributes to psychic numbing, moral apathy, and a deficit of compassion.

When the 2015 earthquake happened in Gorkha, Nepal, I found it hard to wrap my mind around the enormity of the disaster. As the death toll climbed, the numbers stunned me. It's not that I didn't care—I did—but I couldn't begin to grasp the human reality. The day after the quake, my phone started ringing—close friends in Nepal were trying to get tarps and food supplies into the hard-hit areas, and they needed help. I immediately supported their efforts, even though I still couldn't come to terms with the magnitude of the tragedy.

What woke me up, however, was a small photograph on Facebook of a little monk I had met some months before in a village monastery in the Gorkha area. The child looked scared and drained. The trails to this region were destroyed. The kids from this monastery had no food or shelter. Knowing this, I felt I had to help this child. It was personal, one person to another. In short order, we were able to support my good friend Pasang Lhamu Sherpa Akita to hire a helicopter to fly into the quake-ravaged mountains to evacuate thirteen little boys out of the mountains and resettle them in Kathmandu.

When I read the story about their rescue in *The New York Times*, I felt enormous relief. One child's face, and I could not turn away from the reality that all were suffering. It was this one face that mobilized me. Then other faces of men, women, and children I had met in the region began appearing on my social media feed, along with faces of the young Nepali rescuers who were doing courageous work, some of whom were close friends. At first, Upaya was supporting large NGOs that were doing earthquake relief. But we shifted our strategy to supporting individuals who were doing direct work on the ground. This felt more "real" to us, more efficient, closer to the heart.

When our compassion is blocked by numbness or by fear, judgment, or distraction, or the unreality of numbers, we may stay stuck in the unhealthy manifestations of the Edge States, including moral apathy. To find our way out, we need to acknowledge the obstacle to our compassion. We then discern how we can respond appropriately to whatever is present. We must deeply examine our response to suffering, while letting go of self-judgment.

Falling In and Out of Compassion

Eight months after the tsunami in Japan, writer Pico Iyer traveled with His Holiness the Dalai Lama to a small fishing village in Japan that had been devastated by this terrible natural disaster. His Holiness offered love and support to the survivors, yet when he turned from them, his eyes were wet with tears. Iyer did not miss this moment. He later wrote that "The only thing worse than assuming you could get the better of suffering, I began to think (though I'm no Buddhist), is imagining you could do nothing in its wake. And the tear I'd witnessed made me think that you could be strong enough to witness suffering, and yet human enough not to pretend to be master of it."

"Human enough not to pretend to be master of it. . . ." Like most of us, I have been overcome by suffering, my own and others, and, as a result, have fallen in and out of compassion. Along the way, I learned something about what compassion is and isn't. I saw that when I have been caught in empathic or moral distress in response to another's suffering, I did things that were more about relieving my own discomfort than about serving the suffering other. Sometimes, my "over-caring" actually inhibited the person's experience, as I slipped over the edge of altruism into pathological altruism. Or I responded with a show of care in order to take care of myself and not so much the person I was there to serve.

Other times, due to my distraction, numbness, or denial (all forms of apathy), I missed the fact that a student or colleague was suffering. Often in these moments, I was feeling tired, harried, ungrounded, or stressed from work or travel and could not access the emotional resources to appraise the situation and respond with compassion.

Or I fell into futility because I felt I had nothing to offer or did not have the wherewithal to face the suffering of one more person. Maybe, I would simply avoid the vulnerable person or overlook their suffering altogether. In the best of circumstances, my sense of moral responsibility reasserted itself and turned me back toward what might serve.

Or I found myself caught in the grip of moral outrage at the treatment of a patient or a prisoner. Ideally, this moment of anger would alert me to an unjust situation. I usually saw that being stuck in moral outrage was not healthy, and I would drop into an exploration of what might have contributed to the suffering and then work to try to bring relief to the person or situation.

When I was caught in the gaps between kindnesses, I sometimes could turn my eyes toward what was missing. Oddly enough, compassion became more visible by its absence. These moments also showed me that compassion is not a single thing but a suite of braided processes that emerge from the relationship between the mind and body. Compassion is also influenced by the environmental, social, cultural, and relational contexts in which we are embedded. These transits over the edge into the swamp of my own confusion helped me come to know compassion more intimately. They showed me that through compassion, we can lift ourselves out of pathological altruism, empathic distress, moral suffering, disrespect, and burnout.

V. MAPPING COMPASSION

THE MORE I SAW THE suffering caused by the absence of compassion, the more I realized that I needed to take a deeper look into compassion, try to unpack it, do the best I could to map it, and attempt to create pathways to access compassion. In 2011, I was invited to spend a few months as a Distinguished Visiting Scholar and Kluge Fellow at the Library of Congress in Washington, D.C. This special opportunity supported me in taking time away from teaching, so I could focus on neuroscience and social psychology research on compassion. My goal was to develop a map of compassion to train caregivers and others more effectively in cultivating compassion as they encountered suffering.

In a thought experiment, I asked myself four questions. First, I asked, *Can we experience compassion if our attention is not balanced, grounded, clear, and sustaining?* I thought about how clinicians are often distracted by their mobile devices and pagers, the pressure on them to meet quotas and their frequent need to move quickly from patient to patient, and more. It's not easy to be present for a patient's suffering when our attention is fragmented in this way. I remembered that neuroscientist Amishi Jha made the point that wherever our attention goes, our brains follow. "Attention is the boss of the brain," she said. Because attentional balance is challenging for people working in complex clinical situations, compassion may also be challenging, as clinicians' attention is often divided, distracted, and dispersed (what I have called "the three Ds"). To perceive suffering or anything clearly, we need attentional balance.

The second question I asked myself was, *Can we be compassionate if we don't feel concern for others?* Again, I was pretty sure that the answer was *no*. If we are feeling apathetic or are in denial about a person's suffering—or if we feel aversion toward that person—it won't be easy for compassion to arise. The meaning of *prosocial* is the opposite of *antisocial*. Prosocial behavior is about positive social connection, being affiliative, being helpful, and benefiting others. If our intention is self-centered, for example, we probably aren't being prosocial. Care, concern, kindness, tenderness, love, generosity, and even humility are all prosocial feelings that can be expressed through the medium of compassion. From what I have observed, compassion is not accessible without prosocial feelings.

Then, I asked myself a third question. *Can compassion arise within us if we are lacking insight into what might serve to relieve the suffering of another?* The answer was *no*. In order to feel compassion, we use insight to discern what would best serve others. Compassion also involves having a deeper understanding of why it matters for us to care and who we really are.

Finally, I asked myself, *Is it important to have the desire to relieve the suffering of another, even if we can't do anything directly?* This time, the answer was a firm *yes*. We can't always take embodied and direct action that might transform the suffering of another, but at least the *desire* to enhance their well-being is essential to compassion.

I remember hearing Matthieu Ricard give the example of an airplane passenger who sees a man struggling in the ocean. What the near-drowning man cannot see is that a bank of fog is hiding an island less than one hundred yards away. Although the passenger in the plane can do nothing to help, she wants the best for the man in the water. Sometimes we are able to take action to serve someone who is suffering; sometimes compassion is simply wanting a positive outcome for that person, even if we can't take action.

Compassion Is Made of Non-Compassion Elements

In meeting with social psychologists, neuroscientists, endocrinologists, and practitioners of Buddhism, and in looking at my own experience, I felt pretty sure that in order for compassion to arise, four conditions must be present: the capacity to attend to the experience of others, to feel concern for others, to sense into what will serve others, and to act in order to enhance the well-being of others (or at least wanting the best for the person, while not being attached to the outcome).

Attention, prosocial feelings, selfless intention, insight, and embodiment are key non-compassion elements that comprise the body of compassion. I also learned from studying neuroscience research that compassion is not located in one place in the brain but is distributed throughout. Moreover, it appears to be emergent, meaning it arises when the suite of features that comprise compassion are engaged.

As Thích Nhất Hạnh writes, "The flower is made of non-flower elements. When you look at the flower, you see non-flower elements like sunlight, rain, earth—all the elements that have come together to help the flower to manifest. If we were to remove any of these non-flower elements there would no longer be a flower." Just as sunlight, rain, and earth make up the flower, so do attention, concern, intention, insight, and embodiment make up compassion.

From this perspective of interdependence, and drawing on my medita-tion and caregiving experience, and studies in neuroscience, social psychol-ogy, and ethics, I ended up creating a matrix that identifies the primary features that allow compassion to arise; in other words, the non-compassion elements that prime the emergence of compassion.

I have since used this model to train clinicians, chaplaincy students, educators, lawyers, and businesspeople in how to foster a field within and around themselves where compassion can be actualized. We prepare the field for the emergence of compassion through training our faculties of attention, cultivating prosocial qualities and an unselfish intention, developing our capacity for discernment and insight, and creating the conditions for ethical and caring engagement. Compassionate engagement is embodied and ethically aligned. It is also characterized by ease, equanimity, and kindness, and it generates a sense of well-being inside us as we serve others.

I called this model "the ABIDE Model of Compassion." I like mnemonics because they can make it easier for us to remember a pattern or process. The *A* in ABIDE stands for *attention* and *affect* (i.e., having a prosocial affect). These two qualities lead to attentional and emotional *balance*, the *B* in ABIDE. The *I* in ABIDE includes *intention* and *insight*, which are cognitive processes that lead to *discernment*, the *D* in ABIDE. The *E* in ABIDE points us to *embodiment*, *engagement*, and Compassionate Action.

At the end of my tenure at the library, I gave a presentation on the ABIDE model. I then began to work on a second phase of the project, which was to develop an application of the ABIDE model that could be easily taught, and whose purpose is to support clinicians and others in cultivating compassion as they interact with others. A map of compassion is useful, but the territory of our everyday lives is where compassion gets real and is our lived experience.

VI. COMPASSION PRACTICE

OVER THE YEARS OF LISTENING to people in all walks of life talk about the stress they experience when they face the suffering of others, I learned a lot about the challenges of being a teacher, nurse, doctor, lawyer, parent, activist, politician, environmentalist, humanitarian aid worker, and CEO—those who encounter others' difficulties and suffering on a daily basis. Maybe this includes most of us. Yet when we meet suffering, it's all too easy to fall into the toxic aspects of the Edge States, but we don't have to make this our permanent address.

Although East Indian religious adepts have long known that we can transform our minds, we in the West have felt like the hand we had been dealt was the hand we had to play, and we are forever stuck with rigid mental patterns. In the latter part of the twentieth century, however, neuroscience research demonstrated that the brain is constantly changing in relation to our experience. Brain circuits can be strengthened or pruned through repetition or lack thereof. This is called neuroplasticity, when the brain reorganizes itself physically and functionally in relation to internal and external stimuli.

Although our biases and habits of mind can run deep, the way we perceive the world and attend to life can shift radically through mental training or meditation, a significant enhancer of neuroplasticity. The brain's plasticity makes it possible for us to spring back from trauma, to learn new mental patterns, for habitual ways of reacting to let go of us, and to increase our ability to be mentally flexible and nimble.

With this in mind, I developed GRACE, an active contemplative practice that builds on the ABIDE model and is focused on cultivating compassion as we interact with others. GRACE is a mnemonic that stands for: *Gather attention. Recall our intention. Attune to self and then other. Consider what will serve. Engage and end.* It includes all the features of the ABIDE model of compassion and is based on the insight that compassion emerges when these features interact with each other.

Practicing GRACE

How do we practice GRACE?

Gather Attention: The *G* in GRACE is a reminder for us to pause and give ourselves time to get grounded. On the inhale, we gather our attention. On the exhale, we drop our attention into the body, sensing into a place of stability in the body. We might focus our attention on the breath or on an area of the body that feels neutral, such as the soles of the feet on the floor or the hands as they rest on each other. Or, we can bring our attention to a phrase or an object. We use this moment of gathering our attention to interrupt our self-talk about our assumptions and expectations and to get grounded and truly present.

Recall Intention: The *R* of GRACE is recalling intention. We recall our commitment to act with integrity and respect the integrity of those whom we encounter. We remember that our intention is to serve others and to open our heart to the world. This touch-in can happen in a moment. Our motivation keeps us on track, morally grounded, and connected to our highest values.

Attune to Self and Other: The *A* of GRACE refers to the process of attunement—attunement first to our own physical, emotional, and cognitive experience and then to the experience of others. In the self-attunement process, we bring attention to our physical sensations, emotions, and thoughts—all of which can shape our attitudes and behavior toward others. If we are feeling emotionally triggered by the person we are interacting with, our reactivity might affect our ability to perceive another with clear eyes and to care. But if we are aware of our reactivity and reflect on the nature and sources of the person's suffering, we might be able to reframe the situation in a nonjudgmental and insightful way. This process of attunement and re-appraisal primes the neural networks associated with empathy and supports a compassionate response.

From this base of self-attunement, we attune to others, sensing without judgment into their experience. This is an active form of Bearing Witness. It is also the moment when we engage our capacity for empathy, as we attune physically (somatic empathy), emotionally (affective empathy), and cogni-tively (perspective taking) to the other person. Through this attunement pro-cess, we open a space for the encounter to unfold, a space where we can be present for whatever may arise. The richer we can make this mutual exchange, the deeper the unfolding will be.

Consider What Will Serve is the *C* of GRACE. This is a process of discern-ment that is based on conventional understanding and also is supported with our own intuition and insight. We ask ourselves, *What is the wise and com-passionate path here? What is an appropriate response?* We are present for the other as we sense into what might serve them, and we let insights arise, noticing what the other might be offering in this moment. We consider the systemic factors that are influencing the situation, including institutional requirements and social expectations.

As we draw on our own expertise, knowledge, and experience, and at the same time remain open to seeing things in a fresh way, we may find that our insights fall outside a predictable category. The discernment process can take time, and so we try not to jump to conclusions too quickly. Considering what will serve certainly requires attentional and affective balance, a deep sense of moral grounding, recognition of our own biases, and attunement into the experience and needs of the person who is suffering. Humility is another important guiding element.

Engage and End: The first phase of the *E* in GRACE is to ethically engage and act, if appropriate. Compassionate Action emerges from the field we have created of openness, connection, and discernment. Our action might be a recommendation, a question, a proposal, or even not doing anything. We endeavor to cocreate with the other person a moment that is characterized by mutuality and trust. Drawing on our expertise, intuition, and insight, we look for common ground that is consistent with our values and supportive of mutual integrity. What emerges is compassion that is respectful of all persons involved, practical, and actionable.

When the time is right, we mark the *end* of our time in this compassionate interaction, so that we can move cleanly to the next moment, person, or task. This is the second part of the *E* of GRACE. Whether the outcome is more than we expected or disappointingly small, we should notice and acknowledge what has transpired. Sometimes we have to forgive ourselves or the other person. Or this can be a moment for deep appreciation. Without acknowledgment of what has taken place, it can be difficult to let go of this encounter and move on.

VII. COMPASSION IN THE CHARNEL GROUND

RECENTLY, I TAUGHT A GRACE training in Japan for those who work in the end-of-life care field. I shared with the participants that life and death are messy experiences. We should not expect perfect outcomes or to have things go our way. A doctor in the training stood up and spoke about the anxiety he experiences every day as he tries to meet the needs of his patients. When one of his cancer patients is transferred off of his floor to the palliative care unit, he feels defeated, like he has failed his patient. His morale crashing, he panics as he realizes that he has no time to deal with his fear and grief—and no time to get through the line of patients who need his help. He feels trapped by a sense of futility that has drained his capacity for compassion and caring and has led him to experience utter despair and to consider suicide—but he does not want to harm his family.

Clearly, this doctor is in a charnel ground, one that is partly of his making and partly of his society's making. Burnout, stress, guilt, low morale, panic, futility, despair, suicidal ideation . . . it's a lethal combination that can lead to death. He told us he had come to the GRACE training to see if he could find a path out of this desperate situation. Listening to him, I was reminded of Tibet and the charnel grounds I have visited there.

Every time I've traveled to Mount Kailash in western Tibet, I have climbed up to the Dakini Charnel Ground, a barren, rocky plateau above the trail on the western side of the mountain. This is the place where dead bodies are offered in a practice known as *sky burial*—or in Tibetan, *jhator*, "scattering to the birds."

There I have practiced walking meditation among piles of bones and pools of blood, fat, and feces. The stench is rancid, even in the cold wind, and I could hear the flap of vulture wings and howls of jackals close by.

The first time I visited the charnel ground, I came upon two faces shorn of their skulls, their bloody hair in a tangled mess. Shaken, I barely managed to stay on my feet as I avoided stepping on these bloody masks of death. A man dressed in a ragged military coat approached me and motioned for me to lie among the fresh remains. Glancing around, I saw that Tibetans were sitting here and there among the body parts; a woman was pricking her tongue and others were pricking their fingers, drawing blood, offerings that symbolized death and rebirth.

The man in the military coat glared at me and again gestured toward the cold, slippery earth. I slowly lowered my body and lay back onto the messy, rocky ground. The man then drew a long, rusty knife from a sheath beneath his coat and began to mime chopping up my body. A wave of fear and disgust passed through me. But then I let go into the realization that I, too, am blood and bone. The aversion left me as I gazed at the snowcapped Mount Kailash, remembering that sooner or later, I, too, will be dead. And the thought crossed my mind: *Why not live fully now? Why not live to end the suffering of others? What else would I want to do with my life?*

In a way, this strange experience is not so foreign. We are made of blood, bone, and guts, as any trip to the ER will remind us. Yet Kailash is a visibly sacred place, and the ritual of symbolic dismemberment is a rite of passage that opens one to the reality of impermanence and of one's own death. For me, this experience was very intense, but not traumatizing. In fact, it was liberating—because it's harder to fear what one more clearly sees.

We don't have to go to Tibet or into a war zone to practice in a charnel ground. The charnel ground is a metaphor for any environment where suffering is present—a Japanese hospital, a schoolroom, a violent home, a mental institution, a homeless shelter, a refugee camp. Even a space of privilege, like a corporate boardroom, the Wall Street trading floor, or a media mogul's office, can be a charnel ground. Really, any place that is tainted by fear, depression, anger, despair, disrespect, or deceit is a charnel ground—including our own mind.

Whatever our profession or calling, charnel ground practice is available; we sit in the midst of subtle or obvious suffering. The mire we fall into when we go over the edge—this also is a charnel ground. It's a place where we have to face our own struggles, and where our compassion for others who are struggling in the depths can grow strong.

When we suffer within our own internal charnel ground, we are vulnerable to pathological altruism, empathic distress, moral suffering, disrespect, and burnout. But when we take a wider and deeper view, we see that a charnel ground is not only a place of desolation but also a place of boundless possibility. My colleague Fleet Maull, who was incarcerated for fourteen years on charges of drug trafficking, compares his experience of practicing meditation in prison to practicing in a charnel ground.

The prison is a tough practice environment, he notes, one where greed, hatred, and delusion are the order of the day. Yet this charnel ground proved something to him. In his book *Dharma in Hell*, Fleet Maull writes, "I'm thoroughly convinced after spending fourteen years in prison with murderers, rapists, bank robbers, child molesters, tax dodgers, drug dealers and every sort of criminal imaginable, that the fundamental nature of all human beings is good. I have absolutely no doubt in my mind." Like Fleet, I believe that redemption is possible, and every situation has within it something that can teach us, something that can lead us to our natural wisdom.

In many Tibetan mandalas, the outer protective circle depicts eight cemeteries filled with corpses, scavenging animals, bones, and blood. There is no better place to contemplate the impermanent nature of our lives than a cemetery. This circle serves as a barrier of entry to the fearful and unprepared; it is also a zone in which our meditation practice can flourish. If we find equanimity in the midst of death and decay, then we may become the Buddha at the center of the mandala.

Harrowing from Hell

This kind of courage, wisdom, and compassion is exemplified by Jizo Bodhisattva, who represents our capacity to maintain balance as we enter the hell realms of the suffering of others and our own suffering. She has promised not to achieve Buddhahood until all hells are emptied. She often appears to be a simple monk, with monk's robes and a shaved head, but sometimes she is in fact female. In her left hand, she holds a wish-fulfilling jewel to light up the darkness. In her right hand, she holds a *shakujo*, a staff with six jingling rings that alert insects and small animals of her approach, so she won't accidentally harm them. The *shakujo*'s six rings symbolize six realms of existence: the god realm, the jealous god realm, the hungry ghost realm, the hell realm, the animal realm, and the human realm.

Jizo is an edge walker. Both a bodhisattva and a monk, both male and female, Jizo knocks with her *shakujo* on the door of hell. When the door opens, she descends into the fiery pit, where she finds herself among a multitude of suffering, tortured beings. Instead of frantically trying to save them, she opens her arms wide, and those who want to be saved jump into the billowing sleeves of her robes.

Like Jizo, we can come alongside those who suffer and offer a way for them to be harrowed from hell, a way for them to take refuge in safety and goodness. Even if we suffer, we might be able to offer others or ourselves our compassion. After all, bodhisattvas do not seek easy situations. But we must have the strength to enter the hell realm in a way that is mindful, determined, and ultimately curious and fearless. We must have the heart of Jizo to stand at the crossroads of death and life, so others can discover the path to freedom.

The Magic Mirror

During a recent trip to Japan, I had the chance to see a "magic mirror" made entirely of cast bronze. Such mirrors are rare and sacred objects produced by only one Japanese family who still practices this ancient, mysterious craft. On the back of this particular mirror was a relief of a dragon, a symbol of power and good fortune. On its highly polished front surface, I saw my face looking in, just as with any glass mirror. It seemed to be a normal, if exquisitely crafted, mirror.

But remarkably, when the mirror was aimed so that light reflected off of its surface and onto a dark wall, an image of Jizo Bodhisattva was projected onto the wall. This image is hidden inside the cast bronze. The dark outline of this shaved monk's head with her robe draped across her chest was surrounded by a pool of glowing reflected light floating on the wall. Rays emanated from her head as if she were standing in the middle of the sun, and her staff seemed to strike the earth in order to open the gates of hell. Although it appears to be solid metal, the mirror holds a secret.

If we are the mirror reflecting the world, then embedded deep inside us is the invisible bodhisattva who liberates suffering beings. Jizo's great capacity for compassion remains hidden until it is revealed by light. But there's another element that must be present: darkness. The image can be seen only when projected onto a dark surface. This marriage of darkness and light, of suffering and redemption, speaks to the conditions that Jizo encounters and that we meet in the hell realms and charnel grounds of our own lives.

Some survivors of terrible adversity resort to causing harm as a kind of revenge against the world. Others enter professions where they can help people who suffer in ways they have experienced themselves. Those who have survived abuse, addiction, bullying, or systemic oppression may be called to step out of the darkness of suffering and, like Jizo, bring others with them. And like Jizo, they may find the great potential within the human spirit to turn toward goodness in the midst of devastation, and in this way, animate their capacity for compassion and wisdom. These are the ones who have found their way back to solid ground, to the cliff's edge, where their vantage point gives them a wide perspective on the truth of the interconnectedness of all beings and things, on the twining of fear and courage.

Standing at the edge, our determination to meet the world of suffering becomes a calling as we discover that compassion is the great vehicle that delivers us from suffering and gives us power, balance, and ultimately freedom, no matter what we have faced. There, we see that all of us share a common life, a common world, a common destiny.

As performance artist Marina Abramović once said, "On the edge, we're really in the present moment. Because we know we might fall." Because the danger of falling reminds us that the present moment is the only real, the only authentic place to dwell. When we are standing at the edge, we cannot turn away from suffering, whether in our inner or our outer lives. There, we must meet life with altruism, empathy, integrity, respect, and engagement. And if we find the earth crumbling beneath our feet as we start to tip toward harm, compassion can keep us grounded on the high edge of our humanity. And if we do fall, compassion can harrow us from the hells of suffering and bring us home.

Acknowledgments

WRITING THIS BOOK HAS REQUIRED the guidance and support of many friends and teachers. I especially want to offer my deepest gratitude to Kristen Barendsen, who was my frontline editor, a wise and balanced critic, and a marvelous contributor to the book.

I also want to thank Arnold Kotler, who brought his editorial expertise early on to the book, and Whitney Frick, Bob Miller, and Jasmine Faustino of Flatiron Books for their editorial expertise and kind encouragement.

My agent Stephanie Tade has been a great source of inspiration, giving me invaluable feedback on the manuscript throughout the writing process. I am so grateful to Noah Rossetter for supporting me throughout the several years of writing; he worked on the citations and kept me smiling throughout.

I am forever indebted to my close friend Rebecca Solnit, who wrote the foreword, and whose work as a social activist and speaker of truth kept me hewing a tight narrative line as this project unfolded. And Natalie Goldberg, whose insights as a writer gave me the courage to jump into the craft of writing wholeheartedly.

My life and this book have been deeply influenced by many courageous social activists, including Fannie Lou Hamer, Florynce Kennedy, Father John Dear, Eve Ensler, John Paul Lederach, Jodie Evans, Sensei Alan Senauke, and A. T. Ariyaratne. Their work and dedication have been a guide for me.

I thank the journalist David Halberstam, who in the 1960s spoke so movingly of the death of Thích Quảng Đức. His words transmitted a world to me that I could not have understood without that moment in Alan Lomax's apartment in the 1960s when he shared with us his experience of being present when Thích Quảng Đức immolated himself.

I am forever indebted to the great anthropologists Alan Lomax, Mary Catherine Bateson, Gregory Bateson, and Margaret Mead for introducing me to cross-cultural perspectives on human behavior and culture. And to Stanislav Grof, whose work with "positive disintegration" opened the "doors of perception" for me.

I am also deeply indebted to collaborators and colleagues in the end-of-life care field, especially Drs. Cynda Rushton and Tony Back for all that they have brought to our training programs and intellectual collaborations over the years. Also, I offer deep gratitude to Frank Ostaseski, Jan Jahner, Rachel Naomi Remen, Gary Pasternak, and Cathy Campbell for their invaluable contributions.

I want to thank the neuroscientist Alfred Kaszniak, who consulted with me on the science sections of the book. As well, the Mind and Life Institute community, its co-founder, Francisco Varela, and members Evan Thompson, Richard Davidson, Daniel Goleman, Antoine Lutz, Paul Ekman, Helen Weng, Nancy Eisenberg, Daniel Batson, Amishi Jha, Susan Bauer-Wu, and John Dunne, whose work has contributed to my understanding of the neuroscience and social psychology of states and traits. I am also indebted to both Christina Maslach and Laurie Leitch; their work on burnout and trauma have contributed to my understanding of suffering encountered in our world today.

As well, I have to thank great Buddhist teachers, whose lights shine throughout the book. Gratitude to His Holiness the Dalai Lama, Thích Nhất Hạnh, Roshi Bernie Glassman, Roshi Eve Marko, Roshi Jishu Angyo Holmes, Roshi Enkyo O'Hara, Roshi Fleet Maull, Roshi Norman Fischer, Matthieu Ricard, Chagdud Tulku Rinpoche, Sharon Salzberg, and artist, translator, and social activist Kazuaki Tanahashi.

I want to acknowledge all that I learned from environmentalists William DeBuys and Marty Peale about living systems, and thank marine biologist Dr. Jerome Wodinsky of Brandeis University, who many years ago invited me into the life of the *octopus vulgaris* at the Lerner Marine Laboratory in Bimini. I also want to acknowledge marine biologist and neurophysiologist Edward (Ned) Hodgson of Tufts University who introduced me to the world of sharks and ignited my love of the sea.

My collaborators in Upaya's Nomads Clinic have taught me so much. I thank Tenzin Norbu, Prem Dorchi Lama, Buddhi Lama, Tsering Lama, Pasang Lhamu Sherpa Akita, Tora Akita, Dolpo Rinpoche, Charles Mac-Donald, Wendy Lau, among many other clinicians and friends who have served in our high-altitude clinics in the Himalayas, and whose dedication and courage are reflected in various stories in this book.

I thank Sensei Joshin Brian Byrnes, Kosho Durel, and Cassie Moore for their invaluable insights regarding homelessness. And Sensei Genzan Quennell, Sensei Irene Bakker, and Sensei Shinzan Palma for upholding the dharma in their work of serving others.

My close friends Brother David Steindl-Rast and Ram Dass have been by my side as guides and inspirators for many years. Their wisdom is reflected in the book.

My great thanks to Upaya's courageous chaplaincy students who have taught me so much, including William Guild, Michele Rudy, and Angela Caruso-Yahne, whose stories are found in the book.

Deep gratitude to psychologist Laurel Carraher, who invited me into the powerful work serving as a volunteer in the Penitentiary of New Mexico.

Art is also an important source of learning and inspiration for me. I thank artists Joe David and Mayumi Oda, and Sachiko Matsuyama and Mitsue Nagase for introducing me to the magic mirror maker Akihisa Yamamoto. As well, I am so grateful for the words and work of writers Pico Iyer, Clark Strand, Jane Hirschfield, David Whyte, Wendell Berry, and Joseph Bruchac.

My love of my biological family can be discovered in various chapters.

I thank my parents John and Eunice Halifax, my sister Verona Fonte and her children, John and Dana, and Lila Robinson, who took care of me when I was gravely ill as a child.

I want to acknowledge a special group of people who have supported my work over the years: Barry and Connie Hershey, John and Tussi Kluge, Tom and Nancy Driscoll, Laurance Rockefeller, Pierre and Pam Omidyar, and Ann Down. Their generous support of my many projects have made it possible for me to expand my horizon and take the risks that have brought me to the edge where I have learned and endeavored to benefit others.

As I share my great appreciation to those who have contributed to the book, I want to apologize for what might be errors in my understanding and, at the same time, take responsibility for whatever I have written in the pages you read. I have written the book out of my direct experience and what I have learned might not always accord with conventional science or traditional Buddhism.

Notes

4 *In her book*: Iris Murdoch, *The Sovereignty of Good* (London, UK: Routledge & Kegan Paul Books, 1970).

13 *May I do a great deal of good*: Wilbur W. Thoburn, *In Terms of Life: Sermons and Talks to College Students* (Stanford, CA: Stanford University Press, 1899).

16 *what I felt was right*: Cara Buckley, "Man Is Rescued by Stranger on Subway Tracks," *New York Times*, January 3, 2007, retrieved January 4, 2007, www.nytimes.com/2007/01/03/nyregion/03life.html.

16 *bombs fall on civilian neighborhoods*: Jared Malsin, "The White Helmets of Syria," *Time*, http://time.com/syria-white-helmets/ retrieved 1 March 2017.

16 *lives of countless others*: Dave Burke, "Hero Tackled Suicide Bomber and Paid the Ultimate Price," *Metro*, November 15, 2015, http://metro.co.uk/2015/11/15/hero-who-stopped-a-terror-attack-fathers-split-second-decision-that-saved-many-lives-5502695/.

16 *Micah survived*: Hal Bernton, "Mom of Portland Train Hero Taliesin Meche Says Her Son 'Had a Lot of Bravery in his Spirit,'" *Seattle Times*, May 30, 2017, www.seattletimes.com/seattle-news/crime/mom-of-taliesin-meche-says-portland-train-victim-known-for-brave-spirit/.

18 *no distinction between them*: Thích Nhất Hạnh, *Awakening of the Heart: Essential Buddhist Sutras and Commentaries* (Berkeley, CA: Parallax Press, 2011).

18 *they have places to go too*: Joseph Bruchac, *Entering Onondaga* (Austin, TX: Cold Mountain Press, 1978).

19 *when they receive them*: Lara B. Aknin, J. Kiley Hamlin, and Elizabeth W. Dunn, "Giving Leads to Happiness in Young Children," *PLoS ONE* 7, no. 6 (2012): e39211, http://journals.plos.org/plosone/article?id=10.1371/journal.pone.0039211.

19 *spent money on themselves*: Elizabeth W. Dunn, Lara B. Aknin, and Michael I. Norton, "Prosocial Spending and Happiness: Using Money to Benefit Others Pays Off," *Current Directions in Psychological Science* (forthcoming), https://dash.harvard.edu/handle/1/11189976.

19 *humans are wired for kindness*: Olga M. Klimecki, Susanne Leiberg, Matthieu Ricard, and Tania Singer, "Differential Pattern of Functional Brain Plasticity After Compassion and Empathy Training," *Social Cognitive and Affective Neuroscience* 9, no. 6 (2014): 873–79, https://doi.org/10.1093/scan/nst060.

19 *enhanced immune response and increased longevity*: Stephanie L. Brown, Dylan M. Smith, Richard Schulz, Mohammed U. Kabeto, Peter A. Ubel, Michael Poulin, Jaehee Yi, Catherine Kim, and Kenneth M. Langa, "Caregiving Behavior Is Associated with Decreased Mortality Risk," *Psychological Science* 20, no. 4 (2009): 488–94, http://journals.sagepub.com/doi/abs/10.1111/j.1467-9280.2009.02323.x; J. Holt-Lunstad, T. B. Smith, and J. B. Layton, "Social Relationships and Mortality Risk: A Meta-Analytic Review," *PLoS Medicine* 7, no. 7 (2010), http://journals.plos.org/plosmedicine/article?id=10.1371/journal.pmed.1000316.

20 *wiped away tears*: Lauren Frayer, " 'Britain's Schindler' Is Remembered by Those He Saved from the Nazis," NPR, May 19, 2016, www.npr.org/sections/parallels/2016/05/19/478371863/britains-schindler-is-remembered-by-those-he-saved-from-the-nazis.

20 *taking no risks at all*: Robert D. McFadden, "Nicholas Winton, Rescuer of 669 Children from Holocaust, Dies at 106," *New York Times*, July 1, 2015, www.nytimes.com/2015/07/02/world/europe/nicholas-winton-is-dead-at-106-saved-children-from-the-holocaust.html.

20 *the more human he is*: Viktor Frankl, *Man's Search for Meaning* (New York: Touchstone, 1984).

22 *would conclude was reasonably foreseeable*: Barbara Oakley, Ariel Knafo, Guruprasad Madhavan, and David Sloan Wilson, eds., *Pathological Altruism* (Oxford, UK: Oxford University Press, 2012).

24 *not seem so easy to "save"*: "The Reductive Seduction of Other People's Problems," Development Set, January 11, 2016, https://medium.com/the-development-set/the-reductive-seduction-of-other-people-s-problems-3c07b307732d#.94ev3l3xj.

25 *moments of pride and guilt*: Héctor Tobar, " 'Strangers Drowning,' by Larissa MacFarquhar," *New York Times*, October 5, 2015, www.nytimes.com/2015/10/11/books/review/strangers-drowning-by-larissa-macfarquhar.html?_r=1.

25 *in the way of financial efficiency*: Jamil Zaki, "The Feel-Good School of Philanthropy," *New York Times*, December 5, 2015, www.nytimes.com/2015/12/06/opinion/sunday/the-feel-good-school-of-philanthropy.html.

27 *wailing people around him*: David Halberstam, *The Making of a Quagmire* (New York: Random House, 1965).

35 *someone living on the street*: Cassie Moore, "Sharing a Meal with Hungry Hearts," Upaya Zen Center, December 6, 2016, www.upaya.org/2016/12/sharing-a-meal -with-hungry-hearts/.

36 *the wholeness of life*: Rachel Naomi Remen, "In the Service of Life," John Carroll University, http://sites.jcu.edu/service/poem (page discontinued).

40 *"an appropriate response"*: Thomas Cleary and J. C. Cleary, trans., *Blue Cliff Record* (Boston: Shambhala, 2005), case 14.

40 *any plan of action*: Gabor Maté, *In the Realm of Hungry Ghosts: Close Encounters with Addiction* (Berkeley, CA: North Atlantic Books, 2010).

43 *not clothes, just ourselves*: Bernie Glassman, *Bearing Witness: A Zen Master's Lessons in Making Peace* (New York: Harmony / Bell Tower, 1998).

47 *retain a measure of grime*: Hong Zicheng, Robert Aitken, and Danny Wynn Ye Kwok, *Vegetable Roots Discourse: Wisdom from Ming China on Life and Living* (Berkeley, CA: Counterpoint, 2007).

47 *without ever knowing it*: "The Holy Shadow," Spiritual Short Stories, www.spiritual -short-stories.com/the-holy-shadow-story-by-osho.

50 *that way she missed love*: Agatha Christie, *The Mysterious Affair at Styles*

51 *roof planks of this ruined house*: Jane Hirshfield, trans., *The Ink Dark Moon: Love Poems* (New York: Vintage, 1990).

51 *a talk she gave in 2016*: Jane Hirshfield, Santa Sabina Thursday evening talk, tran- scribed and emailed privately to Roshi, 2016.

53 *between gift and invasion*: Leslie Jamison, *The Empathy Exams* (Minneapolis, MN: Graywolf Press, 2014).

57 *words for* in *and* pathos: "Henry George Liddell, Robert Scott, A Greek-English Lexicon, ε, ἐμμετάβολος, ἐμπάθ-εια," Perseus Digital Library, www.perseus.tufts .edu/hopper/text?doc=Perseus%3Atext%3A1999.04.0057%3Aalphabetic+letter% 3D*e%3Aentry+group%3D87%3Aentry%3De%29mpa%2Fqeia.

57 *English word* empathy: E. B. Titchener, "Introspection and Empathy," *Dialogues in Philosophy, Mental and Neuro Sciences* 7 (2014): 25–30.

57 *compassion is feeling* for *another*: Tania Singer and Olga M. Klimecki, "Empathy and Compassion," *Current Biology* 24, no. 18 (2014): R875–78.

58 *I myself become the wounded person*: Walt Whitman, "Song of Myself," *Leaves of Grass* (self-published, 1855).

59 *capacity to distinguish self from other*: Jamie Ward and Michael J. Banissy,

"Explaining Mirror-Touch Synesthesia," *Cognitive Neuroscience* 6, nos. 2–3 (2015): 118–33, doi:10.1080/17588928.2015.1042444.

59 *the benefit of his patients*: Erika Hayasaki, "This Doctor Knows Exactly How You Feel," *Pacific Standard*, July 13, 2015, https://psmag.com/social-justice/is-mirror-touch-synesthesia-a-superpower-or-a-curse.

62 *"making the faraway nearby"*: Rebecca Solnit, *The Faraway Nearby* (New York: Penguin, 2014).

63 *rather than stereotypes or outsiders*: A. D. Galinsky and G. B. Moskowitz, "Perspective-Taking: Decreasing Stereotype Expression, Stereotype Accessibility, and In-Group Favoritism," *Journal of Personality and Social Psychology* 78, no. 4 (April 2000): 708–24, www.ncbi.nlm.nih.gov/pubmed/10794375.

64 *sudden turn of events*: Jeff Bacon, "LtCol Hughes—Take a Knee," *Broadside Blog*, April 11, 2007, http://broadside.navytimes.com/2007/04/11/ltcol-hughes-take-a-knee/.

65 *Take a knee, relax!*: Tricia McDermott, "A Calm Colonel's Strategic Victory," CBS Evening News, March 15, 2006, www.cbsnews.com/news/a-calm-colonels-strategic-victory/.

65 *welcome Hughes's soldiers*: "Heroes of War," CNN, www.cnn.com/SPECIALS/2003/iraq/heroes/chrishughes.html.

65 *never firing a shot*: McDermott, "A Calm Colonel's Strategic Victory."

66 *Throughout the body, hands and eyes*: Gerry Shishin Wick, *The Book of Equanimity: Illuminating Classic Zen Koans* (New York: Simon & Schuster, 2005), 169.

69 *experiences in the camps*: Y. Danieli, "Therapists' Difficulties in Treating Survivors of the Nazi Holocaust and Their Children," *Dissertation Abstracts International* 42 (1982): 4927.

72 *a broken leg or arm*: Olga Klimecki, Matthieu Ricard, and Tania Singer, "Compassion: Bridging Practice and Science—page 273," Compassion: Bridging Practice and Science, www.compassion-training.org/en/online/files/assets/basic-html/page273.html.

72 *after the empathic resonance*: Ibid.

72 *compassion surprised the researchers*: Ibid.

73 *children had completely disappeared*: Olga Klimecki, Matthieu Ricard, and Tania Singer, "Compassion: Bridging Practice and Science—page 279," Compassion: Bridging Practice and Science, www.compassion-training.org/en/online/files/assets/basic-html/page279.html.

74 *suffering from empathic distress*: Singer and Klimecki, "Empathy and Compassion."

74 *empathic distress is inevitable*: C. Lamm, C. D. Batson, and J. Decety, "The Neural Substrate of Human Empathy: Effects of Perspective-Taking and Cognitive Ap-

praisal," *Journal of Cognitive Neuroscience* 19, no. 1 (2007): 42–58, doi:10.1162/jocn.2007.19.1.42; C. D. Batson, "Prosocial Motivation: Is It Ever Truly Altruistic?" in *Advances in Experimental Social Psychology*, vol. 20, ed. L. Berkowitz (New York: Academic Press, 1987), 65–122.

75 *other people's point of view*: Jerry Useem, "Power Causes Brain Damage," *Atlantic*, July–August 2017, www.theatlantic.com/magazine/archive/2017/07/power-causes -brain-damage/528711/?utm_source=fbb.

75 *distinguishing the emotions of others*: Geoffrey Bird, Giorgia Silani, Rachel Brindley, Sarah White, Uta Frith, and Tania Singer, "Empathic Brain Responses in Insula Are Modulated by Levels of Alexithymia but Not Autism," *Brain* 133, no. 5 (2010): 1515–25, https://doi.org/10.1093/brain/awq060; Boris C. Bernhardt, Sofie L. Valk, Giorgia Silani, Geoffrey Bird, Uta Frith, and Tania Singer, "Selective Disruption of Sociocognitive Structural Brain Networks in Autism and Alexithymia," *Cerebral Cortex* 24, no. 12 (2014): 3258–67, https://doi.org/10.1093/cercor/bht182.

75 *networks associated with empathy*: Grit Hein and Tania Singer, "I Feel How You Feel but Not Always: The Empathic Brain and Its Modulation," *Current Opinion in Neurobiology* 18, no. 2 (2008): 153–58, https://doi.org/10.1016/j.conb.2008.07.012.

76 *between gift and invasion*: Jamison, *The Empathy Exams*.

76 *an interview with* Harper's: Jeffery Gleaves, "The Empathy Exams: Essays," *Harper's*, March 28, 2014, http://harpers.org/blog/2014/03/the-empathy-exams-essays/.

77 *really bad guide to policy*: Heleo Editors, "I Don't Feel Your Pain: Why We Need More Morality and Less Empathy," *Heleo*, December 16, 2016, https://heleo.com /conversation-i-dont-feel-your-pain-why-we-need-more-morality-and-less-empathy /12083/.

77 *conservative and liberal journalists*: Amanda Palmer, "Playing the Hitler Card," *New Statesman*, June 1, 2015, www.newstatesman.com/2015/05/playing-hitler-card.

77 *no idea how you feel*: " 'I Have No Idea How You Feel,' " *Harvard Magazine*, April 5, 2014, http://harvardmagazine.com/2014/04/paradoxes-of-empathy.

78 *wait for them to give*: Eve Marko, "It Feels Like 8," Feb. 16, 2016, www.evemarko .com/category/blog/page/24/.

87 *according to neuroscientist*: Lutz A, Slagter HA, Dunne J, Davidson RJ. "Attention regulation and monitoring in meditation." *Trends in Cognitive Sciences*. 2008a; 12:163–169. www.ncbi.nlm.nih.gov/pmc/articles/PMC2693206/

87 *paper on attention regulation*: Lutz A. Brefczynski-Lewis, J. Johnstone, T. Davidson RJ. "Regulation of the neural circuitry of emotion by compassion meditation: effects of meditative expertise." *Plos One*. 3: e1897. PMID 18365029 DOI: 10.1371/ journal.pone.0001897.

87 *faster return to baseline*: Gaëlle Desbordes, Tim Gard, Elizabeth A. Hoge, Britta K. Hölzel, Catherine Kerr, Sara W. Lazar, Andrew Olendzki, and David R. Vago, "Moving beyond Mindfulness: Defining Equanimity as an Outcome Measure in Meditation and Contemplative Research," *Mindfulness* (NY) 6, no. 2 (April 2015): 356–72, www.ncbi.nlm.nih.gov/pmc/articles/PMC4350240/.

92 *friend and colleague*: Dr. Cynda Rushton, "Cultivating Moral Resilience," *American Journal of Nursing*, February 2017, 117: 2, S11–S15. doi: 10.1097/01.NAJ .0000512205.93596.00.

92 *being whole and undivided*: *Oxford English Dictionary*, s.v. "integrity," https://en .oxforddictionaries.com/definition/integrity.

95 *above the abyss of harm*: Joan Didion, "On Self-Respect: Joan Didion's 1961 Essay from the Pages of Vogue," October 22, 2014, www.vogue.com/article/joan-didion -self-respect-essay-1961.

95 *youngest of twenty kids*: Kay Mills, "Fannie Lou Hamer: Civil Rights Activist," Mississippi History Now, April 2007, http://mshistorynow.mdah.state.ms.us /articles/51/fannie-lou-hamer-civil-rights-activist.

95 *who often went hungry*: "Fannie Lou Hamer," History, 2009, www.history.com /topics/black-history/fannie-lou-hamer.

96 *since I could remember*: "Fannie Lou Hamer," *Wikipedia*, https://en.wikipedia.org /wiki/Fannie_Lou_Hamer#cite_note-beast-12.

96 *by inmates and then by police*: Tasha Fierce, "Black Women Are Beaten, Sexually Assaulted and Killed by Police. Why Don't We Talk About It?," Alternet, February 26, 2015, www.alternet.org/activism/black-women-are-beaten-sexually-assaul ted-and-killed-police-why-dont-we-talk-about-it.

97 *itself a marvelous victory*: Howard Zinn, *You Can't Be Neutral on a Moving Train: A Personal History of Our Times* (Boston: Beacon Press, 2010), 208.

102 *dealt (the) enemy (a) heavy blow*: Joanna Bourke, *An Intimate History of Killing: Face-to-Face Killing in Twentieth-Century Warfare* (New York: Basic Books, 1999).

102 *cold-blooded break for lunch*: William C. Westmoreland, *A Soldier Reports* (Garden City, NY: Doubleday, 1976), 378.

102 *eventually pardoned or acquitted*: "Hugh Thompson Jr.," AmericansWhoTellThe Truth.org, www.americanswhotellthetruth.org/portraits/hugh-thompson-jr.

103 *against the wall and shoot me*: *My Lai*, PBS American Experience (Boston: WGBH, 2010), complete program transcript.

108 *Ault told* The Guardian: Ed Pilkington, "Eight Executions in 11 Days: Arkansas Order May Endanger Staff's Mental Health," *Guardian*, March 29, 2017, www .theguardian.com/world/2017/mar/29/arkansas-executioners-mental-health-allen-ault.

108 *"in my nightmares," he said*: Ibid.

110 *undermines alliance building*: Rebecca Solnit, "We Could Be Heroes: An Election-Year Letter," *Guardian*, October 15, 2012, www.theguardian.com/commentisfree /2012/oct/15/letter-dismal-allies-us-left.

111 *leading to stricter judgments*: Liana Peter-Hagene, Alexander Jay, and Jessica Salerno, "The Emotional Components of Moral Outrage and their Effect on Mock Juror Verdicts," Jury Expert, May 7, 2014, www.thejuryexpert.com/2014 /05/the-emotional-components-of-moral-outrage-and-their-effect-on-mock-juror -verdicts/.

111 *people in out-groups*: Carlos David Navarrete and Daniel M. T. Fessler, "Disease Avoidance and Ethnocentrism: The Effects of Disease Vulnerability and Disgust Sensitivity on Intergroup Attitudes," *Evolution and Human Behavior* 27, no. 4 (2006): 270–82, doi:10.1016/j.evolhumbehav.2005.12.001.

112 *rather than connection and cooperation*: C. Rushton, "Principled Moral Outrage," *AACN Advanced Critical Care* 24, no. 1 (2013), 82–89.

112 *professor Joshua Greene*: Lauren Cassani Davis, "Do Emotions and Morality Mix?" *Atlantic*, February 5, 2016, www.theatlantic.com/science/archive/2016/02/how-do -emotions-sway-moral-thinking/460014/.

114 *process towards becoming accountable*: Sarah Schulman, *The Gentrification of the Mind* (Berkeley: University of California Press, 2013).

114 *really don't think I'm human*: *I Am Not Your Negro*, directed by Raoul Peck (New York: Magnolia Pictures, 2016).

116 *if it is not faced*: Ibid.

118 *people live on the streets*: Heather Knight, "What San Franciscans Know About Homeless Isn't Necessarily True," *SFGate*, June 29, 2016, www.sfgate.com /bayarea/article/What-San-Franciscans-know-about-homeless-isn-t-7224018 .php.

125 *level of people of integrity*: Thanissaro Bhikkhu, trans., "Kataññu Suttas: Grati-tude," Access to Insight, 2002, www.accesstoinsight.org/tipitaka/an/an02/an02 .031.than.html.

128 *complexity, confusion, distress, or setbacks*: Cynda Hylton Rushton, *Cultivating Moral Resilience, American Journal of Nursing* 117, no. 2 (February 2017): S11–S15, doi:10.1097/01.NAJ.0000512205.93596.00.

132 *we suffer, and will die*: T. L. Beauchamp, J. Childress. *Principles of Biomedical Ethics* (5th ed.). (New York: Oxford University Press, 2001).

132 *it might be respect*: William Ury, *The Third Side: Why We Fight and How We Can Stop* (New York: Penguin Books, 2000).

134 *others that violate integrity*: Tom L. Beauchamp and James F. Childress, *Principles of Biomedical Ethics*, 5th ed. (Oxford, UK: Oxford University Press, 2001).

137 *kind of respect* moral nerve: Joan Didion, "On Self-Respect: Joan Didion's 1961 Essay from the Pages of Vogue," October 22, 2014, www.vogue.com/article/joan -didion-self-respect-essay-1961.

137 *developed, trained, coaxed forth*: Ibid.

137 *either love or indifference*: Ibid.

138 *want to live in peace*: "Pope Francis: Gestures of Fraternity Defeat Hatred and Greed," Vatican Radio, March 24, 2016, http://en.radiovaticana.va/news/2016/03 /24/pope_francis_gestures_of_fraternity_defeat_hatred_and_greed/1217938.

140 *to their traditional ways*: Saul Elbein, "The Youth Group That Launched a Move-ment at Standing Rock," *New York Times*, January 31, 2017, www.nytimes.com /2017/01/31/magazine/the-youth-group-that-launched-a-movement-at-standing -rock.html?smid=fb-share&_r=1.

141 *according to* The New York Times: Ibid.

141 *the moon, and the stars*: Kazuaki Tanahashi, ed., *Treasury of the True Dharma Eye: Zen Master Dogen's* Shobo Genzo (Boston: Shambhala, 2013), 46.

145 *scapegoating of those*: Denise Thompson: *A Discussion of the Problem of Horizontal Hostility*, November 2003, 8. http://users.spin.net.au/~deniset/alesfem/mhhostility.pdf.

145 *others in positions of authority*: Gary Namie, *2014 WBI U.S. Workplace Bullying Survey* (Bellingham, WA: Workplace Bullying Institute, 2014), 10, http://workpla-cebullying.org/multi/pdf/WBI-2014-US-Survey.pdf.

146 *I felt observed, watched*: Jan Jahner, "Building Bridges: An Inquiry into Horizontal Hostility in Nursing Culture and the use of Contemplative Practices to Facilitate Cultural Change" (Buddhist Chaplaincy Training Program thesis, Upaya Zen Cen-ter, Santa Fe, NM: 2011), 46–47, www.upaya.org/uploads/pdfs/Jahnersthesis.pdf.

146 *normalize my work life*: Ibid., 47.

147 *external causes of oppression*: Florynce Kennedy, *Color Me Flo: My Hard Life and Good Times* (Englewood Cliffs, NJ: Prentice-Hall, 1976).

148 *because it's less dangerous*: Gloria Steinem, "The Verbal Karate of Florynce R. Ken-nedy, Esq.," *Ms.*, August 19, 2011, http://msmagazine.com/blog/2011/08/19/the -verbal-karate-of-florynce-r-kennedy-esq.

148 *favors of the ruling class*: Ibid.

149 Workplace Bullying Survey: Namie, *2014 WBI U.S. Workplace Bullying Survey*.

149 *demeaning their own power*: Jahner, "Building Bridges."

149 *into the nursing profession*: Ibid.

150 *higher rates than whites*: Namie, *2014 WBI U.S. Workplace Bullying Survey*.

150 *stage a walkout*: Nicholas Kristof, "Donald Trump Is Making America Meaner," *New York Times*, August 13, 2016, www.nytimes.com/2016/08/14/opinion/sunday /donald-trump-is-making-america-meaner.html.

150 *worry about being deported*: "The Trump Effect: The Impact of the Presidential Campaign on Our Nation's Schools," Southern Poverty Law Center, April 13, 2016, www.splcenter.org/20160413/trump-effect-impact-presidential-campaign-our -nations-schools.

150 *grounding democratic values*: Karen Stohr, "Our New Age of Contempt," *New York Times*, January 23, 2017, www.nytimes.com/2017/01/23/opinion/our-new -age-of-contempt.html.

151 *if they are persecuted*: Michelle Rudy, email message to the author.

151 *we go high*: "Michelle Obama: 'When They Go Low, We Go High,'" MSNBC, July 26, 2016, www.msnbc.com/rachel-maddow-show/michelle-obama-when-they -go-low-we-go-high.

153 *colonizes, excludes and marginalizes*: Bill Ashcroft, Gareth Griffiths, and Helen Tiffin, *Key Concepts in Post-Colonial Studies* (London: Routledge, 2000), 173.

156 *no mercy to living beings*: Thanissaro Bhikkhu, trans., "Angulimala Sutta: About Angulimala," Access to Insight, 2003, www.accesstoinsight.org/tipitaka/mn/mn .086.than.html.

157 *path of the Dharma*: Ibid.

158 *patient safety, hierarchy, and culture*: Arieh Riskin, Amir Erez, Trevor A. Foulk, Kinneret S. Riskin-Geuz, Amitai Ziv, Rina Sela, Liat Pessach-Gelblum, and Peter A. Bamberger, "Rudeness and Medical Team Performance," *Pediatrics* (January 2017), http://pediatrics.aappublications.org/content/early/2017/01/06/peds.2016 -2305.

159 *from outside the military*: Personal communication with the author, 2016.

166 *threaten your own safety*: Thích Nhất Hạnh, *Interbeing: Fourteen Guidelines for Engaged Buddhism*, rev. ed. (Berkeley, CA: Parallax Press, 1993).

168 *Mara would flee*: Thích Nhất Hạnh, *The Heart of the Buddha's Teaching: Transforming Suffering into Peace, Joy, and Liberation* (New York: Broadway Books, 1999).

168 *a stone a clay pot*: *Collected Wheel Publications*, vol. XXVII, numbers 412–430 (Sri Lanka: Buddhist Publication Society, 2014), 140.

169 *I give up Gotama*: Lord Chalmers, *Buddha's Teachings: Being the Sutta Nipata or Discourse Collection* (Cambridge, MA: Harvard University Press, 1932), 104–05.

174 *expert on burnout*: C. Maslach and M. P. Leiter, *The Truth About Burnout: How Organizations Cause Personal Stress and What to Do About It* (San Francisco: Jossey-Bass, 1997).

176 *rot on the vine*: David Whyte, *Crossing the Unknown Sea: Work as a Pilgrimage of Identity* (New York: Riverhead Books, 2001).

176 *truly serving people*: Jennifer Senior, "Can't Get No Satisfaction," *New York*, October 24, 2007, http://nymag.com/news/features/24757/.

176 *"in a lifetime," Cori said*: Cori Salchert, "How One Mom's Extraordinary Love Transforms the Short Lives of Hospice Babies," *Today*, June 20, 2016, www.today .com/parents/how-one-mom-s-extraordinary-love-transforms-short-lives-hospice -t67096.

177 *be loved before he dies*: Leah Ulatowski, "Sheboygan Family Opens Home to Hospice Kids," *Sheboygan Press*, January 2, 2016, www.sheboyganpress.com/story/news /local/2016/01/02/sheboygan-family-opens-home-hospice-kids/78147672/.

177 *also have each other*: Ibid.

178 *production of this neurochemical*: Olivia Goldhill, "Neuroscience Confirms That to Be Truly Happy, You Will Always Need Something More," *Quartz*, May 15, 2016, http://qz.com/684940/neuroscience-confirms-that-to-be-truly-happy-you-will -always-need-something-more/.

178 *reasoning abilities, and vocabulary*: Sara B. Festini, Ian M. McDonough, and Denise C. Park, "The Busier the Better: Greater Busyness Is Associated with Better Cognition," *Frontiers in Aging Neuroscience* (May 17, 2016), doi:10.3389/fnagi .2016.00098.

178 *So far, so good*: Kristin Sainani, "What, Me Worry?," *Stanford*, May–June 2014, https://alumni.stanford.edu/get/page/magazine/article/?article_id=70134.

180 *job to support them*: "Herbert Freudenberger," *Wikipedia*, https://en.wikipedia.org /wiki/Herbert_Freudenberger.

181 *He was a survivor*: Douglas Martin, "Herbert Freudenberger, 73, Coiner of 'Burnout,' Is Dead," *New York Times*, December 5, 1999, www.nytimes.com/1999/12/05 /nyregion/herbert-freudenberger-73-coiner-of-burnout-is-dead.html.

182 *might even consider suicide*: "12 Phase Burnout Screening Development Implementation and Test Theoretical Analysis of a Burnout Screening Based on the 12 Phase Model of Herbert Freudenberger and Gail North," *ASU* International Edition, www.asu-arbeitsmedizin.com/12-phase-burnout-screening-development-imple mentation-and-test-theoretical-analysis-of-a-burnout-screening-based-on-the-12 -phase-model-of-Herbert-Freudenberger-and-Gail-Nor,QUlEPTYyMzQ1MiZNS UQ9MTEzODIx.html (page discontinued).

182 *exhaustion, cynicism, and inefficacy*: Jesús Montero-Marín, Javier García-Campayo, Domingo Mosquera Mera, and Yolanda López del Hoyo, "A New Definition of Burnout Syndrome Based on Farber's Proposal," *Journal of Occupational Medicine and Toxicology* 4 (2009): 31, www.ncbi.nlm.nih.gov/pmc/articles /PMC2794272/.

182 *what does our life mean?*: Senior, "Can't Get No Satisfaction."

182 *jobs within five years*: Ibid.

183 *2.3 times more likely*: Judith Graham, "Why Are Doctors Plagued by Depression and Suicide?: A Crisis Comes into Focus," *Stat*, July 21, 2016, www.statnews.com /2016/07/21/depression-suicide-physicians/.

183 *tend to burn out faster*: Senior, "Can't Get No Satisfaction."

184 *makes work fruitful*: Thomas Merton, *Conjectures of a Guilty Bystander* (New York: Image/Doubleday, 1968).

184 *That we matter*: Omid Sofi, "The Thief of Intimacy, Busyness," November 13, 2014, *On Being*, https://onbeing.org/blog/the-thief-of-intimacy-busyness/.

185 *Hesse called "aggressive haste"*: Hermann Hesse, *My Belief: Essays on Life and Art* (New York: Farrar, Straus & Giroux: 1974).

185 *stress releases dopamine*: Rasmus Hougaard and Jacqueline Carter, "Are You Addicted to Doing?," *Mindful*, January 12, 2016, www.mindful.org/are-you-addicted -to-doing/.

186 *allotted vacation time*: Brandon Gaille, "23 Significant Workaholic Statistics," Brandon Gaille's website, May 23, 2017, http://brandongaille.com/21-significant -workaholic-statistics/.

186 *abilities and skills suffer*: Cara Feinberg, "The Science of Scarcity," *Harvard Magazine*, May–June 2016, http://harvardmagazine.com/2015/05/the-science-of-scar city.

186 *possibly as a causal factor*: Douglas Carroll, "Vital Exhaustion," in *Encyclopedia of Behavioral Medicine*, eds. Marc D. Gellman and J. Rick Turner (New York: Springer, 2013), http://link.springer.com/referenceworkentry/10.1007%2F978-1 -4419-1005-9_1631.

186 *depression, and cognitive impairment*: Sainani, "What, Me Worry?"

186 *they'd been submerged!*: Senior, "Can't Get No Satisfaction."

190 *challenge he or she faced*: "Impossible Choices: Thinking about Mental Health Issues from a Buddhist Perspective," Jizo Chronicles, http://jizochronicles.com /writing/impossible-choices-thinking-about-mental-health-issues-from-a-buddhist -perspective/. The original article appeared in the anthology *Not Turning Away*, edited by Susan Moon.

193 *with a good spirit*: Norman Fischer, "On Zen Work," Chapel Hill Zen Center, www.chzc.org/Zoketsu.htm.

194 *precisely in that spot*: Clark Strand, *Meditation without Gurus: A Guide to the Heart of Practice* (New York: SkyLight Paths, 2003).

195 *suffering for you and others*: Thích Nhất Hạnh, *The Heart of the Buddha's Teaching: Transforming Suffering into Peace, Joy, and Liberation* (New York: Broadway Books, 1999).

196 *"Not till we are lost"*: Henry David Thoreau, *Walden* (London: George Routledge & Sons, 1904).

199 *Which moon is this?*: Thomas Cleary, *Book of Serenity: One Hundred Zen Dialogues* (Boston: Shambhala, 2005), case 21.

199 *compilation of koans*: Ibid.

199 *lies in peace and harmony*: Dainin Katagiri, *Each Moment Is the Universe: Zen and the Way of Being Time* (Boston: Shambhala, 2008).

200 *develop your own personal life*: Ibid.

200 *flow addiction and burnout*: "iWILLinspire Shonda Rhimes TED Talks the Year of Yes," YouTube video, 19:11, posted by "Ronald L Jackson," February 18, 2016, www.youtube.com/watch?v=XPlZUhf8NCQ.

202 *also craves a human touch*: Omid Sofi, "The Disease of Being Busy," *On Being*, November 6, 2014, www.onbeing.org/blog/the-disease-of-being-busy/7023.

205 *misery of the world*: Shantideva, adapted from the translation by Stephen Batchelor, *A Guide to the Bodhisattva Way of Life* (Boston: Shambhala, 1997), 144:55.

207 *essential for human survival*: His Holiness the Dalai Lama, "Dalai Lama Quotes on Compassion," Dalai Lama Quotes, www.dalailamaquotes.org/category/dalai -lama-quotes-on-compassion/.

207 *growth of compassion*: His Holiness the Dalai Lama, "Compassion and the Individual," Dalai Lama's website, www.dalailama.com/messages/compassion-and -human-values/compassion.

207 *Darwin would agree*: Line Goguen-Hughes, "Survival of the Kindest," *Mindful*, December 23, 2010, www.mindful.org/cooperate/.

208 *man was able to escape*: Charles Darwin, *The Descent of Man* (New York: Penguin Classics, 2004), 126.

208 *mere fellow-creature*: Ibid., 134.

208 *great and dreadful baboon*: Ibid.

209 *why not us?*: "Compassion-Bridging Practice and Science-page 420," Compassion: Bridging Practice and Science, www.compassion-training.org/en/online/files/assets /basic-html/page420.html.

209 *Holt-Lunstad and colleagues*: Julianne Holt-Lunstad, Timothy B. Smith, and J. Bradley Layton, "Social Relationships and Mortality Risk: A Meta-Analytic Review," *PLoS Medicine* 7, no. 7 (2010), https://doi.org/10.1371/journal.pmed .1000316.

209 *rather than self-serving*: Sara Konrath, Andrea Fuhrel-Forbis, Alina Lou, and Stephanie Brown, "Motives for Volunteering Are Associated with Mortality Risk in Older Adults," *Health Psychology* 31, no. 1.

209 *heart rate variation*: K. J. Kemper and H. A. Shaltout, "Non-Verbal Communication of Compassion: Measuring Psychophysiologic Effects," *BMC Complementary and Alternative Medicine* 11, no. 1 (2011): 132.

209 *surgical recovery time*: Lawrence D. Egbert and Stephen H. Jackson, "Therapeutic Benefit of the Anesthesiologist–Patient Relationship," *Anesthesiology* 119, no. 6 (2013): 1465–68, doi:0.1097/ALN.0000000000000030.

209 *improves trauma outcomes*: S. Steinhausen, O. Ommen, S. Thum, R. Lefering, T. Koehler, E. Neugebauer, et al., "Physician Empathy and Subjective Evaluation of Medical Treatment Outcome in Trauma Surgery Patients," *Patient Education and Counseling* 95, no. 1 (2014): 53–60.

209 *terminally ill patients*: C. M. Dahlin, J. M. Kelley, V. A. Jackson, and J. S. Temel, "Early Palliative Care for Lung Cancer: Improving Quality of Life and Increasing Survival," *International Journal of Palliative Nursing* 16, no. 9 (September 2010): 420–23, doi:10.12968/ijpn.2010.16.9.78633.

209 *improves glucose control*: S. Del Canale, D. Z. Louis, V. Maio, X. Wang, G. Rossi, M. Hojat, and J. S. Gonnella, "The Relationship between Physician Empathy and Disease Complications: An Empirical Study of Primary Care Physicians and Their Diabetic Patients in Parma, Italy," *Academic Medicine* 87, no. 9 (September 2012): 1243–49, doi:10.1097/ACM.0b013e3182628fbf.

209 *smoking cessation*: J. M. Kelley, G. Kraft-Todd, L. Schapira, J. Kossowsky, and H. Riess, "The Influence of the Patient-Clinician Relationship on Healthcare Outcomes: A Systematic Review and Meta-Analysis of Randomized Controlled Trials," *PLoS ONE* 9, no. 4 (2014): e94207.

209 *boosts immune function*: D. Rakel, B. Barrett, Z. Zhang, T. Hoeft, B. Chewning, L. Marchand L, et al., "Perception of Empathy in the Therapeutic Encounter: Effects on the Common Cold," *Patient Education and Counseling* 85, no. 3 (2011): 390–97.

210 *stress on clinicians*: "Top Ten Scientific Reasons Why Compassion Is Great Medicine," Hearts in Healthcare, http://heartsinhealthcare.com/infographic/.

210 *being unpleasantly stimulated*: A. Lutz, D. R. McFarlin, D. M. Perlman, T. V.

Salomons, and R. J. Davidson, "Altered Anterior Insula Activation During Antici-pation and Experience of Painful Stimuli in Expert Meditators," *NeuroImage* 64 (2013): 538–46, http://doi.org/10.1016/j.neuroimage.2012.09.030.

210 *greater than novice practitioners*: Lutz A. Brefczynski-Lewis, J. Johnstone, T. Davidson RJ. "Regulation of the neural circuitry of emotion by compassion meditation: Effects of meditative expertise." *PLoS One*. 2008;3(3):e1897.

210 *regulation and positive emotions*: Helen Y. Weng, Andrew S. Fox, Alexander J. Shackman, Diane E. Stodola, Jessica Z. K. Caldwell, Matthew C. Olson, Gregory M. Rogers, and Richard J. Davidson, "Compassion Training Alters Altruism and Neural Responses to Suffering," PMC, www.ncbi.nlm.nih.gov/pmc/articles/PMC3713090/.

211 *state of other-focus*: Emma Seppälä, "The Science of Compassion," Emma Seppälä's website, May 1, 2017, www.emmaseppala.com/the-science-of-compassion.

211 *can't get any other way*: "Georges Lucas on Meaningful Life Decisions," Goalcast, January 6, 2017, www.goalcast.com/2017/01/06/georges-lucas-choose-your-path.

212 *foundation of all ethics*: Marvin Meyer, *Reverence for Life: The Ethics of Albert Schweitzer for the Twenty-First Century* (Syracuse, NY: Syracuse University Press, 2002).

212 *moral identity is compromised*: C. D. Cameron and B. K. Payne, "Escaping Affect: How Motivated Emotion Regulation Creates Insensitivity to Mass Suffering," *Journal of Personality and Social Psychology* 100, no. 1 (2011): 1–15.

212 *inspires us to do the same*: Zoë A. Englander, Jonathan Haidt, James P. Morris, "Neural Basis of Moral Elevation Demonstrated through Inter-Subject Synchronization of Cortical Activity during Free-Viewing," *PLoS ONE* 7, no. 6 (2012): e3938, http://journals.plos.org/plosone/article?id=10.1371/journal.pone.0039384.

214 *non-referential and universal*: Muso Soseki, *Dialogues in a Dream* (Somerville, MA: Wisdom Publications, 2015), 111.

216 *I will be here helping*: C. Daryl Cameron and B. Keith Payne, "The Cost of Callousness: Regulating Compassion Influences the Moral Self-Concept," *Psychological Science* 23, no. 3 (2012): 225–29, http://journals.sagepub.com/doi/abs/10.1177/0956797611430334.

216 *little that one can give*: Will Grant, "Las Patronas: The Mexican Women Helping Migrants," BBC News, July 31, 2014, www.bbc.com/news/world-latin-america-28193230.

216 *could not be more apt*: Ibid.

220 *no-cause comes burning forth*: Attributed to Yasutani Roshi in Robert Aitken, *A Zen Wave* (Washington, D.C.: Shoemaker & Hoard, 2003).

226 *both day and night*: Thanissaro Bhikkhu, trans., "Assutavā Sutta (SN 12.61 PTS: S ii 94)," Access to Insight, 2005, www.accesstoinsight.org/tipitaka/sn/sn12/sn12.061.than.html.

226 *present to whatever arises*: Thanissaro Bhikkhu, trans. "Kāḷigodha Sutta: Bhaddiya Kāḷigodha (Ud 2.10)," Access to Insight, 2012, www.accesstoinsight.org/tipitaka/kn/ud/ud.2.10.than.html.

227 *nature in its beauty*: Letter of 1950, as quoted in *The New York Times* (March 29, 1972) and the *New York Post* (November 28, 1972).

227 *and you miss it!*: Huangbo Xiyuan, *The Zen Teachings of Huang Po: On the Transmission of Mind* (n.p., Pickle Partners Publishing, 2016).

227 *in that very moment*: Sean Murphy, *One Bird, One Stone: 108 Zen Stories* (Newburyport, MA: Hampton Roads Publishing, 2013), 133.

229 *called pity a distraction*: William Blake, *The Book of Urizen*, The Poetical works, 1908, Chapter 5, verse 7 www.bartleby.com/235/259.html.

230 The Shallows, *told* The New York Times: Teddy Wayne, "The End of Reflection," *New York Times*, June 11, 2016, www.nytimes.com/2016/06/12/fashion/internet-technology-phones-introspection.html.

231 *eighty-five times per day!*: Ibid.

231 *Hesse called "the enemy of joy"*: Hermann Hesse, *My Belief: Essays on Life and Art* (New York: Farrar, Straus & Giroux, June 1974).

231 *those who had stopped*: J. M. Darley and C. D. Batson, "From Jerusalem to Jericho: A Study of Situational and Dispositional Variables in Helping Behavior," *Journal of Personality and Social Psychology* 27, no. 1 (1973): 100–08, http://faculty.babson.edu/krollag/org_site/soc_psych/darley_samarit.html.

232 *called this phenomenon "the arithmetic of compassion"*: Scott Slovic and Paul Slovic, "The Arithmetic of Compassion," *New York Times,* December 4, 2015, www.nytimes.com/2015/12/06/opinion/the-arithmetic-of-compassion.html.

232 *'a drop in the bucket'*: Ibid.

232 *disturbing stimuli and stops responding*: K. Luan Phan, Israel Liberzon, Robert C. Welsh, Jennifer C. Britton, and Stephan F. Taylor, "Habituation of Rostral Anterior Cingulate Cortex to Repeated Emotionally Salient Pictures," *Neuropsychopharmacology* 28 (2003): 1344–50, www.nature.com/npp/journal/v28/n7/full/1300186a.html.

233 *rescue in* The New York Times: Donatella Lorch, "Red Tape Untangled, Young Nepalese Monks Find Ride to Safety," *New York Times*, June 19, 2015, www.nytimes.com/2015/06/20/world/asia/red-tape-untangled-young-nepalese-monks-find-ride-to-safety.html?ref=oembed.

234 *"The only thing worse"*: Pico Iyer, "The Value of Suffering," *New York Times*, September 7, 2013, retrieved August 17, 2017, at www.nytimes.com/2013/09/08 /opinion/sunday/the-value-of-suffering.html.

236 *boss of the brain*: "Taming Your Wandering Mind | Amishi Jha | TEDxCoconut-Grove," YouTube video, 18:46, posted by "TEDx Talks," April 7, 2017, https://m .youtube.com/watch?feature=youtu.be&v=Df2JBnql8lc.

238 *no longer be a flower*: Thích Nhất Hạnh, *Peace of Mind: Being Fully Present* (Berkeley, CA: Parallax Press, 2013).

246 *no doubt in my mind*: Fleet Maull, *Dharma in Hell: The Prison Writings of Fleet Maull* (South Deerfield, MA: Prison Dharma Network, 2005).

247 *center of the mandala*: Ibid.

247 *all hells are emptied*: "Kshitigarbha," *Wikipedia*, https://en.wikipedia.org/wiki /Kshitigarbha.

247 *accidentally harm them*: Ibid.

249 *we know we might fall*: Marina Abramović, presentation at the Lensic Performing Arts Center in Santa Fe, August 23, 2016.

Index